CALL NO MAN MASTER

CALL NO MAN MASTER

Joyce Collin-Smith

Introduction by Colin Wilson

Gateway Books, Bath

Published by
GATEWAY BOOKS
The Hollies, Wellow,
Bath, BA2 8QJ

First Printing 1988

9/95

Cover design by Studio B, Bristol

Typeset in 11 on 12½pt Sabon by
Mathematical Composition Setters Ltd,
of Salisbury
Printed and bound in Great Britain
by Billings of Worcester

British Library Cataloguing in Publication Data:

Collin-Smith, Joyce
Call no man master
1. Self-realisation — Stories, anecdotes
I. Title
158'.1
ISBN 0-946551-46-4

(Front cover illustrations, top left, clockwise:
P. D. Ouspensky, The Maharishi, Pak Subuh,
Rodney Collin, Frank Buchman, G. I. Gurdjieff)

In memory of James Webb

Introduction

by Colin Wilson

The 20th century has produced more gurus, sages and messiahs than the previous five centuries put together. The reason is plain enough: the collapse of organised religion has left behind a hunger for moral certainties, a craving for 'hidden knowledge'. "After the war of 1914–18, wherever I went, whether in England, or on the Continent, in America or the Far East, conversation was likely to turn on supernatural subjects." This comment was made by Rom Landau, in a book called *God Is My Adventure*, a study of various gurus and mystics, and it is significant that when it appeared in 1935, it became an immediate bestseller and went through eight impressions in less than a year.

Four decades later, a brilliant young historian named James Webb also became fascinated by this 'proliferation of prophets', from Rudolf Steiner to Billy Graham, from Count Keyserling to Gurdjieff, from Rasputin to Timothy Leary, and set out to record the story in a series of carefully researched books, beginning with *The Occult Establishment*. And it was in 1972 that Webb attended a talk given by Joyce Collin-Smith on the subject of her brother-in-law, Rodney Collin, one of Ouspensky's leading disciples. An immediate and rather strange friendship sprang up—strange because Webb was a total sceptic about 'the occult', and Joyce Collin-Smith—as readers of this book will soon discover—was anything but. Yet she possessed precisely what Webb lacked: first hand experience of the 'quest for certainty' and hidden knowledge. Her influence can be sensed in Webb's most substantial book, *The Harmonious Circle*, a study of Gurdjieff and Ouspensky, which he completed

1

not long before his suicide in 1980. And I suppose it must have been, in many ways, a rather disturbing influence. Webb's attitude to 'the occult' was a rather smart-alecky 'I-know-it-all' kind of rationalism, of the variety that might be expected from a Cambridge undergraduate. Confronted by this extraordinary lady, he must have found himself at first inclined to regard her—with her belief in ESP, astrology and reincarnation—as a self-deluding crank. And then, I have no doubt, it began to dawn on him that she was just as 'tough-minded' as he was himself and that it was perhaps his own approach that was shallow and simplistic. During the period of intense mental stress that he experienced before his death, he admitted ruefully that he had been 'hoist with his own petard'.

I am by no means unsympathetic to Webb's dilemma, having experienced it myself. I was trained as a scientist, then decided that I would rather be a writer of ideas; but my bias remained firmly rationalistic (as it still is). When, in the late 1960s, I accepted a commission to write a book about 'the occult', I had no doubt whatever that it was mostly wishful thinking and self-delusion. I remember spending an afternoon with the Shakespeare scholar G. Wilson Knight, and trying to conceal my discomfort as he talked about spiritualism, and described how he had become convinced that his own mother had communicated with him after her death... Yet the more I studied cases of telepathy, precognition, 'second sight', even reincarnation, the more I became aware that there is a formidable body of scientific evidence. I even began to wonder whether I had not better keep an open mind about astrology when I came across a section in a pocket diary that described the characteristics of the various sun signs (Aries, Taurus, Gemini, etc) and realised that it applied with surprising accuracy to many people that I knew. And, having written *The Occult*, I decided that I would be stupid to try to maintain an attitude of rigid scepticism. I still firmly declined to treat the subject as important, remaining convinced that our business in this world is intimately related to self-discipline and self-knowledge, and that such matters as reincarnation and life-after-death are basically irrelevant. But I also came to accept that there *are* many people who spend their lives on the borderland between two worlds, and that such people can

2

occasionally throw some interesting light into the dark corners of human existence.

I still find myself bumping into my fundamental scepticism as I read Joyce Collin-Smith's autobiography. I know that many children have imaginary playmates who strike them as perfectly real. But it is obvious that when Joyce Collin-Smith talks about her 'brother', she means more than that. If I merely appeal to my own experience, then I would be inclined to dismiss it as imagination. But I know her well enough to know that she is a remarkably honest person, and that she is not indulging in some kind of fantasy; so I have to be prepared to recognise that her early experiences with her 'brother' were beyond anything I have ever experienced, and were nevertheless real and valid. Those who regard 'the occult' as another name for feeble-mindedness will accuse me of credulity. Yet it seems to me that this kind of credulity is a vitally important step in trying to understand some of the bigger issues raised in this book.

Such an issue, for example, raises itself when she speaks of her friend Elsie Abercrombie, who was apparently able to influence people by telepathy. In twenty years of learning about 'the occult', I have come across this kind of thing too often to dismiss it as self-deception. J. B. Priestley, for example, has described how, at a boring literary dinner in New York, he decided to try an experiment in telepathic suggestion, and tried concentrating on a rather severe looking woman, mentally ordering her to wink at him; after a few moments she turned and winked; later, she came across to apologise, and explained that it was merely 'a silly impulse'. So when I came across Joyce Collin-Smith's description of how Elsie Abercrombie made everyone at a dinner party start talking about camels, I was instantly intrigued, and asked her to tell me more about the lady. She told me two fascinating anecdotes. On one occasion, she was sitting with Elsie Abercrombie in a rather cold studio when the old lady murmured: "Cold. Better end it." And a few minutes later, their host remarked: "It seems to have got cold in here. We'll stop early and go in for coffee." Joyce comments: "It might have been a coincidence, but for the wicked twinkle and chuckle which made me sure she had manipulated it somehow."

On another occasion, Joyce had taken the old lady a present of a hydrangea, which survived a long journey by car without problems. But within an hour of being in the same room as Elsie, it had begun to droop. "When I mentioned it, she glanced at it and said balefully: 'I hate hydrangeas.' As I apologised for bringing her an unacceptable gift she stared at it for a long time, then went on talking. Ten or fifteen minutes later I was absolutely astonished to find it had perked up, and was almost visibly lifting its petals, as though exhorted to live after all, rather than hurt my feelings."

A further story about Lady Abercrombie seemed to offer a possible explanation for her peculiar powers. In her mid teens she was thrown from a horse and fractured her spine; her legs became paralysed. One day, she overheard a conversation between her father and the doctor, discussing what to do with her, since it was obvious she would never walk again. This so enraged her that she ordered the Indian servants to put her on the back of an older horse, then set out to control it with her hands and voice. And by doing this again and again, she gradually recovered the use of her legs. I found myself wondering whether this tremendous effort of will had developed in her some strange ability to give 'mental orders'. Then I re-read the story about the dinner party and the camels, and realised that she had possessed her telepathic powers even in childhood; so my explanation had to be mistaken. Yet I cite this example to explain just why I find this book so remarkable and important; it raises questions that should not be ignored, and sometimes points the mind in the vague general direction of the answers.

That is not, of course, the only reason. Most readers will find it fascinating because of her accounts of her first hand experiences with Pak Subuh, the Indonesian 'messiah' who caused such a sensation in the 1960s, and with the Maharishi. When I read a first version of this book, about five years ago, it was mainly about the Maharishi, and I read it from beginning to end with total absorption. When I urged her to try and find a publisher, she explained that several publishers had, in fact, considered it, but the general consensus seemed to be that interest in the Maharishi has now waned so that no one would want to read a whole book about him. I am glad that my enthusiasm made her decide to turn the book into an autobiography, and that she has also spoken at length about Rodney Collin and James Webb, as well as her experiences with the

Ouspensky group led by Francis Roles. But for me, the core of the book remains her account of the Maharishi Mahesh Yogi. Here again, in that anecdote about the irritable lady who complained to the hotel management about the crowds of disciples, I encounter that curious problem of telepathic control. How, otherwise, was it possible for the Maharishi to declare with such certainty that they would have no more trouble from the old lady? But even more fascinating is the question of how the Maharishi succeeded in plunging all his 'initiates' into an immediate state of transcendental meditation—even believing that it should be possible to teach the whole world to 'meditate' in three years. In some odd way, the Maharishi was able to show his followers how to gain what I have elsewhere called 'access to inner worlds'.

Joyce Collin-Smith's subsequent experiences strike me as equally fascinating and important—the strange mental breakdown that caused her to 'see' the past and future of everything she looked at, so that a tree would be simultaneously a shrub, a sapling, and a pile of chopped firewood... The story of her attempted suicide, and her realisation that desperation had revealed to her the trick of holding things 'steady', seems to me of such tremendous importance that even if the rest of the book contained nothing of significance, this anecdote alone would ensure it a certain classic status. But the basic question that it raises is explored further in her discussion of Webb's mental breakdown. Sartre had a similar experience after taking mescalin—clock-faces seemed to be grinning at him, and he had a delusion of being followed by a giant lobster—and this, in turn, seems to support Aldous Huxley's suggestion that our nervous systems are not designed to admit experience so much as to keep it out, to filter it down to an acceptable level. This, in turn, leads me to speculate whether the kind of complacent rationalism to be found in Webb's *Occult Establishment* and *The Flight From Reason* was actually a kind of unconscious defense mechanism, which began to collapse after his exposure to the ideas of Gurdjieff and Ouspensky and of Joyce herself.

But perhaps the simplest way of explaining why I find this book so important is for me to tell the curious little tale of my own unpublished introduction to Webb's *Occult Establishment*. In 1981, I was approached by Richard Drew, the managing director of a small publishing company in Glasgow, who told me that he wanted to bring out a British edition of Webb's *Occult Establishment* (which had so far only appeared in the United States) and asked me to write the introduction. I agreed willingly, and declined his offer of payment, for although I had never known Webb, we had exchanged a couple of friendly letters, and I felt that his brilliant and amusing book ought to be published in England. When Joyce Collin-Smith allowed me to see the letters that Webb had written to her during his mental breakdown, I realised that he and I had shared the same frightening experience of 'panic attacks' (I described my own in a book called *Mysteries*), and that, for Webb, these experiences were a kind of equivalent of the Christian mystic's 'dark night of the soul'. I had described something of the sort in my first book *The Outsider*, in speaking of 'mental travellers' who had seen 'too deep and too much'. I quoted at length from these letters in my introduction (I wish Joyce had done so more fully in the present book). And in September 1981 I sent the completed introduction to Richard Drew. He wrote back to say that the introduction was far too long (in fact, it was shorter than this present one) and that in any case, Webb's wife Mary wanted to delete the whole section about his mental illness. Her feeling, apparently, was that he had simply gone 'dotty' from wasting his time on the absurd irrelevancies of 'occultism', and that she deplored my tendency to take them seriously. My reaction, of course, was to say that the introduction should either be published in its entirety or not at all. Richard Drew's response was 'not at all'. So *The Occult Establishment* finally appeared without an introduction...

Webb himself would have chuckled at the irony of the situation. The aim of his books is to demonstrate that 'the occult' is merely a curious aberration of the human mind, a proof that man has failed to outgrow primitive superstition, and that one of his most incorrigible characteristics is his longing for the comfort offered by fake messiahs and gurus. But his two years of mental illness—'not an experience I would wish on my worst enemy'—left him with a feeling that 'despite the undoubtedly hallucinatory nature of many of my experiences, a residue remains which I simply have to take seriously, although

I can't fit all the altered states of consciousness into one system...' And I state in my Introduction: 'What I am trying to establish here is that Webb's strange visions, brought on by a kind of breakdown between the conscious and unconscious mind, cannot be dismissed as the delusions of a madman; his letters make it clear that he himself remained sane enough to distinguish between delusions and a glimpse of some larger reality.'

The real danger, I am convinced, lies not in this recognition of the existence of a 'larger reality', but in our childish tendency to react to it with fear and mistrust. Joyce Collin-Smith has quoted Ouspensky on the subject of these mystical glimpses, and his comment that 'one could go mad from one ashtray'. But if this remark is read in its proper context—the chapter called 'Experimental Mysticism' in *A New Model of the Universe*—it will be seen that his central point is an extraordinary vision of the *connectedness* of everything that seems to be common to all mystical experience—everything in the universe is seen to be connected to everything else, and the mystic can actually *see* the connections. We all experience something of the sort in moods of happiness and excitement—a kind of mental glow which means that everything we look at or think about somehow *reminds* us of something else—of other times and other places. And this feeling usually brings a curious sense of delight, a recognition that 'all is well'. As Ouspensky looked at the ashtray, it made him aware of so many other things that he felt overwhelmed by the sheer multiplicity of meaning, a sensation that could be compared to a drunkard drowning in a vat of whisky...

This is a sensation I experienced again and again as I read *Call No Man Master*, a tremendous feeling of excitement that made me wish Joyce had been sitting in the chair opposite me, so I could say: 'Yes, but don't you think...' In her first chapter, she describes how Rodney Collin told her that one day she would write a book about 'the miraculous', and that she feels that it must be now or never. And I feel that she is correct in thinking that this book is her 'testament' to others who share her own obscure craving for a 'larger reality'. It seems to me that she has succeeded in saying, accurately and precisely, what she had it in her to say, and that the book has that odd feeling of 'rightness' that ensures that it will be one of those books that will never lack an audience of admirers.

1

Childhood was haunted by an urgent thing forgotten.

Starting up from bed in the old North Oxford House, or a window sill corner behind long velour curtains where I used to secret myself, I would wrack my brains, anxious not to fail some illusive task or duty. Had I omitted to run an errand? Carry a message? Complete my school homework? Wanting always to please, to do the right thing, not to incur the frowns of mother or nursemaids or schoolmistresses, I would feel my heart thumping with continual anxiety. The world was for ever an alien place, in which I sought eternally to find an acceptable mode of behaviour.

I was well into my teens before it occurred to me that I might conceivably be trying to recall some obligation or undertaking left over from 'another time round', a different life all together.

The orderly household allowed no room for strange or unconventional knowledge. I had not heard of esotericism. Reincarnation would not have been admitted as a possibility in the Christian, church-every-Sunday-morning family I was born into. But eventually the thought arose spontaneously: I have been around a long time. I've lived a lot of lives. This is one of a series. What I have forgotten is simply that which I have known before, and must recall at all costs, otherwise something—some task, some purpose—can't be accomplished. In a confused and earnest manner, the thin and nervous child attempted to find again what later seemed best defined as a Way.

My father was Editor of the "Oxford Times". We came from a long line of journalists. Grandfather had worked in Fleet Street, and both great grandfathers on that side were newspaper men, colleagues in the press gallery of the House of Commons with Charles Dickens. Words flowed through me easily, and were soon formulated into vivid imaginings of other worlds and ways, while myths, legends and fairy tales were my intellectual food. It was clear that everything had another meaning. Nothing was quite what it seemed, and everyday life was only a reflection, a kind of mirror image of reality. I seemed to be always trying to turn around, to see the positive of which life in the day to day world was only the negative, to hear the sound of which ordinary voices and noises were the continually reverberating echo.

Retreating into dreams I sought reality in some depth of the mind and heart which, beyond reach of reason and logic and the words of school teachers, I seemed in some sense to know. Here only was a kind of safety from the invasion of foreign presences, onerous tasks, uncongenial surroundings. Though loved and cared for normally by a busy, efficient, committee meeting and socializing mother, a kind and gentle, nervously correct father and the household staff that was customary in those far off days, I withdrew more and more into the realms of privacy and fantasy. Tending to ailments, skeleton thinness, excessive shyness and nervousness, I must have been a tiresome, difficult child. My exuberant and confident younger sister was a much more responsive daughter of the house. Increasingly I slipped into solitude. Fearing rebuffs or incomprehension if I voiced my thoughts, I busied myself with private activities. In a corner of the nursery, the schoolroom, the bedroom I would be occupied in painting pictures, drawing, or making something out of plasticine, a modelling clay for children. I would be writing a story, composing a poem or telling myself a long, imaginary narrative. I was comforted in the making and the doing. It brought results, even if never quite as good as one hoped in advance, while children's games or adult teaching left me with a sense of pointlessness and meaninglessness. Later I wandered round the parks and colleges alone, drifting into churches and university halls and chapels, gradually coming to worship learning. Touching the leather bound volumes in old libraries, lifting them down and poring over them whenever permitted by college librarians in those more easy-going days, I looked for something, anything, that might give me a signposted set of directions, a map, a series of clues, a pattern of living that I could easily follow. Somewhere there must be records that would tell of others like myself?

But for years the only companion was my half-remembered counterpart—an imaginary brother.

I didn't meet Rodney Collin, Ouspensky's pupil and associate, and author of *The Theory of Celestial Influence*, *The Theory of Eternal Life*, etc., until I was already in my thirties.

I was married by then to his brother Derry. Rodney was abroad, in Mexico, and came to see us long after I had become his sister-in-law. So it was a cart-before-the-horse situation, for I had almost forgotten the childhood dreams. When I exclaimed "You are my brother!" with amazement and delight as I looked into the familiar face so like my own, it was a long time after even that late meeting.

We were sitting together on top of the Pyramid of the Sun at Teotihuacan in Mexico when realisation hit me.

"Very likely," he answered amiably, his blue eyes, my own blue eyes meeting, wrinkled against the brilliant midday sunlight, our widebrimmed straw hats tilted to the backs of our heads, our so similar countenances, our tall, thin, narrow-shouldered frames so alike we might indeed have been related by blood and not by marriage.

"One day you'll write all this down," he told me after many months in the strange 7,000 feet above sea level air of the Valley of Mexico, where the altitude and the strong clear light and the philosophically orientated household made joyous sense at last. "One day you'll stop all this novel writing and write something more important." My *Locusts and Wild Honey* and other books were best sellers at the time and the dreams and fantasies of childhood had found their outlet in this convoluted form. "One day you'll write of the miraculous." I had been reading Ouspensky's *In Search of the Miraculous* at night instead of sleeping, for the days were so full of action and eager words. "In your own way you'll give a pointer or two to those who will come after."

I am in my last quarter of life. I've talked, lectured, written, travelled, filled my years with a helter-skelter gallop against time.

I am nearing seventy. 'One day' must be now.

My memory is so long and clear that I sometimes wonder if perhaps, under hypnosis for instance, I might have almost total recall.

I know what it was like to be a baby in a pram lined with white leather which smelled of summer warmth, and above me a green silk canopy hung with fringe to give me shade. I recollect the first experience of causation. If you bumped your legs up and down the pram shook and the fringe danced. If you lay still it didn't move. It was a different and more interesting type of cause and effect than every baby's instinctive knowledge that crying brings attention, voices, arms, comfort. This was simply doing something for its own sake, realising one had power to make things happen. I lay thinking about it, still too young to sit up unaided or utter any word. Perhaps I was five or six months old.

My 'brother' appeared in my imagination when I was two and a half. Mother was expecting a second child. I had been told this, and that she had to go away for a few days to fetch it.

Already I knew of a boy, so like my own self that he seemed my other half. I awaited his arrival with acceptance and confidence. They took me to the nursing home and showed me a newborn baby in a cot, among a row of other cots in a long room.

"This is your little sister" they said. "A dear little girl."

Confusion filled me.

"No. I want my brother."

"A sister, darling, not a brother."

The next cot held a boychild with family round admiring and referring to the small scrap as "he". I moved across, looked through the bars with puzzlement and demanded that we have this one instead. I knew that babies grow. Though not as I imagined, this must be the expected one. The sound of adult laughter resounded everywhere as I was gently pulled away.

"That one! That one!" I shouted in impotent bewilderment and dismay. Though rarely smacked, my illogical screaming and stamping brought stern commands for quiet and a sudden sharp and unexpected slap which reduced me to wailing and eventually to silence. Planted firmly on an upright chair and told to behave myself, I wouldn't look at the babies, or go, when told, to Mother in her pink bedjacket reclining among pillows.

She held out her arms and called me. I looked obstinately at the floor, my small feet dangling, my tears still running. Now suddenly the world was an empty place.

Creative imagination has always intrigued me. From a young age I could visualize, see faces, hear voices, make people, places and situations in my mind. They were as real as my every day surroundings, and there were times in young childhood when I had difficulty in distinguishing between the two modes of experience and was accused of lying. Lacking the brother in the nursery, the 'remembered one' as a playmate, I set about recreating him in my mind.

Slowly he grew tall. Though his face was never entirely clear to me, I knew 'the shape he cut in space.' That was how I defined it to myself. Gradually he became older than I, tall, thin, long-faced, narrow-shouldered, quick and gentle, full of comprehension of all my difficulties. I held long conversations with him in my mind, asking him questions, getting mumbo-jumbo answers that were no more than soothing comfortable sounds. It was like the talking of frogs in ponds in the hot African nights that I experienced later on—or the Raudive tapes, which have the same illusive quality of meaning something that is for some reason not entirely intelligible. I would talk, and listen inwardly, and be at peace.

Only once, in early schoolgirl days, did I hear actual words. My brother appeared to me as though agitated and distressed, walking up and down a room with rapid strides and crying "It breaks my heart. I am heartbroken". He seemed about sixteen or seventeen. Unfortunately I never checked with Rodney Collin whether he had any recollection of some incident that tallied with this event—whether it was true telepathy. It might have been.

Normally his presence was like a reassuring extension of myself, and by my teens I had quite ceased to invent stories of his eventual coming. For years the place on the wide window sill where the curtains concealed me and I commanded a view of the garden gate and path, had been my refuge and my private hermitage. Hearing the creak of the iron gate, I would close my eyes, pretending, pretending furiously, that the footsteps on the driveway were those of the tall thin boy. My parents would greet him with delight. "Here is your long lost brother!" they

13

would call, in the dramatic manner of characters in fairy tales. But the postman, the milkman, the neighbours, my mother's friends and my father's colleagues called once too often and the childhood game wore out.

One day I 'thought him up' for the last time. I was a young reporter on the "Reading Standard", shortly before the outbreak of war. In a spare hour I had wandered into the Forbury Gardens, where the ruined, ivy-clad granite walls of the Abbey are a home to rooks and jackdaws. The medieval round, "Summer is i'cumin in" was written here, and the facsimile of the original MS was under glass on a stand in the central clearing. Poring over it I could hear the round in the ears of my imagination, those subtle strata of the mind which give shape and colour and sound and taste and scent to objects that are not present at the time in reality. I perceived the monks chanting, smiling, rubicund, enjoying a little light relief from their more earnest offices.

"He would like this", I thought suddenly, and was at once filled with such a desolation of longing for the tall, thin young man, now visualized as being fully adult and unattainable in this life, that tears suddenly poured down my cheeks and fell in droplets on the glass-topped pedestal housing the ancient musical score with its barely decipherable words.

The ivy rustled in the wind as the great black birds moved in and out about their inscrutable business. For a few minutes the world seemed again a dreadfully lonely place in which to live. Then I made some sort of decision to be done with all that, to put away childish things and try to be more at home, of necessity, among my fellow human beings on this earth.

2

Rudolf Steiner's *Knowledge of the higher Worlds* was the first esoteric book I ever saw. At about sixteen, browsing round the City Library I found it under Religion and Philosophy, read it in a quiet alcove with a sense of excitement, and finally bore it home, to continue in secret under the bedclothes by torchlight after my sister and I had been told to turn our lights out at night.

The idea of different levels of reality, different modes of consciousness, higher beings who knew more than ordinary men didn't fit in at all with the rector's sermons at St. Peter le Bailey Church where we went on Sunday mornings. The whole notion of discarnate intelligences was new to me and exercised my mind to such an extent that I went to see the rector personally on some pretext or other and tried to question him.

The Rev. Christopher Chavasse, later Bishop of Rochester, was a personal friend of my father and therefore approachable. But he disappointed me by answering my eager questions as though to an importunate child and ended by telling me to say my prayers like a good girl and God would look after me.

"Prayers don't do anything", I protested. "They're only a lot of words."

He laughed amiably.

"Well, we all have times when we find we are saying 'Our Father which art in Heaven' and thinking at the same time what's for breakfast. Sometimes I even find myself saying ABCDEFG or counting to twenty by mistake, because I'm not really paying attention. Even I do that when I'm not really thinking about God properly. You have to pay attention and think about God."

"How can you think about God properly? He's too....." I

15

meant "far away, defying definition. Or perhaps there are many gods, many levels, or many modes of God." But I couldn't express my embryonic ideas.

Dr Chavasse was sitting at his desk in his study at St. Peter's Hall, the Mastership of which went with the living of St. Peter le Bailey. Beside him on the wall was a reproduction of Dürer's hands at prayer. My eye slid away from his face and his useless words and I contemplated the attitude of the fine-boned hands, with a sudden sense of understanding the nature of prayer for one brief moment. I decided Dürer knew something the rector didn't know. ABCDEFG indeed! What a ridiculous and shame-making confession!

Afterwards I tried the Rev. Bryan Green, later a canon and a television personality, but at that time another Oxford rector and also a personal friend of my family. His approach was evangelistic and emotional, and he could fill the church at St. Aldate's with undergraduates and get them queuing in the aisles to approach the altar and give their souls to God. It was easy to be moved to do the same. But in the end my soul still seemed to be a nebulous piece of equipment, not mine to give or keep. And Bryan, though he listened with attention to my stumbling, ill-formulated queries, could pass on nothing save his own emotional attachment to the idea of Christ crucified. This thought—the dying body on the cross—had not taken off at all in me. Nor had "gentle Jesus meek and mild". The "pale Galilean" of Swinburne's poem.*

Only some people had souls anyway, I thought. I'd known that in some way as a small child, seeing the presence or absence in their eyes.

Uncle Reggie Carroll had been in Tibet with Sir Francis Younghusband. He was the first person I recognised in this way. He visited us when I was very young—not a real uncle, but a boyhood friend of my father. He brought Indian silk to make dresses for us little girls, and gifts for my mother and father from the Orient.

Laughing, he draped a length of blue shimmering stuff round

---

* 'Thou has conquered, O pale Galilean,
  The world has grown grey with thy breath.'
                                    Hymn to Proserpine, A.C.Swinburne

me, turning me about and tucking it under one arm and over my shoulder like a sari. Delighted by its frail beauty, I fingered it and looked up into his face. He was a tall, smiling gray-haired man, kind in his touch. His eyes were luminous and had a quality in them I had never yet encountered. I looked deeply into them and he returned my stare with a steady and suddenly quite serious look.

"If you were a little Indian girl you'd wear a silk sari like that always."

"I was once", I said, with unconsidered certainty. He regarded me with immediate gravity, and I gazed up in a long and awestruck look. Later we were alone in the drawing room. "What do you remember?" he asked when no-one else could hear. "Do you really remember being a little Indian girl?"

At once I was unsure and hung my head in silence.

"Try to recall it! Do you remember any name? Any place where once you lived? Perhaps very long ago?"

Standing with my hands on his knee and his own hands capping them, I seemed to get a strange, sweet heavy scent, to visualize the perfumed smoke rising from a shallow dish, to feel myself transported to a dimlit place where everyone was sitting on the floor.

Without conscious thought I sat down cross-legged, a normal position in which I used to sit and think, and then took one foot in my hand and tried to place it on my knee. It didn't go there easily and I let it drop back. Reggie Carroll watched me. Presently he said: "You remember the lotus position," and sitting on the floor himself with easy suppleness, he assumed what I now know to have been the half lotus and then the full lotus posture. At the time it looked very strange, and yet familiar. I tried to copy it and couldn't. Man and child regarded each other in a long silence. No-one entered the drawing room for several minutes, and when they did he rose in an easy movement, touched my forehead, and watched me jump up and gallop off.

I don't remember ever having the chance to talk to Reggie Carroll when I was old enough to discuss reincarnation with any understanding. Perhaps he had died by then, for though he was still agile, he was possibly fairly old. But I thought of him often with a sense of having met somebody who knew strange

17

things and who had recognised me 'soul to soul'. When the blue silk dresses were made up they were frilly and puffed-sleeved and no longer meant anything much. But I would touch mine in the wardrobe cupboard, closing my eyes and letting the folds slip softly through my fingers for comfort. Locked up in the silk somewhere was an echo of a memory.

Tibet was spoken of occasionally because Reggie had been there, and had brought us two tsampa dishes which were used for sugar or something in our household. But it was at school that I first heard of the Dalai Lama, the successive incarnations, the Potala—the enormous ancient lamasery built deep into the rock above the mountain city of Lhasa. We were shown pictures of it. I knew I had seen it before.

I ran home to tell my mother I was going to Tibet when I grew up. Fired by all the new information I had been given in class that day, I re-created an ancient, holy land. In my imagination I heard the prayer flags on the stone cairns blowing strongly in the continual wind. I ran along in thickly padded garments, very different from the light silk Indian sari. Long boots encumbered movement. The cold was intense. I turned the prayer wheels on the walls in passing, hearing them clatter as they revolved. The flat note of the lamasery bells that had no resonance seemed audible. The icy air stung my red cheeks and a gale whistled through the valley.

Somewhere above me in a granite monastery I knew my brother lived and worked, studied and chanted long, long prayers. The school lesson had elaborated itself into a seeming memory.

Dawdling to a standstill by the entrance to the University Parks not far from home, I recalled my present state with a sense of frightened shock. To calm down I entered the park gates and sat down on a bench to think about it. Now I saw myself young and fat and padded, carrying a bowl of cherries in my hands, holding it carefully, to take to my brother. I could glimpse him through lattice work on which blue flowers grew. He would come and stoop, a tall robed figure who received me with quiet affection. For some reason I had often thought of giving my brother cherries. Now it seemed a memory of Tibet. The brief outline at school had triggered off something deeply embedded in my subconscious mind. I reached home at length, entered the kitchen and started to tell it all.

"Where on earth do you get these wild ideas?" Mother answered, busily whipping up cake mixture for some church or garden fete.

"I heard it at school. Uncle Reggie went there. I'm going there too."

"White women don't go to Tibet," she answered firmly. "Its a closed country, closed to foreigners. Uncle Reggie only got in once, on Younghusband's expedition and that was long ago. You'll never go there. Don't be silly."

I felt as though a door had closed sharply in my face. Running up the Banbury Road from school it had all seemed so clear, so certain. I wished so much that Uncle Reggie would come, but he was presumably on his travels again. He would have known. He would have understood. Lacking help I put Tibet away from my thoughts for years.

When I was quite adult I began to realise that a belief that one has lived once in Tibet is quite common among those who seem to recollect other lives. Some watered down influence from that mysterious, ancient culture, the secrets held in the lamasery archives far back in history, seems to go on and on, finding harbourage wherever there is a mind that holds dim memories of other incarnations. I felt sure all Tibetans had souls in those far off days. But in Western people in twentieth century life they seemed a much scarcer commodity to me.

I began to think everybody must have an embryonic one, but in most people it never developed into anything much. Uncle Reggie's eyes were the only indication that it could develop fully in a living man. I thought of him for peace and reassurance for many years, long after Christopher Chavasse and Bryan Green had been dismissed and left to their sermonizing and their flocks of Christian worshippers. It was the Orient that called me now.

I went on to the "Oxford Mail" and "Oxford Times" staff straight from school, and after a couple of years, got myself the job on the "Reading Standard."

Growing in confidence I soon found that the inbuilt family aptitude fitted me without great effort into the mould of newspaper reporter.

We worked a thirteen day fortnight—one whole day off every two weeks, but plenty of freedom between the assignments of the day. It was before the days of National Union of Journalists power, and each person worked long hours on his own responsibility. Coming and going about my duties, usually free for part of each day, especially if there was an evening function to be covered, I felt a sense of purpose and enjoyment. I liked the quick, alert, enquiring minds of my fellows, their absence of narrow prejudice. I was the only girl. Except in Fleet Street, women journalists were not numerous then.

My duties took me to meetings covering every political party, every 'cause' or project, every line of thought, protest or aspiration which the times produced. From the extreme left, to the British Union of Fascists on the right. From the Anti-Vivisection League to the Total Abstinence Union: from the Federation of Women's Institutes to the Society for Psychical Research I wended my way, reporter's book in hand, taking my shorthand note, rushing back to the office to bang out a 'story' on my typewriter and be off to the police court sessions or a Town Council meeting; or perhaps to be diverted to an accident, a warehouse fire, the death of a local celebrity or an unexpected development of some kind.

I had an idealistic view of the newspaper world. Honesty in reporting, the straight story, the cool, unslanted presentation of events was the custom of the press in the main in the 1930s. In particular the provincial papers prided themselves on covering everything at length, unbiased, "bringing the world to the world", as the Gaumont British News slogan defined it.

To be unprejudiced is fairly easy when young and inexperienced and continually presented with honesty opposing views on every subject that exercises the human mind. People get very heated about their causes, I found. Often my personal as distinct from my professional interest was angled for, with requests to put my name to petitions, write special articles, get in some way involved.

But already I was thinking that none of the 'causes' about which people shouted at each other in extremes of fury and conviction of their own rightness had anything to do with real, bare bones causation, basic cause-and-effect activities. Push down trouble in one quarter and another would pop up elsewhere immediately. Alleviate one cause of injustice and others would suffer somehow as a result, especially if there was government or local government interference in the apparently 'natural' scheme of things.

In my idle times, I read the metaphysical poets, listened to classical music with a group of young friends, went to the theatre or to social 'bring-a-bottle' parties, and integrated myself with reasonable ease into the structure of society in Reading, while still keeping a footing in the Oxford University circles I had cultivated in my late teen years.

The wide spectrum of those few pre-war journalistic years formed the rubble of the roadway I have trodden all my life since then, I think. The Fates were kind. I had a very good grounding for someone inwardly yearning always to find a 'Way'.

Eddie Armstrong, the chief reporter on the Reading Standard was a member of the Oxford Group—Moral Rearmament as the movement later came to be called. I 'pulled his leg' about his desire to confess his sins to all and sundry, and was not particularly impressed when taken to a meeting at which the founder, Dr. Frank Buchman, was speaking on one of his flying visits from the United States. He was an ex-Lutheran Minister, round-faced, round-eyed, round glasses, beaming with bonhomie, and he had an easy flow of words which did not at first hold my attention much. But suddenly it seemed all the youngsters in the circles I moved in were getting 'changed'— the Buchmanite terminology for a sudden conversion to the Christian faith.

In the course of work I had met Eric Kennington the sculptor, later one of the official war artists, and known also for his friendship with T. E. Lawrence and his illustrations of the Arab chiefs for *Seven Pillars of Wisdom*. Sent to interview Eric about his effigy of T. E. Lawrence which was to be installed ceremonially in St. Martin's Church at Wareham in Dorset near the site of Lawrence's death, I struck up a friendship with this mild and quiet-minded craftsman, and used to go and sit with him in his studio at Homer House near Reading as he chipped away,

21

putting finishing touches to the effigy. He must have been in his late forties I think.

Celendine Kennington was a rather formidable lady. While apparently having no objection to the presence of the gawky young girl I still was, in her husband's studio, she often descended on us and led me off through the extensive grounds to tea up at the house. There she talked interminably about Moral Rearmament, in which she too was now deeply involved.

"What on earth do you and Eric talk about?" she demanded crossly. He's not interested in MRA or anything much except his work. Usually he hates people there when he's working." She seemed unable to have any conversation with her husband, perhaps because she tended to dominate everyone around too much.

I found I didn't know what we talked about. "Sometimes about T.E. I suppose." He was obsessed with thoughts of Lawrence. His respect for the depths of T.E.'s thought amounted to a sort of reverent love. "But really mostly we just don't talk at all. I had been accustomed to go in because he always said "Come again on Wednesday" or some such command. He wouldn't stop work. We were usually silent.

But one day he took me into the house and into his Lawrence room, where he showed me T.E.'s Arab robes, the curved scimitar that had been the gift of the Emir Feisal and various of his possessions. Then he placed in my hands the MS of *The Mint* on which Lawrence had an embargo of 25 years or so after his death before it was to be published.

I had read and appreciated *Seven Pillars* when my father, at Lawrence's brother's request, prepared the English edition for publication from the limited American version with its different spelling. There was something very appealing to me about the Arab adventures and the perfect prose in which he expressed the depths of his thought. But the convolutions of his mind in later years, when he enlisted in the ranks of the Army as Private Ross, and later in the RAF as Aircraftman Shaw were quite beyond my immature thought at that time. I saw the tormented mind, but not the reasons for it. I turned the pages of the Mint without understanding, and set it aside and returned to the studio. The continual stress in Lawrence and the tranquility of Eric Kennington who had loved him, were in sharp contrast. I

22

remember a moment of visualisation of the difference between those who struggle with life and those who take it easily, flowing with the stream in some profound way, and I have pondered on it many times all down the years.

I would sit on the window ledge and watch the sculptor's hands at work and think long peaceful thoughts. That was why I went there, in a way, for the long, peaceful thoughts. It is discoloured now, that monument, made shiny by the touch of inquisitive or reverential fingers in the little Dorset church where visitors have flocked to see it over 50 years. Then it was pristine fresh.

Sometimes Eric looked at me and once he said: "I shall model you one day, in clay, and we'll cast it in bronze." But the war came and it was never done.

Meanwhile Celendine, because she was more sophisticated than my fellows and also more determined, talked me round and got me into the Oxford Group by slow degrees. She was one of the older adherents. Mostly they were youngsters who 'shared' their follies by continual public confession.

Basically it was no more than evangelistic Christianity. The groupers were exhorted to live up to four ideals of behaviour: Absolute Honesty, Absolute Purity, Absolute Unselfishness and Absolute Love. The fact that such perfection was beyond attainment necessitated the continual round of confessing and 'sharing' one's shortcomings. I tended to opt out of all this: it was too embarrassing and seemed a bit juvenile to me even then.

What got me was the 'Quiet Time' concept. This was fundamental to Buchman's ideas. It was a method of prayer that was to be cultivated for half an hour at a time at intervals during the day. The discipline of this—so much more demanding than anything I had encountered in conventional church-going, had a certain appeal. Besides, strange things happened when you started the practice known to MRA as 'Listening to God'.

First, the mind was to be emptied of thought. There was to be a notebook and pencil to hand. In quietness and emptiness, messages would come. These were the words of the Lord and must be written down at once, and when appropriate, acted upon.

23

Eddie Armstrong was always going off into a 'Q.T' in his corner of the reporters' room, ribbed or ignored according to who was present. He smiled his way benignly through disapproval or contempt, was amiable and helpful to everyone and lived a good and useful life.

It was a bit much for the staff when I got the bug too. No-one else was 'changed'. But the young circles in Oxford grew and quickened, lively and eager as nineteenth century revivalists, earnest as Puritans, gentle as Quakers, cheerful as Boy Scouts and Girl Guides as they went about their good deeds for the day.

The great meetings and confessions with Frank, as Buchman liked to be called, smilingly placing an arm round people's shoulders, were the Billy Graham phenomenon of the late '30s, I suppose. Frank preached a good and sincere proselytising sermon, laced with Americanisms.

"What is it to pray?" he called. "I will tell you! 'Perfect Radiograms Always Yours.' That is what happens when you listen in to God."

Everyone was jolly and happy. There were summer camps and winter conferences. Because he felt strongly that the coming war could be averted if only enough people listened to God and were changed, he set us all on a scheme to beard the high-ups of the land in their dens and convert them. This high-pressure salesmanship idea was based on the notion that if you got the big names the others would follow. Years later I encountered the same theory when with the Maharishi Mahesh Yogi. He believed too that if TM, his Transcendental Meditation, could be introduced in Buckingham Palace and 10 Downing Street, the world would be saved from the folly of its ways.

Lacking a personal introduction to the prime minister or the Sovereign we youngsters embarked—though with some embarrassment on my part—on a campaign we privately called 'mayor-baiting'. It involved taking MRA leaflets along with us wherever we went and drawing the attention of the mayor and corporation and any local dignitaries to their contents. In this Eddie and I were judged especially useful, as we had access to so many places in the course of our duties.

Celendine concentrated on the more exalted county circles, and at Homer House we had meetings to compare our successes. In spite of the presence at 4 Hays Mews off Berkeley

Square of Beverley Nichols the author—a brief adherent—and Bunny Austin the tennis player, who sacrificed the remainder of his Wimbledon career to further the aims of Moral Rearmament, few well-known people joined the ranks in an open-handed way. But I dare say as many were privately and discreetly practising the Listening to God technique as now practise TM. There is a certain similarity of approach.

In the studio, Eric worked away, untouched by the goings on up at the house. "Don't you want to listen to God, Eric?" I asked.

"He gave me hands to chip with. I shall chip", he answered. After a long silence he added: "You'll see what will happen to those young people in the end. They'll do less and less in life, and end by doing nothing but interfere with their neighbours."

It was true that Eddie seemed less and less inclined to leave his office corner except when a 'sharing meeting' or a mayor-baiting prospect loomed. But by this time I'd made a new boy friend and was more concerned with affairs of the heart than with the avuncular friendship I had had with him.

Roger Ranson had land north of Oxford which he had inherited and began to farm there after coming down from University. He moved in the Oxford rather than the Reading circles, but we all got together for the great campfire gatherings at the property of his neighbour, Brigadier-General C.R.P.Winser.

Roger and I went back to Spelsbury Downs Farm, where his housekeeper provided lunch or supper, and had our 'Quiet Times' in one another's arms by the wide log fire. It was all very innocent. He was a shy young man, earnest in his endeavours, but possibly with a leaning towards his own sex, as the prima-donna-like jealousy of his financial partner should have indicated to me. I knew nothing of homosexuality however. It was not spoken of openly in those days, and young girls were remarkably ignorant about sex. We were taught nothing by school or parents. I was quite content with the apparently rather slow-to-develop situation. We talked religion hand in hand by the hour and only got marginally closer when Roger's partner left us on our own.

The whole question of what actually happens when one attempts to open the mind, or empty it entirely, in an effort to

25

communicate or to receive communications from a higher source kept us enthralled. But gradually it led to greater and greater uncertainty.

If there are no ritual words, no object of contemplation, no basic concept to hold the mind steady, no mantra, no phrase or idea to focus on, strange things could certainly happen.

With most people initial results were interesting, as though the semi-conscious or sub-conscious barriers were easily broken or by-passed by the simple act of 'listening'. Occasionally new thoughts or ideas arose. One's feelings of knowing something that entirely materially-orientated people did not understand was strengthened.

One summer evening Eddie Armstrong and I went over to Pangbourne on the river Thames after our day's work, and climbed a hill together. As he moved off with his notebook and settled some distance away with his back to me, I assumed my usual crosslegged posture. I had always sat like this, even in nursery days when I would wriggle down to the end of the bedstead and grasp two round brass knobs in my hands, and with closed eyes in the darkness think my difficult thoughts. Now I could do the half Lotus, but the full Lotus position was never truly mastered, perhaps for lack of perseverance when I was young enough.

There on the hillside, late sun in my face, the smell of wild thyme and the downland flowers carried on the warm air, I went into the customary 'listening' state. After a few minutes the outer world faded and the inner consciousness began to awaken more. Suddenly as though in a trance I seemed to understand the Trinity. Not the Father, Son and Holy Ghost Christian concept, but a very ancient male, female and issue picture, nearer to Cabalistic teachings. The sense of deep reality—that duality and then the Trinity were the first mani-festations of an Absolute, unmanifest First Cause—was so strong that I attempted to put it into words in my QT notebook. But it proved an impossibility, being neither the Western nor the Hindu Brahma, Vishnu, Siva Trinity of which I had read. I could only get down: 'Three in One, One in Three', and was left with a sense of frustration and helplessness to express anything.

The realisation that one could never define the indefinable in words grew stronger from that time. Later I understood what Gurdjieff meant when he stated with apparent ambiguity: "the truth can only be told in the form of a lie." Ouspensky, struggling with the thoughts induced by experimenting with mescalin, concentrated on an ashtray on his desk and wrote his profound impressions. Later, released from the drug, he found to his chagrin that he had penned the ridiculous words: "A man can go mad from one ashtray".

The deeper the QT became with me, the more the tendency was to go beyond logic and reason into hitherto unexplored regions of the mind, but to be unable to bring anything back from that area into the world of every day.

But it was not long before a hotch-potch of ideas of an exceedingly mundane kind began to invade one's open mind—with nothing to stay their progress. Earnest groupers found that God was advising them on every detail of their daily lives, from what they should put on to where they should eat their lunch. In case of doubt, we were told to "check our guidance" with others. Some of the excesses of silliness were dismissed laughingly as mere peccadillos on the Lord's part. One was thankful to find it was not after all necessary to tell the mayor one had kissed one's boyfriend behind the Town Hall when the car park attendant was not looking, or confess from a public platform that one had once avoided a compulsory PT session when a fourth former at school.

"All the same, its getting a bit ridiculous," I said to Roger, after the jolly junkettings of a campfire gathering in one of General Winser's fields—American evangelistic songs and sausages roasted to a frizzle in the dying embers. "I feel I'm back in the fourth form myself." There had been a lengthy 'sharing session' after the campfire, in which there had been some embarrassing washing of dirty linen in public by leaders of the group, and a long hysterical outburst by a neurotic girl who confessed to hating her seemingly innocuous mother. The poor woman was sitting head in hands listening to this airing of a hundred minor childhood grievances.

Roger had been glum for some days. He had not even opened his mouth to sing the rousing MRA song:

"Fathers we had who dared to storm the last frontier,

They faced the cost and fared Westward where their vision
beckoned clear.
Shake us Divine unrest, and set us in the paths they trod,
Our passion the will to fashion a hate-free nation under
God..."

I had always previously rather liked the camaraderie of the
summer evening gatherings. They were mostly Oxford undergraduates, their shining young faces filled with warmth and
generosity and hope for the future. We stirred each other up in
innocent idealism. Each generation has its version of the MRA
syndrome I suppose, and I have seen it repeat and repeat since
then, from Flower Power and TM, to Billy Graham, to
Bhagwan Rajneesh and a host of minor cults. It is a phenomenon of untried youth, holding experience of life at bay. It dies
in almost every individual with the years.

Roger had a different reason for glumness and eventually it
all came out in a torrent.

"At Hays Mews they've got records on all of us. In a filing
cabinet. Like a sort of police record or a doctor's file. They were
looking someone up, discussing his past, reading out all the sins
he'd shared—that sort of thing. When I was left alone for a
while I looked mine up. And yours. I glanced at them. Then I
tore them up."

I was horrified. It was like a 'trusty' in prison doing the dirty
on the guards. When I said that, Roger answered: "Guards?"

We looked at each other. And suddenly the whole set-up
seemed quite alien and sinister to us both.

Eventually my journalistic instinct came to the fore in a big
way, and I wrote a lengthy article for the Oxford Times and put
it tentatively on my father's desk. He had made no comments on
my connection with the group, but when he had read it he said:
"Not bad. Not bad at all", and published it uncut on the leader
page.

It was a fair assessment for a nineteen year old, I think,
pointing out the value and the dangers, the interesting
phenomena, and the dubious and silly as well. As was the
custom on provincial papers at the time, the article was signed
with my initials only. The day of the big by-line had not yet
come.

To my amazement the article aroused an enormous amount of correspondence and comment. Learned dons, elders of the church, Canon John Stansfield of Christchurch, the local vicars, down to housewives and anxious parents who felt they had 'lost' their children to the MRA movement, were moved to write in with such profusion and verbosity that the letters page was filled with nothing but comments on the Group for weeks—until Father had to terminate it with a "This correspondence is now closed" footnote.

On the whole it seemed that the churchgoers approved the movement. Canon Stansfield wanted to know who on earth JYH was that 'he' could dare to criticize a method that was nothing more nor less than a modern version of Brother Lawrence's *Practice of the Presence of God*. General Winser, also unaware of the authorship, berated the writer for deriding a movement that had done nothing but good "to redeem the young of this generation".

Others, however, complained like parents of the Moonies in the '80s, that their offspring had ceased to be interested in pursuing their studies or their careers and did nothing but sit idle, notebook in hand, or run around embarrassing their neighbours with spurious confessions of sins, unnecessary personal revelations, and tormenting the unconverted with evangelistic zeal and a plethora of religious books and tracts. Their conviction of having a monopoly of Truth was not unlike that of the Jehovah's Witnesses. They too thought they were Chosen People.

For a while I had a foot in both camps. I didn't want to lose my circle of young friends. But increasingly I found myself out of sympathy with them.

One day Peter Farrow, a pleasant young curate whose company I found perfectly acceptable, took me out to a wood near Oxford. We parked at his instigation in a leafy clearing. Here we were to have the usual QT, so out came our notebooks. Peter had, I remember, given me a new and beautiful leather-bound looseleaf one as a birthday present. Side by side in the car we closed our eyes in obedient listening.

After some minutes I was suddenly aware that Peter's breathing had become a little heavier, and his hand groped for mine. Then firmly turning me towards him he said with shining confidence:

"We've received the same guidance, haven't we? I'm to marry you and we shall work for Christ and change the world together".

I was horrified. "No, no! I've received no such guidance at all."

"Listen again, Joyce. He is telling you this, loud and clear."

Both exasperated and suddenly alarmed at his urgency and the arms that were now attempting to enfold me even more closely, I pushed him off and opened the door of the car.

"We must be listening to different Gods", I said.

"Don't be silly! There's only one God. You know that quite well."

"I'm not so sure. Anyway, if I marry anyone, I shall marry Roger", I shouted, jumping out in haste. Peter looked at me in disappointment and disapproval, reduced temporarily to silence. Then:

"You'll never marry Roger—I can tell you that", he called after me as I strode away among the trees to seek the main road and a bus back to Oxford.

In this last prophesy at least he was quite right. War broke out in a few weeks time, Roger enlisted in the RAF as a bomber pilot and was killed the following year in a raid on Cologne.

As for me, I left the Oxford Group, saw MRA as an interesting experiment no more, and turned my attention to other things. Moral Rearmament had not worked, for the conflict in Europe had broken out just the same, and clearly I too must serve in the armed forces before long.

But the idea of listening to an 'inner voice' of some sort remained with me as a constant to my thought, and at times of stress I sometimes called upon it with success.

3

War corrupts everyone.

The innocent, idealistic youngster with notions about truth and beauty, a sense of the high calling of journalism, and no experience of sex beyond a tentative embrace or two enhanced by dreams and fantasies of love, soon gave way to a uniformed aircraftwoman, 'square-bashing' and drilling by the hour, bullied by sergeants, finding the world a considerably tougher place in which to live.

When I got my commission I served with the Polish bomber squadrons operating from a bleak Yorkshire airfield. I shared their desolation at the loss of their homeland to the Germans and the Russians, as Poland was gradually squeezed between the two. I formed attachments and they were broken rapidly by death. Time after time two or three of the Wellingtons failed to return to base after a raid.

Night duty in the operations room, the briefing of the aircrews before each sortie, the hours of waiting in anxiety, and the de-briefing of exhausted men in the early hours, marked the long months. They trooped in, in their sheepskin-lined jackets and boots, sat unwillingly around the intelligence officers' desks as we were forced to continue with our questions to ascertain the success of each raid on the armaments factories of I.G.Farben at Essen, or the workers' homes where the women and children of Frankfurt and Cologne were the innocent victims of our bombing tactics.

I was then moved on to a secret Combined Armed Services establishment where our duty was the interrogation of high-ranking prisoners of war—those whose will had been broken in the notorious London Cage, and who were sufficiently senior to be judged worthy of further attention. They were to be

31

pressurized and tricked into revealing troop positions, strategies and anything of use to our secret service.

As a journalist I was required to 'knock into shape' the assorted material that came from bugged cells where frightened and sometimes garrulous men or unhappy, tight-lipped long-term detainees talked freely to one another on the whole, almost always totally unaware of the then quite new listening-in techniques about which they appeared not to have been warned in advance. Though no-one was tortured, there was a systematic breaking down process that was forerunner of the more sophisticated brain-washing methods of postwar totalitarian states.

Material of use to us was wheedled and bullied out of prisoners by divers means, apart from the random recording of conversations. It was sent through for translation into English and then in my department we waded through the many duplications, eliminated the rubbish, compared notes and put together the documents that were disseminated to various war department sections.

In those years my thought became shallow, circumscribed by events, limited by fatigue, disciplined out of existence by the knowledge of other people's suffering which sometimes seemed too hard to face and bear, and by the inaccessibility of books and the absence of congenial companionship. We lived always for the day, in an 'eat, drink and be merry' atmosphere. Tomorrow we too might die.

Some time after Roger's death I had sexual experience with a young airman and eventually married him. At once he got me pregnant, determined to possess me wholly in this way, against my own instinct that this was not the time to start a family. But after five limited and frustrating years with him, in which the war ended and we struggled into poverty-stricken peace, he abandoned me for someone else, and left me with a small daughter to bring up alone.

I found a war widow with a son of my own child's age, installed her as housekeeper and got a job in Fleet Street. In due course there I met Richard Collin-Smith, whose brother was known in the philosophical and literary world as Rodney Collin, pupil and close associate of P.D.Ouspensky, and author of books based on the Gurdjieff method of psychological development. Rodney had developed his own line of thinking after Ouspesky's death.

I had had nothing to do with religion and philosophy for some years. My mind and heart had hardened through experience of life in war and the discovery of infidelity and parting, duplicity and cruelty and loss. Richard, for some reason, thought my expression appealing: "You always look so sad. I want to make you happy", he said.

When Rodney and Janet Collin-Smith came over from Mexico we were living in an old house at Westerham in Kent. I was writing vigorously and had made a success of my first novel, *Locusts and Wild Honey* which had been started during an extended honeymoon trip to South Africa and Rhodesia. My pen still flowed readily and historical research led easily to characterization and plot. The BBC dramatized *Locusts* and it went into various overseas markets and satisfied me with its success. I was a minor celebrity. My knowledge of the world had matured. My hunt for half-remembered things had been converted into creative imagining.

I am a tall woman, six feet without shoes, but Rodney was much taller. I looked up into a pleasant, undistinguished face and kissed my new in-laws dutifully and greeted my new schoolgirl niece Chloe with a maternal embrace. I had absolutely no premonition of what was to come.

My daughter Ann Veronica by my disastrous first marriage was a shy eight year old, given to clinging to me and reluctant to meet strangers. I had told her we had not met Uncle Rodney and Aunt Janet before. To my surprise she went at once to Rodney, took his hand, sat beside him and wouldn't be parted from him throughout the day. He held her to him benevolently while speaking mostly to my husband and myself. Her eyes didn't leave his face—as once, I suppose, my own eyes couldn't leave the face of Uncle Reggie Carroll.

"Mummy, why did you say we hadn't met him before?" she asked in puzzlement as I tucked her into bed.

"Do you think we had?"

"Of course. When I was..." she hesitated and thought about it. "When I was little, he was always here", she said.

Rodney and Derry, as my husband Richard was known in the family, were the sons of a curious marriage between a retired

33

businessman and a girl in her mid-twenties. Frederick Collin-Smith had made a considerable fortune as a wine importer but had remained a bachelor, in spite of the twinkle in the eye which suggests to me he had not been uninterested in women. Before the first world war he bought a Georgian house on the high Marine Parade in Brighton and drove up and down in a dogcart with two highstepping ponies. His bride was the beautiful daughter of the proprietor of the Royal Crescent Hotel.

There was four years' difference in age between the boys. Curly-headed young Derry remembered going round the antique shops in the Lanes in Brighton with his tall, thin elder brother, browsing in bookshops, exploring old churches, sitting on the dolmen stone in the churchyard of St Nicholas, from which the original Brighthelmstone was named.

Rodney was interested in megaliths, stone circles, in pre-historic man, the beginnings of civilizations, the relics of the past and all that might lead to an understanding of the nature of God and man.

Like myself as a child, his upbringing was fairly conventionally Christian, though his mother read Theosophy and in her years of widowhood had allowed her mind to wander in less narrow confines of thought than those of the social circle in which they had previously moved. But as a youth, Rodney had heard nothing much of esoteric ideas and pursued his own line. As an eighteen year old he walked round Spain with a rucksack and a few pounds in his pocket, earning his way; and came back to write *Palms and Patios* which was a good beginning to a writer's life, for which he had an obvious aptitude.

He and Derry both embarked on careers in journalism. But though competent, Rodney found himself decreasing in purpose and drive, and ultimately a sense of desolation filled him. He told me later that the continual inner question: "Who am I?" plagued his younger years.

Seeking a cause to follow, he joined Toc H and worked for Tubby Clayton its founder: enlisted in the Peace Pledge Union and struggled with their propaganda against war: worked briefly as PR man for a number of minor good causes: and finally joined a team engaged on researching and writing the Daily Express Encyclopedia. The wealth of knowledge he acquired during those years of endeavour proved as useful to him in his later work, as my own reporting experience did to me.

One day, sitting on an upturned packing case in a flat into which he was moving, he found himself so overcome with despair at his inability to find companionship or a way of living that satisfied his hunger for reality, that he remembered the moment all his—alas, not long—life.

"I started looking about the empty room for some sign, some omen, some portent that might mean I had done well to move here", he told me. "There was a crumpled newspaper on the floor that had been used for packing. I happened to see the name Oberammergau. It was the year of the passion play, the last one before the war as it turned out. I thought I might as well go to it. Perhaps something interesting would happen to me there."

In fact he met his future wife, Janet Buckley. She was nearly ten years older than himself. Her father Wilfred Buckley had been Minister of Milk Production in the first world war. He was an authority on Venetian glass, and bequeathed the vast Buckley Collection to the Victoria and Albert Museum, where it is still displayed. Janet had grown up in luxurious circumstances, an adored only child, educated by governesses. She had developed a leaning towards Buddhism and Eastern ideas, and because of her longer span of living was way ahead of Rodney in her thought.

They fell in love. Because of the age difference she hesitated to agree to marriage. But soon her objections were overcome and the two remained together and were rarely parted.

Janet's exploring mind led her into divers fields of religion and philosophy, and eventually Rodney accompanied her to hear the Russian philosopher—Ouspensky—who had recently parted from Gurdjieff and was lecturing in London.

Rodney's first reaction was, as he told me: "This is the most interesting man I have ever encountered. But I'm not ready for him." However Janet attached herself to the Ouspensky following and Rodney gradually came into the circles himself, pondering more and more on the ideas that Gurdjieff had called "the Work", or the "Fourth Way".

Ouspensky, himself also a journalist, had published his

35

Tertium Organum and *A New Model of the Universe* as a result of his own researches into the nature of man. His basic theme was the growth of consciousness: that man's possibilities lie in this direction and that all efforts towards this end would be of immense value, leading on to the Fourth Dimension and other dimensions of experience.

Through the strange Caucasian Greek Gurdjieff, whom he encountered back in Russia, his own country, after lengthy wanderings in search of masters in India, he learned of methods and techniques and a pattern of development which could possibly bring into being the progress towards higher consciousness which had already become his aim.

Ouspensky's *In Search of the Miraculous* details the development of the relationship between the two men, and their eventual parting during the Russian revolution.

Ouspensky owed much to this teacher, whose knowledge was mysteriously profound and came from sources which have never been satisfactorily explained. Perhaps it was of Sufi origin. Perhaps it came from enclosed communities in the East, even in Tibet, where Gurdjieff professed to have travelled extensively. Perhaps Gurdjieff had invented his 'system' himself.

The apparent scientific basis of his thought, his knowledge of physics and chemistry, his wide familiarity with ancient oriental traditions that Ouspesky himself had been delving into for some time, together with his psychological insight and understanding, appealed to Ouspensky greatly.

But the many apparent contradictions in Gurdjieff's personality and his actions disturbed him. There were a number of instances of prevarication or deception which could scarcely be dismissed as mere peccadilloes, or an attempt to teach by allegorical means. In addition Gurdjieff's ruthlessness troubled Ouspensky more and more.

"It is better to die making efforts than not to make efforts", he said, when Ouspensky protested that he drove his followers too hard, too drastically. "For a man to wake up, become conscious, a big stick is necessary."

The exercise in attention known as the 'stop' exercise caused Ouspensky concern by the manner in which Gurdjieff imposed it on his followers. The demand was that, whatever the pupil might be doing at a given moment, on the command "stop" he

36

should at once become motionless in his present situation, "remember himself" as Gurdjieff put it.

Ouspensky saw it applied when a man was lifting a boiling hot glass of tea. Continuing to hold it in mid-air he suffered burns to his hand. Gurdjieff laughed, and recounted a tale of his own master—real or fictional—who according to him had called "stop" from within a tent in the Gobi Desert at a moment when one of his followers had his nose and mouth under water in the river, trying to retrieve some object. The aspirant remained motionless to a point of near suffocation until the order to continue was given.

Ouspensky saw the value of the 'stop' exercise, and continued to use it with his own followers later. But he was a more moderate and temperate man altogether, and no-one was to come to harm at his hands.

When the Revolution broke out Ouspensky remained within reach of Gurdjieff, deciding against escape to the west while the going was good. He followed him and his group to Georgia in South Russia. His devotion to Gurdjieff was such that, lacking transport or local accommodation, he frequently walked twenty miles in the snow at night and twenty miles back again, in order not to miss one of Gurdjieff's lectures. "There was often no room in the carriage, so there was nothing else to do", he said about this period later on.

The turning point appeared to come when Gurdjieff sent a follower back to Moscow at a time when his life would clearly have been in considerable danger. "I would not have sent a dog to Moscow at that time", Ouspensky wrote later.

After much pondering, and clearly in a state of deep inner distress, he parted from Gurdjieff and went to London. Around the same time Gurdjieff departed for Paris and eventually set up his headquarters at La Prieré, in Fontainebleau, near Paris.

"I confess I felt very foolish", Ouspensky wrote. "I had given up my career and all my prospects to remain with G. and I had ended by parting company with him."

Ouspensky found a patron in England and established himself there in his own right, lecturing regularly, and gradually attracting a fairly large following from among the intelligentsia in London. Gurdjieff had apparently always had a very mixed bunch of followers of various nationalities, and tending to what

Ouspensky described as "that stratum of lower middle class society from which nothing very interesting could be expected".

By contrast, Ouspensky attracted and cultivated the aristocratic, the literary and artistic levels of society, and above all the more intelligent and devoted types who were really more serious as far as personal development was concerned.

When Rodney Collin joined his ranks he was living at Gaddesdon, but subsequently moved to a country house called Lyne Place at Virginia Water. Janet, who was financially very comfortably placed, bought a large modern house in wooded grounds nearby. There she apprenticed herself to her master Ouspensky, working every day at menial tasks in the kitchens at Lyne Place, doing the 'stop' and 'self remembering' exercises and attending every lecture, taking the system of self-development very seriously indeed.

Rodney, working in Fleet Street by day, attended lectures spasmodically but spent more time working in the Lyne Place gardens, cultivating vegetables and fruit for the house.

By this time the idea of esoteric school had taken root in his mind. He was naturally a self-driving man, a self-actualizing man, to use Abraham Maslow's terminology. Once he got the bit between his teeth, he worked hard at everything he did, even at times to the point of exhaustion.

It was one of Gurdjieff's concepts that vigorous self-driving is necessary, and that if a man could work himself to the point of collapse and then get his 'second wind' and still continue, he would eventually cease to function on the normal store of energy that is available, and tap what he called 'the big accumulator." Here a finer type of energy would become available and accessible and would enable him to see what he is, to observe the various functions of the mind, and to develop in some way.

Rodney took to this idea more readily than to the lectures, and imposed upon himself rigid disciplines and exercises far beyond anything required of Ouspensky's followers.

By the time the second world war came, Ouspensky was an ageing man. He parted company temporarily with his wife, always known in the 'Work' circles as Madame. She decided on a move to the USA with as many of the followers as preferred her own, more extreme, more Gurdjieffian approach.

Ouspensky himself seemed more hesitant about the future. Then he broadcast his intention of joining Madame, and the remainder of the followers gave up their jobs, sold their houses, and went with him to Southampton. At the docks he suddenly announced he was not going. "I thought to take a holiday, but now I've changed my mind", he said. The assembled company was thrown into hysterical disarray. Some boarded the ship without him, others returned, homeless and jobless, to their own areas and in anxiety awaited the master's orders.

For a while Rodney and Janet were separated, he electing to stay in England, and she to go to the USA as previously planned, with their baby daughter. As well as the inheritance from her father, Janet had considerable resources in the USA from her American mother's estate, and these were largely diverted to help with the purchase of Franklin Farms near Mendham, New Jersey.

The work there with Madame appeared to grow more and more bizarre. People were subjected to almost absurd lengths of discipline or public humiliation in an attempt to break down what Gurdjieff had called the "false personality" behind which everyone hides his real nature, and to enable the true self to emerge.

Once the assembled company, dressed formally for dinner, were required to change clothes, donning each others' garments and jewellery at Madame's whim. People were frequently addressed publicly at the dinner table with contempt or extremes of rudeness. They were forced to endure all manner of deliberate methods of embarrassment. Janet accepted it all with fortitude, sure that through the ruthless method she was growing in self-understanding.

Madame frequently spoke in riddles, copying this from Gurdjieff whose tales and fantasies were by this time almost folklore. At one time Gurdjieff had assured Ouspensky that he was preparing a great pageant or masque to be called the Struggle of the Black and White Magicians. Any number of apparent preparations were made for the masque before Ouspensky realised that it was not a theatrical performance but a symbolic description of world events in the days ahead. Madame delighted in the same kind of invention, with allegorical or hidden meanings behind her words, which kept

39

people on their toes, puzzling over meanings which sometimes didn't even exist at all.

My friend Irene Nicholson, author of a number of books on pre-Columbian civilization in South and Central America, once arrived at Franklin Farms from London uninvited, and sent in a message "Miss Nicholson requests an interview with Madame and will wait". She waited and waited and waited. After some hours a secretary arrived with the reply:

"Madame says to Miss Nicholson, 'I am not here to help the weak but the strong.'"

Shattered, full of chagrin, Irene departed and returned full of distress to Ouspensky's household in England. It was not until some years had passed that, as she told me, long after Madame's death, it occurred to her that Madame had not in fact refused to help her at all. She had only to send back the message: "Miss Nicholson is still waiting", and she would almost certainly have been admitted. She had labelled herself as weak.

Eventually Ouspensky decided to leave England before war conditions made it increasingly difficult or impossible. Rodney and the remainder of the band sailed with him. During a lengthy and uneasy period at Franklin Farms, Rodney and Janet and their small daughter Chloe were together in the joint household.

Rodney was of course of an age to be drafted into national service, and in an attempt not to avoid this duty altogether, he got himself enrolled into the British Purchasing Commission and was sent to Mexico. Very shortly he was transferred back, apparently spontaneously, to New York, and resumed residence at Franklin Farms. He thus had an easy war, while his younger brother Derry served in the British Army in West Africa and Burma.

When speaking of this period to me later, Rodney said that he had resumed his self-appointed task of gardener, growing vegetables for the household at the end of his day's work. He was still an erratic attender at meetings and lectures.

Ouspensky was now lecturing regularly in New York in the evenings. Though Rodney hardly ever went, he would lie awake in his bedroom until he saw the lights of the returning car swing into the driveway. They were reflected on the walls of the room. Ouspensky would then enter the kitchen and sit drinking wine with whoever had been with him or had waited up for the opportunity to be in the master's company.

One night it occurred to Rodney with a sudden sense of revelation that he went to bed instead of to lectures, for a very different reason than he supposed. It had been easy to say that, after a day's work with the Purchasing Commission and the evening digging potatoes, he was too tired. Now he saw that, just as he had once said: "This is the most interesting man, but I'm not ready for him", he was again shirking some inner demand of his nature.

He told me: "I leapt out of bed, flung on my dressing gown without even bothering to fasten it and tie the cord, and ran downstairs and flung open the kitchen door with a crash". This was completely different from the exceedingly controlled and disciplined behaviour that was customary in the household, and contrary to his own normal behaviour too.

He quite expected to find a number of people sitting drinking wine together. He was still a junior member of the household and would not usually have joined them uninvited. It so happened Ouspensky was quite alone, sitting at the end of the long table with a bottle and a glass of wine. He was drinking fairly heavily by this time. Rodney said: "Before I lost courage and before I could control my words, I shouted at O"—as he always called Ouspensky in later years—"Why am I afraid of you?" O looked at me calmly and said: "why do you say 'I'?"

It was part of the teaching of the 'system' that people consist of many disunited 'Is'. The 'I' who goes to the office is different from the 'I' who is husband and father, or the 'I' who has aspirations to other personal aims. People even assume different 'Is' with different companions. In this sense, Gurdjieff said, "only God can say 'I', since only God is unity".

This comment of Ouspensky's, fairly commonplace as it may seem, hit Rodney with a sense of profound revelation: a typical Maslow or Colin Wilson 'peak experience'. It proved a turning point. From that moment the 'Work' took on new meaning in his life.

Invited to sit at the table with the master of the household, Rodney apparently poured out torrents of ideas while Ouspensky drank and listened. Eventually they repaired to his study, where he showed Rodney his collection of antique pistols, a hobby of which he was proud.

Some time during those hours Rodney told him: "I am a journalist. I want to write".

"You have nothing to write about", Ouspensky answered. "But stay with me and later we shall find you something to write."

When the war ended Ouspensky returned to Lyne Place, and Rodney, Janet and Chloe returned there together. Their house at Virginia Water had been commandeered by the Army and a gun emplacement had been planted in the rose garden. They took up temporary residence in a caravan in Lyne Place grounds.

By this time Rodney was much closer to Ouspensky, to the chagrin of older and more long-term followers. There appears to have been constant bickering and jealousy, and the interminable jockeying for position that occurs in any communal household round a master figure.

It is only right to say that Ouspensky never styled himself a master, as Gurdjieff had done. His approach to Work ideas was always humble. Having put forward a theme based on his own *Theory of Man's Possible Evolution*, he would always tell his followers not to believe what he said, but to "experiment, observe, find out for yourselves".

It was his followers who thought of him as a master. Longing, as do so many aspirants, to sit at the feet of a teacher, they addressed him always as Mr. Ouspensky, and showed respect amounting at times to reverence. Once a woman, in an impulsive move of humble adoration, dropped to her knees before him. He snapped at her sharply: "Get up at once! Never do that again". And turned from her in apparent extreme disapproval and contempt rather than embarrassment at the dramatic gesture.

Ouspensky's health deteriorated slowly. He seemed to like Rodney to be in attendance, treating him more as a son than as a disciple.

He embarked on a series of strange ventures, continuing almost to the day of his death. Rodney would be required to get the car out, and help, at times almost carry, Ouspensky into it. He was told to drive round all the old haunts, all the places

Ouspensky had lived in, or lectured in, or visited. At each place there would be long pauses while the dying man made attempts to memorize all observable details for 'next time round'.

The doctrine of recurrence which Gurdjieff had instilled into him was not the same as any normal version of reincarnation. Gurdjieff had told them it was useless to consider reincarnation as a practical study, since, even if it could be proved to have reality, the knowledge of it would serve no purpose.

"What if you have lived many times before? You have to work on yourself as you are now."

Recurrence, however, was a theory based on the idea that the essence of a man will recur in the same circumstances, experience the same things, until his level of consciousness grows to a point where he need not suffer the same trials and tribulations as before. He will then 'recur' in slightly better circumstances. He has no power to change his circumstances as such. But by changing his attitude to them he is doing something positive. Ouspensky was therefore apparently determined to remember everything he had done. He was determined to die consciously.

One night, sitting in the car outside the house, he demanded that his two cats be brought out to him. He held that cats had astral bodies, that they were the only animals so endowed. That was why they were used as witches' 'familiars'.

All night the old man sat in the back of the car with the cats, while Rodney sat in the front in silence. At intervals inquisitive, anxious or exasperated members of the household peered from the windows of the house or came out on to the porch and stooped to look into the car. Ouspensky acknowledged no-one. The cats sat side by side on his knees and he stared into space.

Later, in Mexico, Rodney showed me some private papers referring to this time. They contained certain details of his relationship with O that are not public knowledge. I presume that they were later destroyed, for his daughter Chloe has no knowledge of them. It has been suggested that the relationship was of a homosexual nature. Rodney was not homosexually inclined, and I do not think this to have been the case. Nevertheless the intimacy of the relationship increased, and with it the exasperated jealousy of the household.

So many people have claimed that Ouspensky died in their arms that they almost equal the number of beds in which Queen

Elizabeth slept. Rodney and Janet both talked openly of their version, and it is important when assessing Rodney Collin's two principal books, which were both published within three years of Ouspensky's death. His other books, *The Theory of Conscious Harmony* and *The Mirror of Light* are collections of extracts from his letters and writings put together posthumously by Janet. I am by no means sure he would have wished them all to see the light of day—but they have all remained in print continuously since 1956, finding a readership with successive generations. Not so a little series of booklets which Rodney published himself under the imprint *Editiones Sol* which show the strange state of his mind just prior to his death.

Ouspensky died on 2nd October 1947 in his bed at Lyne Place, in the presence of several people. A few hours before the end he had said to everyone around him: "I abandon the system. Start again for yourselves".

Rodney told me that he himself was supporting O in his arms when he died. Shortly after he breathed his last breath, and had been straightened out and covered, Rodney left the weeping group and entered the adjoining dressing room. He locked the door behind him. Here he remained for what has variously been reported as three, four or six days, responding to no knock or call or rattling at the door from without. In the meantime Ouspensky's body was removed from the bedroom and taken in due course for burial at Lyne church.

Janet told me that, after several days in which the household was in turmoils of distress, Dr. Francis Roles, a Wimpole Street lung specialist, who had been a close and faithful follower of Ouspensky's for years, assumed command of the group.

They began to consider whether they should indeed "abandon the system", or whether these were the rambling words of someone no longer in command of his own thoughts.

At the same time a growing anxiety for Rodney, shut in, silent, responding to no-one with any sound from within the small dressing room, caused increasing agitation. At Francis Roles' instigation, a ladder was placed up to the window of the room and somebody started to climb up in an attempt to look in. The prolonged silence had by this time alarmed everyone to such an extent that various people thought Rodney might be dead.

Suddenly the sash window shot up. Rodney's hand came out and with a violent push, sent the ladder hurtling back towards the ground.

Janet said: "At least everyone knew then that he was alive. I had tried to persuade Francis to leave him alone to his vigil, and after this he did".

Eventually the bell that Ouspensky had been accustomed to ring for attention, peeled loudly and continuously in the basement kitchen. No-one knew what exactly to expect. Janet was sent for and went to the bedroom, into which Rodney had moved. He was seated cross-legged on Ouspensky's bed, unshaven, emaciated, dirty.

According to Janet, he had neither eaten nor drunk during his long vigil and she maintained there was no water in the dressing room. Others have said there was, and that he could not have existed without liquid for anything like the length of time in which he is supposed to have been incarcerated. At any rate he was extremely thirsty. He asked for lime juice and Janet brought it to him.

"He looked very strange and childlike", she told me. "I had difficulty in communicating with him. I told him he must wash and shave. I brought him a comb and put it in his hand. He sat looking at it for a long time, turning it this way and that. He said 'this is the most beautiful comb I have ever seen'".

The comments Rodney made then and in the next few days sound almost like those of someone high on drugs. Aldous Huxley said in *The Doors of Perception* that when he experimented with mescalin he recollected having sat for a long time examining the tweed material of his trouser leg and believing the weave to be a most beautiful and remarkable creation.

In speaking of the vigil to me years later in Mexico, Rodney said that O had invaded his being in some way. That he felt his presence and thought he was being given direct messages of an extraordinary power and depth. Nothing mattered except that he attend to the inner experience consciously, minute by minute. He knew he must not be disturbed until it was over.

He perceived four interpenetrating levels of existence which he later called "the four worlds" and used as the basis of *The Theory of Eternal Life*. These were the mineral world, which responded to a very, very slow evolutionary process, worked to very slow vibrations: this he thought of as Hell. The cellular world, the world of the flesh, responding to a different time scale, faster vibrations, and representing Earth. The molecular world, the world of scents and sensual perception corresponding to Paradise. And the electronic world, equalling the speed of light, and loosely labelled Heaven. The worlds were not only interlinked and interpenetrating; they were conjoined by a time scale developing logarithmically, and by the logarithmic time scale man's essential nature and his development from conception to birth, to death or judgement, could be measured.

When he wrote *The Theory of Eternal Life*, Rodney painted the four worlds as four swirling circles of red, green, blue and gold, touching at a central point, and imposed the logarithmic time scale in a series of developing tubular patterns. Richard Giatt later repainted it, but it has rarely been reproduced in colour, and makes little impact without colour and clarity. A large copy of Giatt's original adorns my study wall and always excites attention by those who recognise what it is.

In recent years Tad Mann, the American astrologer, has taken Rodney Collin's logarithmic time scale theory and used it as the basis of his own astrological work in the *Round Art of Astrology, Life* Time Astrology* etc. He is a highly intelligent man whose work I value greatly. He finds it to be astrologically and possibly scientifically provable.

Shortly after leaving Ouspensky's room, Rodney asked to address the assembled household. There have been several versions of this event, which aroused excited interest in some and bewilderment or distaste in others. Clearly from the accounts he was still 'high'.

Within a short while he expressed a wish to leave Lyne Place. Janet found and rented a mansion flat in St. James' Street, London and they moved into it.

"At last O. has given me something to write", he said. And while Janet held many callers, importunate, inquisitive or urgent, at bay, he shut himself in his study and began.

4

By the time Rodney Collin visited us at Westerham *The Theory of Eternal Life* and *The Theory of Celestial Influence* were both in print and he was getting quite a following.

Francis Roles had taken on the remnants of Ouspensky's Lyne Place group, and the London followers who had been accustomed to attend the lectures at Ouspensky's headquarters next to the Royal Ballet School in Colet Gardens. There the various disciplines designed to bring about the development of the human potential were followed still, with the addition of various buttons and bows added from time to time by Dr. Roles himself.

Ouspensky had formed and registered a body called *The Society for the Study of Normal Man*, later changed by Francis Roles to the *Society for the Study of Normal Psychology*.

This innocuous sounding title which gave his studies and work an acceptable image, was based on Ouspensky's idea that man continually deviates from the 'norm' which ought in theory to be a state of balanced serenity and alert intelligence.

Gurdjieff was still teaching in Paris that "man is like a house wired for electricity but not yet connected to the mains". Great, even violent efforts were needed to enable him to cease groping about in his own property in the dark and "light up the rooms" so that he could begin to use his full possibilities.

Clearly only a small part of the human mind is accessible and in conscious use as yet. But Ouspensky in his later days had begun to say, that he was getting nowhere, was disappointed with his results and with his following. He believed that some sort of 'direct method' from outside himself needed to be found.

The Gurdjieff concept, which Ouspensky had accepted, was that several levels of 'man' already exist, from the primitive to the technologically advanced, and these he had labelled Man

47

Nos. 1, 2, 3 and 4. The effort required was to develop Man No. 5, an increasingly conscious man, more in control of his own destiny than the lower states. But beyond this, there must also exist in theory, Man No. 6 and Man No. 7, both of them slightly nebulous concepts of higher states of being.

The idea of a direct method had held Rodney from early days, hence his vigorous personal efforts and attempts to raise both the level of his knowledge and the level of his being—what a man is, in himself.

These two lines must, Gurdjieff had said, keep abreast with one another. Where knowledge outran being one got the chaos inherent in modern society, where scientific and technological knowledge is wielded by men of little inner stature who are leading the world into an increasingly dangerous state. Where being outran knowledge however, the result would be what Gurdjieff described as a "stupid saint". Such people would tend to do nothing towards man's development in the long run, since they would become increasingly inactive and content with the status quo.

Rodney, ever active and vigorous, resolved to keep the two lines equal and to develop in his own way according to his own inner convictions. Soon after emerging from the intense period of writing in the St. James' Street flat, he decided to go and live in Mexico, to which he had been drawn during his travels for the British Purchasing Commission. He was still to some extent on a 'high' and appeared to have a childlike, innocent and trusting attitude in his dealings with others, rather at variance with his previous apparently slightly peremptory manner.

Those who wanted to carry on with Ouspensky's work exactly as he had left it were mostly content with Francis Roles. Francis however distrusted the transformation in Rodney and was troubled by the way people seemed to be drifting over to him. Rodney in fact was not seeking disciples. He was a man who was set on 'going somewhere', and if others cared to string along they could do so, but he was largely indifferent as to whether they did or not.

Francis was a cautious and careful man. He gradually developed a marked tendency to restrict his followers. He told them who they should or should not have dealings with and what they should or should not read. Eventually there was a list of proscribed books almost like that of the Roman Catholic Church. These included the writings of Maurice Nicoll whose *Commentaries on the Teachings of Gurdjieff and Ouspensky* and *The Mark* were thought unsuitable reading. And all the work of J.G.Bennett. Both these intelligent and clearly 'self-actualizing' men had been pushed out by Ouspensky to develop their own lines rather than toeing anyone else's.

Rodney Collin's *Theory of Eternal Life* and *Theory of Celestial Influence* were soon among the forbidden reading, apparently on the grounds that their contents were by no means provable and might be scientifically inaccurate.

Also all those people who had once worked with Ouspensky and had since left, or who still worked with Gurdjieff, were declared persona non grata, and soon Rodney Collin's followers were added to the list.

The situation developed to such an exaggerated extent that husbands and wives, parents and children in different branches or splinter groups of the Work were forbidden to communicate.

Sergei, the anglicized son of an elderly erudite Russian lady, Madame Kadloubowsky, was told he must no longer talk to his own mother. Madame K. as she was affectionately known was exceedingly scholarly and very well respected. She had translated the *Philokalia* into English. She had access to all Ouspensky's lecture notes, many of which she had herself prepared. She gradually sorted and edited them, and eventually published them as a large volume under the simple title *The Fourth Way*.

The name came from Gurdjieff who had described the various methods of development that he was familiar with as: 1. The Way of the Fakir: development by physical means. 2. The Way of the Yogi: development by mental means. 3. The Way of the Monk: development by way of the emotions. And the Fourth Way: an amalgam of all three, which would enable a man to fulfill himself in the world, in life, instead of by withdrawal into recluse-like states.

When Ouspensky had said in his last days "I abandon the system" he had also instructed those about him that nothing further of his writings or his lectures was to be published. Francis Roles was therefore very heated and angry at Madame K's action, which he regarded as direct disobedience of the master's wishes. Madame K. in her wisdom disappeared from the scene, and from her flat in Edwardes Square, Kensington, just got on with the job she had set herself. Her son Sergei, an architect who had abandoned his Russian name and was now known as George Kadleigh, was in some distress, and he and his wife Lesbia were torn between the desire to follow Francis Roles and their instinct that son should not be parted arbitrarily from mother. Many other relatives and erstwhile bosom companions on the Way were likewise tormented over their personal attachments—as were the Scientologists, and 'the Moonies' later on.

Once a couple of years later I asked Francis Roles about these problems with relationships, and he answered that it was his duty to "keep the system pure" and to "protect people in the Work".

"Why have you banned Rodney's people? Not one could be a more faithful follower of O."

"He's a violent man", Francis Roles said. "He will die a violent death."

Recalling Rodney's mild and gentle manner, I probed further and learnt that on one occasion in the past Rodney had lost his temper with Francis and had thrown a coffee cup at him. There was also the matter of the ladder pushed away from the window. He had a third story, involving Rodney slapping the side of his face so hard in the course of some awareness or endurance exercise that his eardrum was split. This tale was retold by my friend James Webb in *The Harmonious Circle*, with the added information that Roles had been permanently deafened as a result.

I never saw the slightest sign of violence in Rodney myself. Nor do I personally recollect Francis Roles suffering anything save the slight deafness of old age in his later years.

When I first met my brother and sister-in-law, it was Janet rather than Rodney who interested me in the Work ideas. Less clear headed than Rodney, however, she muddled her way through explanations of growth of consciousness etc. and was unable to explain the system with any clarity.

Rodney and I talked of journalism, of books, of art, of philosophy and religion in a generalized way and with no apparent purpose or pattern behind the series of conversations, at Westerham and later in the mansion flat which they had retained in St. James Street. I found him easy and congenial company. I was glad to know him. But I recognised nothing remarkable and nothing familiar or significant about him.

Like Celendine Kennington some years before, Janet set about a vigorous proselytising effort, and eventually got me to visit Francis Roles in Wimpole Street. Here I was admitted into a small, afternoon group of beginners. I could not attend evening meetings for my daughter was still at day school and I had to get home to Kent in time to look after her.

The first question Francis Roles asked me was: "What do you want?" This was apparently a standard opening gambit to enquirers for information as aspirants for entree into the now increasingly enclosed circles of the esoteric teaching. After a moment's thought I answered: "To go back where I came from. To go back to God".

People apparently tended to give answers ranging from: "To be perfect"; "to attain unity"; "to help the evolutionary process"; "to understand God"; "to understand myself"; or "know what it's all about", and a variety of others.

By focussing the attention of the individual on his own wishes, his own needs, Francis got everyone going on disciplines and exercises of observation. The drastic 'stop' exercise had been abandoned, but there had been a build-up of the 'self-remembering' technique.

To practise this, the student would, as often as possible during the day, be aware of himself in the time and place in which he found himself; of his posture, his feet on the ground, the feel of his clothes upon his body, the people and objects around him; and use his senses to the full to record everything seen, heard, smelt, tasted or touched in that moment of time.

While this may sound relatively easy, it soon becomes apparent that it is a state that can't as a rule be sustained for more than a minute or two. Almost at once vigilance is relaxed as some object of attention—a word, a sound, an item of furniture—attracts attention and one becomes 'identified' with that one thing and only marginally aware of everything else.

Ouspensky recorded that he had once resolved to "remember himself" while walking down the Nevsky Prospect in Moscow while working there with Gurdjieff. He had set out in an alert state, observing the horses and carriages, the pedestrians and the buildings on either side of the road. An hour or two later he again "woke up", remembered himself", back in his own apartment. In the mean time he had called at his tobacconist and ordered his special cigarettes, had been to a stationer and bought some pens and done a couple of other routine errands, all in the state of 'waking sleep' in which most of the day's activities of ordinary men and women are carried out.

The state of 'waking sleep' or 'identification' in which people bustle about their day-to-day affairs is indicative of the generally low level of consciousness of the individual, which in turn is reflected in the low level of order and purpose or unity in the nation or in the world at large. Tommy Steele, in Moscow in the days of his rock and roll youth, commented that all its citizens "look as though they are hurrying to Woolworths to buy a pot of paint or something, and all they can think of is 'Woolworths—paint'". One might of course say the same of London or any other city. Each person is locked in with his own individual problems and ideas and intent on his immediate purposes.

I liked the self-remembering exercise. Naturally observant, perhaps as a result of my journalistic background, I found it relatively easy to maintain for a few minutes at a time. I was also conscious after a while of being rather more observant as a general rule than many of the pleasant assortment of people in the group, who surprised me by not being able to recall on demand what they had had for breakfast that day, exactly the position in which they had parked their car, or what route they had taken on their way to work.

It soon became apparent to me that it was not only the 'inner voice', the 'listening to God' sort of technique that was needed in order to find out who one really was, and what one should be doing; it was also the cultivation of the world around by the full and constant usage of the senses.

Once, sitting on a table in the sixth form common room at school as a thin, long-legged teenager, while we schoolgirls discussed our adolescent philosophy, a sudden small peak experience caused me to burst out with: "Anyway, there are two different ways of doing it. One is like the nuns here, walking about with their heads down and hands in their sleeves, not looking at anything, not touching anyone, always looking for God somehow inside. The other is going round with your head up and looking at everything, and getting involved, and—and love and sex and all that sort of thing and really wanting to be part of the world, because that's God too."

Going up in the lift to the flat in Wimpole Street where Dr. Roles held those afternoon meetings in his private apartment above his consulting rooms, I thought one afternoon of that moment suddenly with an opening up of a new channel of understanding. Through 'listening to God' and through self-remembering—experiments far apart from each other, and bridged by the war years and my personal and private tragedies, I had grasped the nature of the two modes of the Creator. God immanent and God transcendent had suddenly become comprehensible to me.

In spite of rules and regulations, I managed to keep in touch with Rodney and Janet and remain in Dr. Roles' group as well, for quite a long time. I soon discovered that, though he had inherited a most interesting and ancient teaching, it was becoming successively watered down through each new leadership. The present adherents, though growing in number—Francis Roles had a couple of hundred followers when I was with him, and laid claim to over a thousand at a later stage of his endeavours—there was an uninspired mediocrity in almost all who followed him.

They were mainly professional people, mostly middle-aged, and unlike the Moral Rearmament Movement, keen and lively youngsters were rarely admitted at all. In fact the enclosed nature of the Work activities meant that outsiders of any kind were viewed with a certain amount of suspicion. It was considered an activity of major and on the whole undesirable proportions to "bring anyone into the Work".

The Work people had been taught, in Gurdjieff's terminology, that they could not "do". That is, that everything just happened to them, since they lived entirely under the law of chance, and only by the positive breaking down of their 'false personality' could they begin to grow. To this end they must offer themselves wholly to their new master, obeying his whims and wishes with humility and not questioning his motives or his laws.

No longer was there Ouspensky's liberal 'don't believe what I say, find out for yourselves' attitude. Neither was there the ruthless and vigorous authority of Gurdjieff, who clearly really knew many things above the normal level of man's understanding of life. Instead, a petty despotism was developing. Roles was therefore attracting those who wanted a master, rather than a teacher or adviser with knowledge beyond their own. This meant the intake, though carefully vetted, was essentially confined to those who wanted to be told what to do. There was a passive obedience in them. It was easy to tell them what not to read, who not to see, where not to go. They asked his permission for almost every action, even in their private and personal lives, sometimes not accepting an invitation of any kind without first seeing if he agreed. I invited a number of people to Westerham, but only those who were 'trusties' were permitted to accept.

There was no such obedience in me. I wanted to go to the source of any knowledge that might be within reach. I therefore read everything I could get hold of by Gurdjieff and Ouspensky themselves, and Rodney's writings, Nicoll's and Bennett's. Rather than cause a furore of disapproval, I simply got on and did it. In the same way I continued to see everyone I wanted to know, but kept my mouth shut about it.

One of my friends was Lady Abercrombie, widow of Sir John Abercrombie who had been in the Diplomatic Corps in India. They had lived in circles into which she had been born, for her father had himself been in the Indian diplomatic service and she had spent her girlhood there.

Elsie was old enough to be my mother, and wise enough too. Her physical health was failing, but mentally she was exceedingly alert, spiritually much more advanced, I thought, than the bulk of Work people, as well as being much more widely read. As a girl in India she had constantly sought a master. Once, out riding alone, she had been impelled to stop her horse and climb over the wall of a Maharajah's estate, convinced there was something of consequence to her on the other side. There, sitting in the lotus posture under a tree was a holy man. She had met many such, and usually they turned out on further investi-

54

gation to be rather disappointing. However her enquiring mind caused her to go through what she knew to be the courteous method of approach.

She sat down on the ground herself, a considerable distance off, not looking at him, and waited quietly until he invited her to come near. She then rose, gave him the Hindu respectful palm to palm greeting, and seated herself a little nearer. In the course of an hour's conversation—she spoke fluent Hindi—she heard him say: "No, I am not your master. Your master is in the West. Go now and seek him. He awaits you". There were certain other indications which made her feel she would recognise the right man when she saw him, and these led her to P.D.Ouspensky. She had worked with him and under his direction in London with disciplined devotion. But she had been one of those who had been first to see and recognise that Rodney Collin had experienced something and should now be followed with confidence. While maintaining polite contact with Francis Roles and all her former friends, she also cultivated Rodney and other deviant groups privately and with discretion, and kept her own counsel.

I learnt much more from Elsie Abercrombie than from anyone else in the Work groups in London. We developed a close and valued friendship in which we repeatedly discussed our experiences and ideas. Both of us had become increasingly conscious that only a small part of the human mind is in use as yet. In certain circumstances extra powers, extra knowledge, extra strength can be drawn upon. The question was, how could one achieve this by intention or will? Mostly it occurred only by apparent chance.

Although slight in build, Elsie had an extraordinary recollection of once having carried her fully adult six foot brother on her back. When riding in India his horse had bolted in dangerous terrain and the fall had broken his leg. In going to his assistance she had lost her own mount, both animals having been apparently frightened by the scent of tiger. She dared not leave him while she went miles back on foot to seek assistance. In the same way that men have been known to lift a car single-handed off a trapped child in their desperation, Elsie lifted and carried the tall young man the whole way home. Physically the deed would have seemed impossible, and afterwards she had no recollection of how she had mustered the strength or bent her will to it.

Elsie was also full of stories of her childhood which intrigued me by the knowledge that she had certain natural powers that other people did not have the use of. At an early age she had discovered it to be possible to influence other people's words and actions. Once in India, banished by her mother from a formal gathering, she had returned to her schoolroom and set herself in pure mischief to influence events downstairs. They would all start talking compulsively of something silly, something irrelevant, and be unable to stop, she determined.

Her mother, knowing her gift, came up sternly half an hour later and shook her: "Stop it at once, you naughty girl! They're all talking and talking about —"

"Camels?" said Elsie with an innocent look. And so it proved to be. On many other occasions in her later years she had attempted to use this ability to useful purpose. Frequently it worked. People she desired to contact, telephoned. Events turned out for her, or for her friends, to good advantage. She once appeared to support and guide me away from disaster, driving in heavy snow at night near her Hampshire home. But she had no idea how she did these things. She had simply 'seen' me approach a blind corner where the camber was bad and had 'steered' me.

Such episodes greatly strengthened my longing to find a method which would awaken latent possibilities. And I was beginning to think that the Work ideas, disciplines and practices, though interesting, were unlikely to achieve anything much this side of the grave. Only in successive incarnations or 'recurrences' would one perhaps get results.

I resolved therefore to go and visit my brother-in-law in Mexico.

5

I flew in over the Gulf of Mexico just as the sun was going down. In the late afternoon the sunbaked landscapes of Georgia and South Carolina were visible below. Then the aircraft swung out over the sea, circled and began the descent to the strange Valley of Mexico 7,000 feet above sea level, surrounded by mountains reaching to nearly 18,000 feet.

Because of the altitude, Mexico City has a curious effect on the new arrival. Having descended from the air, one has no sense of height until it becomes apparent that breathing is altered and that steps and stairs must be taken slowly, running avoided. The rarified air takes several days to get used to.

Rodney and Janet met me at the airport and took me at once to an outdoor restaurant which was their favourite eating place. Although they, in common with most English and American families, kept servants, eating out was largely the custom. Restaurants stayed open till midnight or two in the morning, when the night was cool, and were always thronging with people. Mariachis—singers with wide sombreros and Mexican Spanish guitars—serenaded the diners in most places. The haunting Spanish type music with its curious mixture of European and Mexican-Indian rhythms, even now when I hear it on radio or television, transplants me mentally to the atmosphere, the scents and sounds and memories of patio gardens strung with coloured lights in the trees, warm night air, and the heady taste of tequila sipped with a touch of salt and a slither of lemon, in the custom of the country. Hot chilli sauce on chicken molé, the lush, semi-tropical fruits, the flat tortillas like unleavened pancakes are all built into my taste buds in perpetuity.

I had by now not only read Rodney's books, but corresponded with him extensively. But I remembered him personally only as the mild and amiable man I had known for a few weeks on his visit to England a couple of years previously. Whether through flight fatigue, altitude or the tequila, I began to feel within an hour in his company here in Mexico that I was dealing with someone totally different from my recollection.

He was wearing a vivid blue shirt open at the neck and hanging outside his trousers. The sunbrowned skin accentuated the now greying, longish hair that curled up and away from his face. He seemed exceptionally tall. His eyes, like Elsie's and my own and those of a number of people who all seem to me to be part of the same group soul or some such thing, were of an exceptional blue. Sitting opposite him at the restaurant table in the patio garden I found we were looking deeply into each other's eyes. And his had, without any doubt at all, the same look about them as those of Reggie Carroll.

At first in Mexico City I talked my head off, asking questions and expressing my opinion on everything. I felt always slightly lightheaded. Rodney had round him a group of those English men and women who had followed him from London, but these were now outnumbered by the Spanish-speaking Mexicans. As a result, he lectured mainly in Spanish, and almost all group meetings were in that language too. This exasperated me, for I felt I had no time to learn the language fluently. I felt left out. In fact the more demanding I became, the more I felt that, though friendly, no-one was really interested in me at all and that I would be taught nothing in the long run. Everything was going on round me at a great pace, but little was explained.

Rodney had started the only English bookshop in Mexico City, the Libraria Britannica. It still flourishes. He had acquired a mine in the largely unexploited mountainous interior of the country, and was exploring it with a group of peons. It could yield silver, salt and various nitrates. But like most such projects in those days, the absence of roads and the intransigence of the authorities combined with the dilatoriness of the workers to make the mineral-rich mountain areas not really a very viable proposition.

He had bought an old hacienda and installed there a group of peasant women to weave the brilliantly coloured Aztec design blankets and serapes that the American tourists dearly coveted. He had tried to get an export licence for them, but once again bureaucratic stubbornness thwarted the enterprise after a year or two.

His other big project was the building of a planetarium, high in the hills twenty miles or so out of Mexico City. The City is the third largest in the Western hemisphere, and is a hotchpotch of American skyscrapers, wide, five-line highways of fast-moving traffic, Mexican-Spanish architecture, some of it ornate and rather beautiful, and districts of shady boulevards and modern residences in tree-lined gardens. There are also large areas of tenement blocks and slums occupied by the poorer Mexicans and the Indio peons.

Just beyond the boundaries of the city, the wide, cactus-strewn and arid-looking lands stretch out. And beyond that, the snow-capped mountains of Popocatepetl and Izztaccihuatl are almost always visible. To leave the high valley, you must go up through the mountains. Then you drop down then into the tierra calliente, the semi-tropical hotlands. Here, colour abounds—in the flowers, the blossoming trees, the fruits, the clothes that people wear. Though the peons out in the wild country dress soberly in dark skirts and rebosos over their heads and the men in white with a serape folded over the shoulder, on the many fiesta days they appear in an assortment of hues and variants of the Spanish style and Mexican national costume. In the clear, light air beyond the city colour is everywhere. There was no smog in those days though at times it plagues the city now.

The planetarium site had been cleared and work was going on apace. Rodney had recruited a team of peons to hew into the volcanic rock that forms the basis of much of the land inside the circle of mountains. He had designed a building to consist of two interlinking circles below ground level. These were to be the Chamber of the Sun and the Chamber of the Moon. Between the two was a small circular space where a large upturned shell on a pedestal caught the sun through an aperture above at the summer solstice.

Around the two chambers, hewn deep into the relatively soft rock, was a narrow, curving passage way. The walls were being adorned bit by bit with mosaics showing the development of man, from the primordial forms of life to the perfect man. Rodney worked daily cutting and placing the mosaics, while the peons continued to build above ground. Here, the upward continuation of the underground chambers was to become a lecture hall, with a floor suitable for ritual or national dancing, exercises and the Gurdjieff-style 'movements' which were used to develop concentration and attention. The other chamber was to be a library, to house Rodney's now enormous collection of esoteric books. The planetarium itself, onto which a moving programme of the starry heavens could be projected, was to come in due course under the great domed roof. No definite plans for the completion of the project however were ever actually prepared.

Rodney laboured against odds in many ways. Janet's money was more than adequate. But he trusted everyone too readily, and first the foreman and then other employees milked his resources—including one large swindle—and progress was very slow. He had supervised the laying out of a long, steep, winding road as an access way from the only nearby motor road. He set beside it boulders on each of which he hewed out a Sign of the Zodiac and began to paint them in clear colours. I remember him kneeling in the hot wind and the dust working away, a red shirt open to the waist, a sombrero on the back of his head. Seeing the chisel, I thought of Eric Kennington in the studio at Homer House long ago, saying: "God gave me hands to chip with, I shall chip". While Francis Roles' people were intent on examining their own inner natures, Rodney was determined to get on and *do* something with his life.

Seeing the poverty and lack of health care for the peasant workers, Janet meanwhile opened a clinic and employed the services of a doctor from the city to attend there. The women and children queued for his arrival twice a week. Janet and Chloe, now aged eighteen, and a band of helpers sewed bright, full skirts and frilly blouses to give to the poorest, who were pretty much in rags.

Water was piped up at last, and gardens were laid out. They were planted with vegetables in narrow terraces, and with small shrubs and young trees to give shelter from the hot sun. The volcanic soil proved very fertile.

At the time of my visit, work at the planetarium was gradually taking over from all the other projects. We drove up there most days. Rodney's creative drive and imagination, and his manual skills, were considerable, and his energy seemed boundless. He was also so much in demand to answer comments and questions and deal with matters of a philosophical nature, that it was difficult to get a word with him at all. To do so one must pick up tools or implements and work with or beside him on whatever was then demanding his attention.

I felt that I wanted to learn from him. There was a quality of dignity and authority in him. His lectures, as much as I could make out of them, were veering further and further away from the Gurdjieff and Ouspensky teachings, and getting into a sphere where action and giving service to the people of the world, attention to the needs of the planet, were of paramount importance.

Increasingly agitated by the difficulty of communication, the sense of something important eluding me, I eventually managed to button-hole him one day in his study at the large apartment in Rio Nazas which was then their home. A previous communal household at a hacienda at Tlalpam, had been abandoned just before I came, as having run its course.

Rodney normally sat cross-legged or in the half-lotus when teaching or when talking at home, the posture that I always assumed myself. He was seated thus in a wide chair, with the white, slatted Venetian blinds cutting the hot rays of the afternoon sun and striping everything with light and shadow. On his large desk were an assortment of papers, letters and manuscripts. On a wall to one side was a huge painting of Ouspensky sitting with his two cats on the arms of his chair, which Rodney himself had done.

I sat on a long sofa and tried with increasing urgency and exasperation to question him about the basis of his present day thought.

"I don't understand anything! I am waiting to get some sort of revelation what your work is actually all about", I burst out finally. The blue eyes regarded me benignly.

"Joyce, nothing can happen until you are quiet", he said.

Until that moment I had not realised the depth and extent of my own inner agitation.

I made some effort to relax my body in an attitude of

self-remembering: to listen to the inner voice in MRA style: to be more fully aware in some way of the present situation. We remained in silence.

Suddenly the room began to swim in a rather alarming way. I thought the slatted light and shadow might be about to give me a migraine headache, to which I have always been slightly subject. I said shakily: "Could you close the blind, Rodney?"

He reached behind him and pulled the cord. The lines of black and white disappeared and the room became marginally dimmer. Still we looked at one another and nothing was said.

Then slowly Rodney's face began to change in shape and type. I couldn't understand what was happening.

"You look like an old man", I blurted out. "There's a growth of a bit of a beard —"

"It's only because I haven't shaved for a few days", came a voice out of Rodney's mouth that was not Rodney's voice at all.

Frightened, I glanced about the room in confusion. Then I looked back again. The face of the man crosslegged in the chair was the square, heavy-jawed, bespectacled visage of Piotr Damianovitch Ouspensky, Rodney's beloved master, always known in the household now simply as O.

"You are Mr. Ouspensky!"

"I was called that," answered a different, guttural voice.

In a few moments, the O face faded completely, and like a television programme in which one picture is panned in over another, an oriental face appeared.

"You're Chinese now."

"Tibetan", he answered.

Then with great rapidity, a series of different faces superimposed themselves one on another—dark-skinned, middle-eastern, Mediterranean, northern European, of several different apparent ages and types, some wearing headgear of one kind or another. My heart thumped as I watched.

"Who are you?" I asked at last.

"All these and many others too", answered the voice of Rodney Collin, and his sunburned, grey-haired, blue-eyed twentieth century face appeared as normal as if it had been there all the time.

"Your other lives?"

"The curtain of time grows thin", he answered me.

62

Later, I cross-questioned myself and examined and re-examined in my mind the strange phenomenon. Had it been perhaps just a trick of light and shadow? A neurological migraine-type visual disturbance? Sheer imagination? Eventually I asked several other people in the household and among the many followers who came and went constantly, if they had experienced something similar with Rodney.

To my consternation, no-one had. Then I found in a little while that the phenomenon was centred in myself. Janet, seated on her bed, combing her hair, suddenly assumed a series of other faces, and as I began to speak of it, she turned into a Tibetan child.

"I think I'm your daughter", her voice—Janet's own voice—said. "You promised to do something for me, about the weight. You said you would bear it for me."

I had been having increasing problems with my own weight recently. From a thin young girl, I had grown decidedly plump after the birth of my only daughter and the breakdown of my first marriage. This had grown even more of a problem in recent years, so that I was now on an almost perpetual diet and was thought to have a possible hormone imbalance. At once it seemed to me as though a half memory was stirred. The high valley of Lhasa again, the lamasery bells—how did I know, so very well, the curious flat note they made? The constant wind, the prayer wheels, the flags blowing on the stone cairns. And I, an old woman now, with a fat round, middle-aged daughter, padded and quilted, distressed about her weight. "I wish I could bear it for you", I seemed to have said.

I am aware now that this phenomenon, known generally in psychic circles as 'transfiguration', is a known occurrence, not particularly uncommon in those who are a little clairvoyant. It occurred again and again in Mexico, repeated itself intermittently on my return to England, and eventually became something I could occasionally—though by no means always—induce at will.

Later a woman in the Work in London saw different faces in mine, as I reclined in bed in her flat in Sussex Gardens, reading a book, propped among pillows.

"You look Grecian," she said suddenly. "I can see you down to the waist and you're wearing a white robe." And a moment

63

later: "Now you have an Egyptian face." Both times I heard myself answer "yes", as though from a dim memory in the depth of my being. I had felt the pull of a heavy white linen garment across one shoulder and felt my hair was pulled back and banded high. Then I had felt the heavily made-up Egyptian face, black kohl accentuating the eyes. In a moment it was gone. I could put no name or place or period to it.

After the incident in Rodney's study everything began to move very fast indeed. I had the curious impression that time had expanded in some way, so that every sixty seconds was filled with a great deal more than a minute's worth of experience, every day with as many impressions as one might normally take in in a week. I seemed to be continually slotting in and out of time, to see myself and those around me in a variety of different roles, all old roles, all familiar ones.

Rodney commented in answer to my question: "I think it may be that there is such a thing as a group soul. We incarnate within reach of each other, but in different relationships. Former lovers are now mother and son, father and daughter, or just friends and co-workers—that sort of thing." Still the moment of recognition of Rodney himself did not come. I was concerned not only with the mysteries of other possible identities, but also very much with the question of my own identity. Who was I? What had I to do?

A number of people flew down from the United States to see Rodney. There were in fact continual visitors flying in from all over the place, and Rodney would be closeted with various people talking privately. In the evenings the household and guests would usually go out somewhere to dine around eleven or midnight. There might be any number from four of us to twenty. The talk was always of philosophy, of growth of being, development of knowledge, awakening of consciousness, and methods and ways leading to this end.

Rodney had tried marathons of endurance, walking long distances in the heat, without water and rest, sometimes continuing for several days. His faithful second in command, John Grepe, who was then running the Libraria Britannica, and an assortment of others would accompany him, keeping going as long as they could before collapsing.

There was something a bit extreme about these experiments,

and they appeared to be having little or no effect on anyone save Rodney himself. He was becoming increasingly exhausted. Somehow one was always conscious that he was a very 'big man'. Not that he gave any indication of feeling this himself, for his attitude was modest and humble in the extreme. But he was very impressive, attracting attention everywhere.

One evening the restaurant party included Hugh Ripman, who had worked with both O. and Madame in New York and had arrived on a flying visit.

We were seated opposite one another at the long table. A shy, controlled, self-disciplined man, he was, I thought, a little difficult to talk to. This applied to many of the long-term Work people. They developed such strong self-awareness and serious purpose, that their lives became circumscribed in some way and they had absolutely no small talk whatsoever.

I was asking Hugh something about the nature of consciousness, the real meaning of the Work in the Gurdjieff sense. What was the Big Work? Gurdjieff had said that in order to be "in the Work" a man had to be of use to himself, and of use to his master, and of use to the Big Work.

Hugh Ripman began a careful explanation of his understanding of this somewhat abstruse subject, which Gurdjieff himself had never clearly defined but which was generally thought to have something to do with the evolution of mankind. I was watching him and listening intently. He was an intelligent man who had been making great efforts over a good many years. However he had, as many people seemed to have, difficulty in formulating the basis of his own beliefs.

Suddenly the intentness of our concentration on one another had a curious effect. Hugh said: "I would very much like to help you. I am trying to explain —"

At this point his words became completely lost in what appeared to me like a vast and instantaneous opening of the inner doors of my mind. I remember saying:

"I know! I know! I've always known. I had simply forgotten. How could I have forgotten what is so obvious?"

I felt that I had expanded in myself to fill the room, to fill all space available. That I was centred everywhere and nowhere. That I was part of everyone and everything around me. That in some sense I myself was God. After an unknown period, perhaps only a few seconds, I descended again to the normality of the restaurant, the noisy chatter at other tables, the waiter clattering the plates. Hugh's expression was a half-smile of nervous embarrassment. He had evidently said a number of things to which I had not attended at all, but none of them warranting this loud, emotional outburst. I felt tears in my eyes.

"You have given me a key that will unlock all doors", I said. He cleared his throat and said anxiously that he was very glad if he had helped to clarify anything.

I have tried a great many times in vain to recall the details of the words that passed between us. I never saw Hugh Ripman again. He can have had no personal feeling for me, nor I for him. But the obvious gathering together of all his resources in a disciplined attempt to help, had apparently combined with my own depth of hunger and need, to trigger off some inner reaction in my mind. For a moment I 'knew'. But the conscious mind still did not grasp the nature of the secret, or understand the source of its own sudden great rush of happiness.

I felt for days afterwards that I knew something, but I didn't know what I knew: a curious paradox familiar to those who have been through the doors of perception and glimpsed the truth of things. Like fairy gold, it turns to pebbles in the morning. It is not the currency of everyday living, and can never be used as a gift or as payment for anything.

All the same I now 'knew' what was the nature of the 'urgent thing forgotten' which had so haunted my childhood days, even though I was unable to communicate its nature to others. The best I could do was to say: "It is something to do with the stream of creativity: with conscious co-operation with all that flows out from the Creator, so that we the 'creatures' become aware of our own innate nature, and turn deliberately back again towards the source of our being."

From then on I was immensely happy for all the remainder of my months in Mexico.

Rodney took a few days off and announced that he would take me and several others to one of the Aztec and Toltec sites, Teotihuacan, the City of the Gods. The extraordinary pyramids and the remains of the old civilizations that are scattered in largely uninhabited country throughout Mexico were of great interest to me, and he had already shown me several. He held that the Aztecs, who had ritually slaughtered prisoners on top of some of the pyramids, were the debased remnants of the much older Toltec culture. The Toltecs were the people who knew, whose complex, verbally transmitted teaching had come down only as fragments from the pre-Spanish Conquest days. Golden towers and domes had risen from the islands in the waters of the then flooded Valley of Mexico, and long causeways had linked them to the land around. The beautiful golden City of Tennochtitlan, which Hernando Cortes and the Conquistadores robbed and desecrated, had evidently been a place of a very high, ancient culture.

Jewels, and the great feathered headdress of Monctezuma, the last emperor, still exist. And the huge, stone Aztec calendar, twelve feet across, preserved in the Academy of Fine Arts in Mexico City is evidence of a complex and profound knowledge of planetary movements and of the nature of time.

On the eve of setting out on what was to be our special expedition to the city of the gods, I sprained my ankle badly. It swelled up enormously, and though I strapped it tightly, being used to sprained ankles, I had the greatest difficulty in putting it to the ground. The party thought of leaving me behind, with my foot up on the sofa and the maids to look after me at the apartment.

I was determined to go. I hopped to the car. Janet, sensibly enough, objected that I was too incapacitated to be able to cope with the rough ground at the only partially excavated city. But Rodney said: "Joyce is to come", and helped me in beside him.

The layout of Teotihuacan consists of a long roadway with the great Pyramid of the Sun—larger than the Great Pyramid of Giza—at one end, and the much smaller Pyramid of the Moon at the other end. The road is known as the Roadway of the Dead. On either side are half-excavated buildings, mostly with underground chambers with murals and carvings of the curious, angular type that the Aztecs created. They portray the gods of the elements: the Rain God, Huitzzlipochli, for example. And great, stone heads with plumes, dating from an ancient order known as the Knights Eagle and Tiger. Rodney was knowledgeable about the significance of this apparently religious order, which appeared to link the creatures of the earth with the creatures of the air. He was also full of tales of

Quetzelcoatl, the white god who should come from the East, and whom Monctezuma felt he had recognised, with tragic results. The emperor welcomed the visitors with gifts of gold and jewels. In a few days the Eastern god turned very nasty and the robbery, pillage and bloodletting began.

Driving along I confess I felt very happy and interested. But once we reached the place, I had difficulty. The party scattered, looking at things. I stood on one leg, looking at the Pyramid of the Sun.

"What do you want to do?" Rodney asked.

"Get to the top", I said, gritting my teeth.

"Oh Joyce, don't be tiresome," Janet said with a certain exasperation. "Even we are not going to make that climb. We'll all just go up the Moon Pyramid, and then we'll come back here to the car and have our picnic lunch with you here. Just sit in the shade here and wait for us."

I looked at Rodney. He held out his hand, ignoring Janet.

"Come along then," he said, "if that's what you want."

Painfully, hopping and struggling step by step, I got to the pyramid with him, and we began the long, hard climb up the many, many steps hewed into the pyramid's side. It seemed to go on for ever. Rodney held my hand in a firm grip, lifting, pulling me steadily up with him at a pace I could sustain.

Half way up at last we paused and rested. To my amazement at that moment a peon bearing trinkets appeared from nowhere, walking along a ledge towards us with a broad grin.

"Bienes Tardes, Senor, Senora! Will the Senor buy something for the Senora? It will make her happy."

"I'm happy already!" I answered. But we looked in the tray and selected a Mexican silver ring like a coiled serpent and put it on my finger. I have worn it for over thirty years now, in memory of that day.

At last we managed to reach the top, and sat there under the sun. Away down at the other end of the Roadway of the Dead we could see the tiny figures of the rest of the party, grouped on the top of the Pyramid of the Moon.

We sat in silence. I got up once briefly, to look at the view from the other side. Rodney rose to help me. His shadow was cast across the top of the great stone structure—a tall, narrow-shouldered, rather wide-hipped shadow that looked familiar in a distant kind of way. A shape cut in space. We sat down again and put on our straw hats and looked into one another's faces.

Suddenly I knew: the most immediate and extraordinary sense of recognition, coupled with amazement that I had not known long before. This was the tall man, the tall thin youth, the tall little boy, the loved one.

"You're my brother! You're my brother!" I cried.

"Very likely," Rodney answered. "You are very, very familiar to me. There is certainly a Karmic link."

It was so long since I had thought of my "brother" that the whole thing had receded deeply into my mind. But now it began to bubble like a stream undammed, and I almost shouted my joy and delight at the wonderful moment of re-union.

"The air is full of angels!" I half laughed, half cried. It seemed to me that strange, benign, discarnate presences circled and touched us both with gentle wings.

From then on we always walked side by side, hand in hand or arm in arm, our long, swinging strides matching, our feet always in harmony. The conversations were easy, free and flowing. He was full of wisdom, full of common sense.

"There is no 'ought'", he said, when I demanded whether I ought to take a certain course of action, whether it would be beneficial.

"Take what you like, and pay for it", he would often say. "There is time for everything, but no time to waste," he advised me when I seemed in undue haste. "Don't pour out so easily, lest the creative pressure falls in you", he said when I turned out reams and reams or words on my portable typewriter. "Wait. You will write about all this later on."

These possibly not very remarkable comments, because of the context in which they were originally uttered, have been to me like lighted beacons, flashing at intervals, whenever, through the long years since, I have needed to get my bearings. They sound within me, resonating in his well-remembered voice.

Soon Rodney suggested some of us should make an expedition that had long been mentioned—to see the sunrise from the heights of Popocatepetl. Popo, and Izzta, as the twin mountain of Izztaccihuatl was called affectionately, are the Smoking Warrior and the Sleeping Woman, in translation. The former looks like an Indo peon wrapped in a serape, perpetually smoking his pipe—the thin blue plume of smoke rising always from the never quite extinct volcanic crater: and the latter appearing to be a naked woman lying on her side. The old chief waits contentedly for his woman to awaken.

You can drive up a rough track, through lava dust, until you come out not far below the Cortes Pass, where the Spanish Conquistadores looked down in 1519 on the City of Tennochtitlan. Now you gaze down from the great height onto the colossal modern city built on the dried-up lake beds and based on lava dust.

Rodney and I went up to the steep precipice to look over it, as usual hand in hand. But as I stepped forward confidently, he surprised me by drawing back abruptly, saying: "Don't look down".

"Why not?"

He didn't answer. He took two or three steps backward. I pulled my hand from his and went forward and looked over the edge at the magnificent view. The small incident remained somewhere in the back of my mind, to be recalled vividly as having great significance when only a year later we were faced with the tragedy of the manner of his unexpected death.

On that day everything seemed joyously happy and alive. We climbed on, outstripping the rest of the party. Above us we could see the snow-line looming near. Rodney had once climbed up through the snow, to the point nearly 18,000 feet above sea level where the great, mile-wide crater opens out. Deep down inside it, smoke issues from wide fissures in the flat, grey bed. But the air is so rarified that one really needs an oxygen mask. Rodney had climbed without one, having to pause every few steps to draw a laboured breath for the last hour.

"I had meant to climb down into the crater and walk across it, as I know others have done", he told me. "But a strange thing happened. The lack of oxygen affected me, giving me a state of euphoria, but not enabling me to hold my purpose in mind. After staring at it, and recalling that on the way up I felt I was coming out into Heaven, I began to think I was looking at what was the main entrance to somewhere quite different! Luckily I had enough sense left to turn eventually and come down again."

That day we were not to go quite to the snowline. Though I

70

was pressing to climb on, Rodney said it was far enough. The rarified air, which was already making me gasp, would soon begin to affect us too much.

The climb was no more than a scrambling walk. It was still only half light, very early morning. He led us to a point where we looked across mile upon mile of uninhabited mountain country, strange and wild-looking as some other planet than the earth. In the distance, as the sky lightened, the great, bronze orb of the Sun began to rise, pulsating and vibrating in the clear air, behind the great Peak of Orizaba, the highest point in Mexico.

"Its like the dance of Siva", I said in awe. I was recalling the Hindu gunas and the oriental tradition in which we were both well versed. We stood apart from the rest of the group hand in hand, in a deep and private silence of communion with nature, with one another, and with the glory of the Sun God rising silently in majesty.

Rodney had always maintained that to us, here on earth, the Sun is essentially God, since without its light and heat there could be no organic life on earth at all. It would be a cold, dark place incapable of sustaining any form of development. Therefore we could and should worship our God in humility and reverence—even though he is not the king of all the universe.

If one speaks of peak experiences, mine was a peak indeed. I felt that nothing more could be desired, but to live and work beside my beloved brother for evermore.

I did not realise at all that I was getting into a state of increasing euphoria. The strange experiences of the last months, together with the continual effect of the Mexican air, was putting me gradually into a perpetual 'high'. I found I could not sleep. I was so full of energy and ideas, my head could scarcely contain them. Logic and reason were slowly being taken over by something rather different.

Seeing my lack of steadiness and calm, Rodney took me down to the Tierra Calliente, to Cuernavaca for a week. There among the semi-tropical plants, the bougainvillea, the heavy-scented white jasmine, the scarlet flame trees, the blue plumbago and the glory of the tree called cups of gold, I was to rest and relax in a tourist hotel with a shady garden and a swimming pool.

71

Instead of studying, writing or relaxing by the pool, I found myself sociable and garrulous to a fault, talking to the American tourists, visiting the market and keeping long, strange vigils in the ornate Roman Catholic churches.

Rodney had said it is important to pray, and did so constantly himself. I lit candles and knelt among the Mexican people, who pray readily, popping into the church on the way to market to light their candles and ask a blessing of the Madonna. As Roman Catholicism was imposed by force after the Spanish conquest, it is of course technically a Catholic country. But a mixture of old knowledge and old superstitions seems to move the worshippers. On fiesta days they dance for hours in the piazzas, drinking pulque—the crude stuff of which mescalin is made—until the inner doors of the mind appear to open as their bodies eventually reach a state of exhaustion. Then, as often as not, they enter the church, fall on their knees and with adoration worship the Christian God and pray Our Lady for forgiveness of their sins.

This curious mixture of paganism and Christianity fills the churches with an extraordinary atmosphere. My attempts at prayer of a kind that would go well beyond the unsophisticated 'listening to God' technique, threw me into a curious state of self doubt and confusion.

I also seemed to come down from my exalted adoration of Rodney and all his works, and to consider him against a background of events which I have not so far described in this narrative.

Shortly before my arrival, there had entered the circles close to Rodney a rather beautiful Mexican woman named Mema Dickins. Her husband, Toby Dickins was of the Dickins and Jones family. He worked for Kodak in Mexico City. He used to say that he had been shown Mema's photograph by a friend in England many years ago, and had at once known this was the woman he was going to marry. He went to Mexico expressly to meet her, and did so. They had been married for years and had three growing sons.

Mema was a devout Roman Catholic. She was also a natural medium. It was her custom to take communion every day, and to make her confession regularly.

According to her own story, Mema began to receive visitations from a man who appeared to her clairvoyantly, commanding her to "go to the philosopher Rodney Collin". For a while she dismissed or was simply non-plussed by this command. Eventually, however, she told her confessor. He recognised Collin's name, knew him to be resident in Mexico City and found out his address. He advised Mema to obey 'the voice' and go and see what came of it.

When Mema was first shown into Rodney's study she saw the large painting of O. that adorned the wall and exclaimed:

"That's the man who sent me!" She recognised the face, while knowing nothing, it seems, of the man it represented. Mema then proceeded to give a variety of 'messages' to Rodney, purporting to come from O., then from Gurdjieff, and later from other, usually historical, personalities.

Rodney accepted her with his childlike grace. She became a daily visitor. She poured out messages of varying depth and value to everyone around.

The household had been thrown into disarray some short while before my arrival by her advent, and this was evidently the true reason for the abandonment of the communal household at Tlalpam, in favour of an apartment in Rio Nazas. Some people disliked Mema on sight and distrusted every word that came out of her mouth. Some were unable to differentiate between the words and opinions of Mema Dickins herself, and the words that flowed through her from—who knows what source, or what levels of different sources.

A hard core of followers, centred mainly round Janet, found that they had been given a direct hot line to the Almighty, and worshipped the oracle with increasing reverence. Her most trite or everyday comment was thought to be a command from the masters and acted upon with alacrity. The remark: "You shouldn't eat so much cream" was translated as "Mr. Ouspensky says we shouldn't eat cream." Her comment at an art exhibition that she found Turner pallid and incomprehensible became: "Mr. Ouspensky did not approve of Turner's style".

When I had been in the apartment a few weeks, as I was sitting reading one day, I heard a man's footsteps approaching down the long drawing room. Glancing up from my book I was astounded to perceive that the 'man' was in fact Mema, walking with a heavy, measured tread, unlike her usual small-stepped feminine walk. Drawing up a chair in front of me she sat down, her knees apart, a totally uncharacteristic posture for so feminine a woman, and her hands planted firmly on her knees as she surveyed me. Looking at her with some surprise, I perceived that her face was changing slowing into that of Gurdjieff. In a gutteral voice, the apparition addressed me. The impact of the words was less profound than the impact of the appearance. He/she told me that I was vain and arrogant; that I only wrote books because I wanted acclaim: and that I should wear heavy costume jewellery instead of the light necklaces and bracelets I preferred.

In a few moments, Mema crossed her feet, relaxed her hands in her lap, looked at me in a perfectly normal way and enquired if I had had a good day and if I was reading an interesting book?

So many and varied were the experiences of all kinds that I was receiving at that period, that the Mema Dickins phenomenon seemed to fit in, at first, as one of a variety of interesting and new developments, and I did not give the matter very serious thought. Mema was, however, to prove in the end to be Rodney's undoing.

It had occurred to me that quite a number of the people who had originally thrown in their lot with Rodney were no longer around. Enquiries about them drew rather evasive answers. Clearly they had left him. They were brushed under the carpet with comments that they "had not agreed with the way the Work was developing".

Although most of the visitors from afar were apparently mainly concerned with Rodney's books and with the Work ideas, there was a close circle round Rodney that I was rather unsure about. They were mainly Mexican, and Mema Dickins was central to their work. They would gather in Rodney's study behind locked doors, tape recording—something. I was not invited to join them, and as the proceedings would have been in Spanish this seemed quite natural and did not trouble me in the least. I had more than enough to think about without desiring entry into a small group which had evidently been working together for some time on some specialized project. But soon I began to discover that it was the activities of this group that had been the basis of the disappearance of many of the original followers.

One day Rodney told me that, with the advent of Mema, it would now be possible to find the traces of Fourth Way School through the ages, and put together a document that would be of great value for the future. He was intending to go soon to Europe and the Middle East and follow up evidence that was accumulating. I found this an interesting idea, and would have liked to be in on the project. However it was clear that I had to get home to my husband and daughter soon.

When I returned to Mexico City from Cuernavaca I was in a cooler frame of mind altogether. I began to wonder a good deal about a number of aspects of Rodney's work and activities and about what might be happening to him personally. He seemed exceedingly tired. He was still working very vigorously and continuously, but it looked to me as though his resources might in some way be running out. He had got in the habit of putting himself at everyone's disposal, even rising from the meal table or from bed to attend to anyone who asked to see him. Once, seeing him leaving his lunch unfinished once again to talk to a rather garrulous lady whose purposes didn't seem to warrant such lengthy attention, I asked him if he ought not to rest more, finish his meals in peace and get me or someone to hold some of his callers at bay.

"The more demands that are made on me the better", he answered. "I must do what I have to do."

"And what is that?"

"Obey O.'s will."

I wanted to say something about his own will, his own needs, his own contribution to the Work. But there was a touch-me-not expression on his face that I was beginning to know well, and I thought it best to make no further comment. All the same the idea of obeying the will of a master beyond the grave gave me a certain sense of disquiet. I thought he could lose his sense of direction that way.

We all flew out of Mexico City together and parted company in New York. Rodney, Janet and Chloe, Mema and one or two others were to go on to Paris and I to London.

Chloe was a very pretty eighteen year old, lively but quite pliable and obedient. She adored her father. For some time Mema and Janet together had been hatching a plan for Chloe to be married to Tony, Toby and Mema's eldest son who was the same age as herself and in his last year at a public school in England. This marriage was, they said, at the will of O. and G. The young couple would carry on the Work together in due course. Chloe was not consulted in the matter, but was simply led along, apparently complacently, in the direction of an eventual marriage to this really quite presentable and pleasant boy, when the time was right.

However in the last few months she had attracted the attention of the boys at the American College in Mexico City which she still attended on a part-time basis. They wanted to take her out. I remember in particular one nice youngster who offerred to teach her to drive. All her requests to accept this quite innocuous invitation were vetoed by Mema and her mother, who kept her fully occupied at home and at the Planetarium site, and reminded her constantly that she was affianced. I wondered about it, but did not give a great deal of attention to this arranged marriage. I supposed Chloe would assert herself and make her own will known in due course if necessary.

I returned home, having lost all my surplus weight, confident and with a sense of renewed purpose: but no longer in a highly elated state. I went to see Francis Roles and asked if I might resume attendance at the London meetings. After hesitation he agreed, providing that I did not distract his followers by telling them anything about the Work in Mexico, as "Rodney is going an entirely different way".

When I told Elsie Abercrombie this she remarked in the forthright language she used when exasperated by Roles: "What the Hell does that matter—as long as he's going! Francis is getting completely shut up in a box of his own opinions."

In a few weeks Rodney wrote from Athens asking Derry and me to go together and meet him and his party in Rome on a certain date. This was a planned holiday for Derry. But for some reason Rodney had written a completely wrong date in his letter for our meeting, and as a result we missed each other, could not make contact at all out there, and the planned meeting and the joint vacation never took place at all. Later he said: "O. evidently didn't intend it to happen". Instead, he and Janet and Mema would come to England in a month to see all their friends.

When they arrived, Chloe wasn't with them. She had been left behind in a convent school near Paris. "O. and G." had advised or desired her to be left there to learn Latin and Greek so that she would be able to help Rodney with his work. As she had been accustomed to dress and use make-up like an American teenager at home, this sudden reversal to schoolgirl status —gym tunic, long knee socks, scrubbed face and unvarnished nails—must have been quite hard for her. She was permitted to fly over and spend Christmas with Derry, Ann and myself at Westerham. She was courageously cheerful and was applying herself to the task set her. But she looked pinched with cold and stress at the Spartan conditions of the convent: and so excessively pleased to see us that I felt she was having rather an unhappy time.

Although bright and quite artistically creative, she was not naturally studious or scholarly, and would almost certainly not of her own choice have devoted a year to learning Latin and Greek.

Chloe was going to be a considerable heiress on her mother's death. Tony would inherit little, for his father's small resources would be divided between all the sons, and Mema had nothing of her own. Mema's 'voices' had manipulated a very satisfactory match for Tony. It was clearly essential to the plan that she be kept on ice in a safe place until the boy was ready for her. That thought, when it struck me, seemed a bit disloyal to Rodney and Janet who presumably wanted what was best for their beloved only daughter. All the same, it troubled me. The children were fond of one another and it might be a perfectly suitable marriage. But it was clearly not a spontaneous love match. They were encouraged to correspond with one another regularly, but there was no shining-eyed look when Tony's schoolboy type letters arrived. She accepted the situation like a pliant, obedient child.

In late 1955 Rodney, Janet and Mema again arrived in England and booked into the Adelphi Hotel on the seafront at Brighton, not far from Rodney and Derry's childhood home. I went down to spend the day with them. Rodney had written me a number of long letters during the course of their travels, extracts from which appear in *The Theory of Conscious*

Harmony. From some of the letters I gathered that the oracle had directed his party and had shown them some interesting things. They had been to Paris: to Seville for Holy Week: to Athens: back to Rome: On to Istanbul: back once again to Rome, in answer to the messages Mema was giving them.

Rodney felt he had found traces of "school" in a number of areas, and wrote a good deal about Cosimo de Medici, about the House of Lorraine and about Leonardo da Vinci, and various other well known historical figures, artists and writers in particular, whom he claimed had been "schoolmen". Mema's voices had sent them to look at places, to pick up clues, to make discoveries, which were apparently part of a vast and complex pattern of underground occult activity, stretching into political, literary and artistic fields over many generations. They had in fact touched upon many fields of esotericism later unearthed by James Webb and researched diligently for his three books: *Flight from Reason, The Occult Establishment* and *The Harmonious Circle*. These overlap to some extent the slightly different investigations and conclusions drawn by Henry Lincoln, Richard Leigh and Michael Baigent in their book *The Holy Blood and the Holy Grail*.

Rodney was both excited and yet a bit uptight about his discoveries. Like most mediums, Mema's 'messages' inclined to vary in accuracy. They would consist of something like: Go back to Rome. Go to such and such a library. In such a position, on such a shelf, third from the left you will find a book bound in red leather. Its title is so and so. Turn to page such and such and you will read how the Fourth Way came to Florence and the names of those who brought it to the Medici family.

The party would fly back at considerable cost from some other research area—Iran, for instance. The library would be located, the shelf found, and there sure enough was the book of the name given. But on opening, it proved to be on quite a different subject and nowhere did it contain any reference at all to the matter referred to.

It was therefore becoming a more and more frustrating search, as though no high master, but a sort of Robin Goodfellow character was leading them a merry dance, amused by their obedience and their simplicity.

I had much less experience of mediumship at that time than I have now, and I was as puzzled as Rodney himself by the strange phenomenon. I confess that, though intriguing, I thought it was exhausting Rodney needlessly and might in the end prove a complete waste of time.

One interesting thing came of it for me. Mema, hearing me say that I had always been interested in whatever came out of Tibet suddenly went into one of her semi-trances and answered: "Why not, since you were born there? It was 1620. Your name was HAON." She wrote this down on a scrap of paper. Then again taking up the pen, wrote rapidly a few words in what Rodney described as an eighteenth century hand, and signed it Ivan Ivanovitch. This message made my hair stand on end. I had known the name Ivan Ivanovitch all my life, and had used it as a sort of incantation or invocation when I was a child, thinking it to be a name of power. It could get me off things I didn't want to do, make things go my way. "Ivan Ivanovitch, make me get spots so I don't have to go to that party." "Help me find my pencil case." "Get me through the exam."

When questioned, Mema said that Ivan Ivanovitch was "one of the teachers of Gurdjieff, very tall and blonde, wore a blue tunic buttoned high at the neck, had very blue eyes." I asked Rodney if he could verify this, and in a letter he wrote:

"Ivan Ivanovitch, we have been told, was a mysterious figure who came from Tibet early in the nineteenth century, who moved unseen behind the schools in Sicily, in Florence and in Rome, who inspired Ibsen and Stevenson and Nietzsche, who returned to Russia about 1885, gave Krilov his fables, helped Philemon translate the Philokalia, moulded the Russian ballet, taught Ouspensky's grandmother and Gurdjieff in his youth, and disappeared whence he came on the eve of the 1914 war." I did not feel very sure of the historical existence of this 'mysterious figure', but I kept an open mind for a long time. Rodney was quite tranquil and complaisant about these 'messages'. He was convinced that he was doing good and useful work completely in accordance with his master's wishes. However the 'voices' grew stranger and wilder, and at Brighton he added, with seeming complete unawareness of the oddness of the statement from a man of previously considerable intelligence and discrimination:

Ivan Ivanovitch is Master Atlas, who upholds the world. He

was also St. Luke: St. Luke, the teacher of Cleophas and Simon, the disciples at Emmaus. And he is also St. Christopher, the teacher of Saints Cosmo and Damian. As Ivan Ivanovitch he was teacher of Gurdjieff and Ouspensky. He was the unknown teacher of Kunrath and Dee. The names change with the centuries, but the beings are eternal. He was also the 'other disciple' who was known to the High Priest. And he was with us recently, in twentieth century Paris."

This considerable hotchpotch of information left me exceedingly disquieted and unsure. There are indeed two minor saints of Asia Minor, acknowledged by the Roman Catholic Church, named Cosmo and Damian, who worked together in a medical capacity—and Ouspensky had apparently been christened Piotr Damianovitch at his grandmother's instigation. There was therefore a slim link with the name Damian, and with the churches of Asia Minor, the churches traditionally descended from St. John and the Magdalene, who figured to a lesser extent in Mema's 'messages'. But the pattern that lay behind it came from a shadowy and mysterious land indeed.

Rodney and I walked up and down the seafront at Brighton talking of these matters together.

"As soon as we have transcribed all this I'll let you have the tapes", he said.

In fact time was now very short. I never heard them.

We strolled back to the Adelphi Hotel, and as I had already said my farewells to the rest of the party, I reached up and kissed him goodbye. We stood for a moment in the porchway in the sunshine arms round one another in a quiet embrace. As I stepped back I gave him a last look. Against reason the now familiar 'inner voice' said to me: "Its the last time."

He was then forty-seven and I was ten years younger. It seemed very improbable. I hesitated, then turned away and got into my car.

I never saw him alive again.

6

Chloe wrote from the convent early in 1956: "Mummy and Daddy have gone to Peru to visit Daddy's group in Lima".

Rodney still maintained links with a variety of people, and although he seemed to have a smaller following than before, and not to be lecturing so much, he was always on the move and kept an enormous correspondence going. There was therefore nothing unusual about this communication. But on reading the words, seated at my kitchen table over a morning cup of coffee, I was immediately filled with an irrational feeling of dread.

Among the many pre-cognitive dreams, apparent memories and half known things from childhood, was the complete conviction that I should die in Peru. I have in fact never been to that country and it now seems improbable that it will be the land of my own death. But "I shall die", came to mind at once, and was then translated as "he will die". I sat rigidly immobile, filled with terror and a sense of inevitability and helplessness. I did not know what exactly to expect. But I knew it was the end.

Rodney, Janet, Mema and two or three others had flown down from Mexico City, visited the people in Lima, and then taken a small aircraft to go high up to the ancient mountain city of Cuzco, which was to the Peruvians 'the navel of the world'.

Before leaving home, Rodney had spent a considerable time putting his affairs in order. In answer to Janet's enquiries about this excessive preoccupation with details of his papers and his personal affairs, he had said: "Something new is about to happen, but I don't know what it is. We have to be prepared".

Janet wrote later that she had been troubled about his health for several months. He had always been rather prone to fainting fits. But this is often the case with tall people, and Derry and I also have this minor problem and attach little importance to it.

However he had had a number of very prolonged blackouts, especially after the exhausting marathon walks that he was still doing occasionally. On one occasion he had led a party the whole way from the Planetarium site to the Zocalo, the Cathedral square in the centre of Mexico City, a distance of over twenty miles, in the heat. He had intended that they should all end their expedition on their knees in the cathedral, for worship and adoration of the Christ and the Madonna was now pre-occupying him more and more. He had recently been received into the Roman Catholic church, at Mema's instigation. He spent long and longer periods in prayer.

However, on this day he had collapsed in a dead faint just outside the cathedral and had not recovered consciousness for nearly twenty minutes. This was obviously abnormal and a cause for anxiety, since the average faint from heat exhaustation or fatigue lasts only a few seconds. On finally coming round, he had insisted on entering the cathedral to complete his intended vigil.

When flying up to Cuzco in a small unpressurised plane, an oxygen mask is necessary because of the great height, but at a certain point, Janet turned round in her seat to speak to him and found that the mask had fallen from his face—he should have been holding it on. He was either asleep or unconscious. She managed to rouse him, in the narrow confines of the small aircraft, and held it in position for him until they landed.

Janet's long account of the subsequent developments, which I still have, goes on to detail all the events of the next three days. She wrote slightly varying versions to a few other friends in England and to Francis Roles. Other people—quick to express an opinion though they had not in fact been present—added adornments of their own to the story, so letters and long narratives flew back and forth between Mexico and London for some time.

The first night in the hotel in Cuzco, Rodney took two Coramine pills for altitude sickness. This surprised Janet, as he was as a rule against taking medication of any sort. He was inclined to endure pain, such as stress pain in the neck and shoulders, from which we both tended to suffer when overtired, with the comment that it was "necessary" or even that "O. wills it". However she made no comment to him about the pills.

82

The following day they looked round the ancient city, and made arrangements to be conducted up to the Inca ruins in the hills. This was an expedition that he had anticipated with pleasure, for he was always deeply involved in the idea of civilizations in the past.

In the late morning, they visited the Spanish colonial type cathedral in Cuzco. While there, Rodney suddenly made an exclamation as though he had recognised something of immense significance. He had in fact made eye contact with a small peasant boy who was badly crippled and apparently nearly destitute. Peru has many such, and there was no official aid or recognition of their plight. They eked out their existence begging, or in any way they could.

Rodney said: "I've seen the boy." Mema appears to have been in on the secret, but Janet confessed herself nonplussed by the apparent emotion visible in Rodney's face. Without speaking to the child at that time, Rodney turned away. But the child followed him, hobbling on his sticks, as though he too was aware of his destiny. He took up a position outside the hotel, and was still there after the party had returned, rested, and ventured forth again.

At this point Rodney approached the boy, took his hand and spoke to him. They talked together privately for a few minutes. He gave his name as Modesto. Rodney told him to come along with him. The sight of the English and American party had apparently already attracted a certain amount of attention, and beggars and sightseers were by now crowding round Rodney. There is of course a tendency in poverty-stricken countries for those who are not adequately fed or clothed to expect largesse from visitors, who all appear to be goldmines by comparison. Seeing the tall Englishman and the crippled Modesto walking hand in hand, the crowd grew bigger, evidently excited by the curious sight and in expectation of money.

Janet's account says that Rodney suddenly stopped, looked round him and said: "You must help yourselves. You must do something for each other. You must give to each other."

A voice from the crowd said contemptuously: "Its all very well for you to say that, Senor. You are rich. But we are poor. We have nothing to give."

Rodney answered: "Everyone has something to give. Everyone can give a smile, a kind word." He then did his best to discourage them from following so closely and led Modesto away. He took him to buy a shirt and trousers to replace his rags. Finding him to be dirty, he led him to a courtyard fountain, and washed the skeleton-thin little body. Stripping off his own shirt, he dried him with it. Once clothed, he took the child to an eating place and bought him a meal, which he devoured ravenously.

Clean and fed now, the smiling child followed Rodney, and was left once more to his vigil outside the hotel. Rodney told Janet later that the boy lived in the bell tower of the cathedral, sleeping there on a straw petate, and earning a few pesos from the priests for pulling the bells for them.

During the course of that night, Janet, who had been sleeping soundly, was wakened by Rodney, who seemed to be in a state of distress. In answer to her anxious enquiry whether he was ill, he said:

"I've done the wrong thing. It seemed to me so important that Modesto should be healed that I have been offering my own life in his place. Now I realise suddenly that I have been prepared for other work."

To calm him, Janet answered: "If there is other work for you to do, you will be shown it, and no words that you may have said will make any difference." She tried further to quieten him. In agitation he said: "I invoked the Trinity. If you do that, what you ask is done."

Eventually Janet calmed him down and he returned to bed and to sleep. In the morning Modesto was again at the hotel entrance and followed them, but apparently Rodney said nothing to him at all.

After lunch, the party retired to their rooms for a siesta, preparing for the arduous day going up to the Inca ruins on the morrow. In the early afternoon heat, Janet slept soundly in the twinbedded room, with Rodney on the other bed also sleeping. She awakened with a start as the cathedral clock was striking three. Glancing at Rodney's bed, she saw that it was empty.

Fifteen minutes later, at exactly 3.15 p.m, a young man driving his car across the cathedral square, glanced up at the clock to check the time. As he did so, he saw a body come hurtling out of the opensided bell tower. According to his story at the subsequent police enquiry, Rodney fell or jumped forward, head up, his arms stretched wide. He apparently turned over in the air, his face coming uppermost. He hit the ground feet first, and was killed instantaneously.

It is noteworthy perhaps that, as the head is the heaviest part of the human frame, an unconscious body apparently tends to turn head downwards during a long fall, and it is therefore unusual for the feet to strike the ground first. The assumption would seem to be that he may have been conscious. Later an autopsy confirmed that the spine had been impacted into the brain. Another witness came forward to say she had seen him fall in an upright position, arms outstretched in the form of a cross, and head back as though looking at the sky.

Rodney's right leg was broken in the fall, and when Janet saw the body at the local hospital a little later, it struck her forceably that the broken leg was drawn up and impacted, making it look exactly like the shortened leg of the crippled boy Modesto.

The body was removed to the house of one of Rodney's followers, where the drawing room was quickly converted into a 'chapelle ardente'. A Franciscan priest came, and all night Janet, Mema and the rest of the party remained kneeling in prayer around the black wooden coffin on trestles, with its glass front through which Rodney's face could be seen. They thought he seemed to be smiling. After the brief police and medical proceedings the following day, he was buried in a corner of the cathedral cemetery, in an angle of the old church wall, among rose bushes. Blue flowers that he had always loved were planted on the grave. The silent party, with Janet drained from weeping, made their way home again to Mexico. The "Daily Telegraph" published a brief obituary based on his published books.

For five weeks there was no sign of Modesto, and eventually the authorities seem to have lost interest in seeking him out. Then one day he was seen hobbling across the cathedral square and up to his shelter in the tower room. The priest was found, the police were told, and he was taken in and questioned. He appeared terrified. He said he had been hiding in the hills, afraid to come home.

"Why?"

"Because the god-man said he would heal me, and then he died. They will say I killed him".

As far as could be gathered from the frightened boy, Rodney had come out of the hotel about three o'clock, taken him by the hand and gone with him to the cathedral. They had climbed the spiral staircase together and entered the tower room. From it, there was a wide view which included a giant statue of Jesus Christ which stands on a small hill overlooking the city.

Rodney—whose fear of heights I have already mentioned— quite uncharacteristically sat down in the open window embrasure from which there was a steep drop into the cathedral square. Seated thus, he began to tell Modesto of the love of Jesus Christ for all His children and to say Jesus would heal him and enable him to walk on two legs like other people.

After some minutes of talk, Rodney, stood up. He then pitched forward through the opening and fell. Under the questioning, the little boy, who was obviously still in fear of some terrible fate befalling him at the hands of the police, suggested that he might have hit his head on the top of the embrasure as he stood up. He might have hit his head and then fallen. He had made some sort of exclamation before falling. He might have been ill, dizzy. He might have jumped. The one thing he was sure of, and kept repeating tearfully was that the god-man had said his leg would be made better. But it had not come true.

In a strange way, however, the promise was eventually partially fulfilled. Rodney's many friends and devotees donated money to open an orphanage and children's clinic in Cuzco. Modesto and other abandoned children were admitted. Modesto's leg was operated on and was, it seems, considerably improved, enabling him to walk with relative normality thereafter.[*]

---

[*] See my *Beloved Icarus, Astrological Journal*, Autumn 1971 Volume XIII, No. 4. A curious sidelight on this event, and in particular Rodney's apparent conviction that he had done something which would result in Modesto being healed, through his "invocation of the Trinity", is the belief of the local people that they had seen Modesto *run* from the cathedral and across the square shortly after the death. He had always needed sticks to hobble with. None of Janet's party saw this, but the tale became local folklore. The miracle, if such it was, did not last. It remained an unexplained and rather interesting mystery.

On the day after Rodney's death, Derry and I received a telegram from Janet giving the bare details, and asking me to go to Paris and break the news to Chloe. I was distraught. I ran from room to room in the house sobbing hysterically. Derry, who had of course lost his much loved only brother, was a tower of strength, controlling his own grief in an attempt to comfort me.

"I waited all my life. I only had him two years," I cried. "I can't bear to live without him. I wish I too could die. It was meant to be me who would die in Peru."

While I packed a small case, Derry telephoned Heathrow to make a reservation for me to Paris. I wept in the aircraft so uncontrollably that the stewardness came to see if I was ill. I arrived late at night. It proved impossible to get out before morning to Note Dame des Oiseaux. The convent was an old mansion that had been the home of Chateaubriand whom Mema had identified as a 'school' man. It was some considerable distance from the city. I therefore booked into a hotel.

Rodney had died on May 3rd. It was now the 5th, and Paris was unduly warm for the time of year. Almost all night I paced my hot room, stood by the open casement windows overlooking the Rue des Saints Pères and the Rue Jacob, or knelt by the bed in some attempt to seek help or reassurance, before I had to face my young niece and comfort her in the morning.

I was almost sure that the death was premature. But it seemed to have a kind of inevitability about it. At forty-eight his life span might have been completed. Such work as he could do, he had done well and diligently. But in recent months he seemed to have lost touch with the old realities and to have turned into somebody who could no longer effectively live and work in this world.

Some time in the early hours, kneeling with my head on my arms, exhausted from weeping, I heard a voice. It seemed to be outside myself. I heard the words: "Its quite all right. Tell her its quite all right." I jumped up at once. I had heard 'voices' several times before, mostly in Mexico, where I had accepted them as part of the strange experiences there. But from this time onward they became an occasional part of my daily life. This time there was no further 'communication' and I was unable to identify the voice at all. However it gave me a sense of not being quite alone. I was able to quieten myself inwardly, and to travel calmly to the convent in the morning.

I spent four days with Chloe. The nuns were exceptionally kind, holding a requiem for Rodney, and encouraging my niece and me to be together. They gave me a room in their guest wing. By day we walked or sat in the grounds, mostly at the round stone bench and table under mauve lilac trees in bloom, where Chateaubriand had apparently sat to work on sunny days gone by. The heavy scent of lilac still takes me back to those early days of mourning for my brother.

Chloe was bewildered by the turn of events, but very plucky. She said: "Why? Why?" And then with childlike acceptance decided that God had willed this unexpected death of her loved father, and that He had changed His mind about wanting her to learn Latin and Greek to work with him. She thought she should fly home. I restrained her as we waited Janet's instructions.

When they came, in a long letter, she described the death as a happy one, and said that Rodney would "now be able to help everyone and reach all those he loved". She expected Chloe to remain at the convent, and return when she had taken her exams in a few weeks' time. It was the kind of letter one schoolgirl might write to another. The immaturity of Janet's thought had often struck me. She had led Rodney into the Work, but he had outstripped her a very long time ago.

Before I left Paris, Chloe and I decided that we ought to break the news to Dr. Albert Rouhier, who ran the Librairie Vega in the Boulevard St. Germain. Dr. Rouhier was a close friend of Rodney's, and had supplied him with many books on esoteric subjects. He had succeeded in obtaining a vast library left by a Dr. Cabrera, which would have been broken up but for his intervention. The Cabrera collection contained many valuable and long out of print books on alchemy, magic, astrology, divination philosophy and religion, and a wide range of related subjects. He had been a scholar of occultism. It was almost priceless as a whole, but much less valuable if broken up and dispersed at auction, of course. Rodney agreed to purchase and the whole lot had been shipped out to Mexico. They were to have been housed at the planetarium.

I had not met the Parisian bookseller before, though I had

heard a lot about him. Later he became a valued friend to me. Albert Rouhier was a big man with a beard, a large stomach, and a blue Parisian beret on the side of his head. He spoke no English, but could understand it in written form. He greeted us with warm smiles, embraced Chloe and kissed my hand. But as soon as we told him of Rodney's death he became grave and preoccupied.

"J'arais aucun pressentiment", he said over and over, shaking his head.

"Mummy said it was a happy death—une mort heureuse—in her letter", Chloe told him.

"No. He will have to pay a high price."

I had calmed myself inwardly in the last days, partly out of the need to support Chloe, and partly at least from a sense that, though there must be more in this than met the eye, it might indeed be "all right" as the voice in the night had said.

"Those of us who loved him will perhaps be able to pay the price for him, in our own lives?" I said in my halting French.

"No. He himself will have to pay. You can't pay for him."

We left the dark bookshop—it used to be the sort of Watkins Books of Paris—in a more sombre mood.

"All the same, we'll love and pray for him, and he'll be all right", Chloe said. And afterwards I agreed it might be so.

7

Back home I found that Francis Roles had telephoned. His prophesy that Rodney would "die a violent death" seemed near enough to the truth to give him confidence. But he was genuinely upset, and had left a message with Derry that I should go and see him if I "needed" him. In any case, he would clearly welcome further details.

I went up a few days later, calm now and composed, although with no certainty of what I should say. I found him snowed under with letters and accounts of Rodney's death from all over the place, many of them highly coloured and totally at variance with Janet's narrative. The general impression seemed to be that Rodney had been going mad for some time, and at the end he had totally lost his reason. It was curious that some of his erstwhile friends were the most vituperative in their abuse of him, or contemptuous in their condemnation of his association with Mema Dickins.

Francis Roles wanted me to read them all. But after glancing through them I put them down, feeling that nothing at all was to be gained by this premature judgement. Nobody even knew for sure whether he had jumped from the tower or whether his heart had simply given out up there.

Later, when James Webb was writing *The Harmonious Circle* about the work of Gurdjieff and Ouspensky, he said to me: "I could not go along with all that Rodney Collin said. But the quality of his life and the manner of its ending appealed to me." This seemed a better comment than all the noisy talk by those who had known him.

Although a certain inner desolation filled me, I continually comforted myself with the knowledge that I had known him, that something of him would clearly survive this life, and that I had learnt enough from him to continue on the Way. I took to holding my head high, saying that Rodney's work appeared to have been completed, and allowing no further conversation on the subject.

I threw in my lot with Francis Roles as far as I could. He was very kind to me now, and we had many sessions of quiet talk together. But he was nervous of any idea, any development that did not echo exactly the teaching he had inherited from Ouspensky, or the way that O. had indicated they should go. His well-drilled troops were obedient and straight-faced. They had an expression of alert watchfulness, which some of us had jocularly called "meeting faces"—e.g. the expression people put on when they are attending a philosophical or religious meeting as distinct from the more relaxed expression of every day living.

I confess that after all my adventures I soon began to feel them to be very boring. However I was prevented from drifting away entirely, by Francis's continual reference to his search for a "direct method"—something that would raise consciousness more quickly than the regular disciplines and practices and bring within sight the attainment of the status of 'Man No. 5'. This, he was sure, had been O's last wish. And such a method might, I thought, enable me to recover and retain more clearly and permanently the understanding that I had had briefly during that evening in the company of Hugh Ripman. I was still trying to remember exactly what it was that I had perceived in that moment of 'enlightenment'.

In 1958 the Indonesian mystic, Pak Subuh, came to London. He was at once taken up by J.G.Bennett and invited to set up his headquarters at Bennett's country mansion, Coombe Springs.

John Godolphin Bennett was an adventurous man who had outgrown Ouspensky and parted company from him in an amicable way. Since few people realised that he had been encouraged to set up house for himself by O., he was generally regarded as a dangerous outcast and to be avoided like the plague. Anyone who had dealings with him was felt to have been contaminated in some way.

In fact during his remaining years Bennett explored, gave hospitality to the Sufi, Idries Shah, returned to Christianity, continued with his thoughts and his writing on the teachings of Gurdjieff, and left a considerable legacy of scholarly and worthwhile books on esoteric Ways. I only met him personally a couple of times, so I shall not digress further to consider his contribution to the Work.

Hearing that Pak Subuh had a 'direct method' of some sort that he was imparting to Bennett's followers at Coombe Springs, Francis Roles resolved to meet him privately. After a lot of secret and hush-hush goings on, he invited twenty of his 'trusties' to gather together with Subuh and his wife Ibu and see if anything could come of the practice which Subuh had named the *Latihan*—the 'exercise'. Francis did not include me among the chosen twenty, probably because he was by no means sure that he could trust me. I might get the bit between my teeth and go off in my own way at any time. He would have been considerably disconcerted if he had had a glimpse into the future at the time of the Subud experiment, for in fact almost every one of the carefully selected bunch defected from Francis's flock—not all to Subuh, but to other teachers or methods —within two years. They had all got a sniff of something different, and like a herd of deer raising their heads to the wind and the scent of fresh fodder, they were off in search of pastures new.

Francis's contact with Pak Subuh was quite brief. He decided the new practice was dangerous and not to be given to the flock as a whole.

I, however, came in on, as it were, the second wave, and proceeded to experiment for myself. Madame Kadloubowsky and I had always kept in contact, and I had been accustomed to visit her, and talk over the wide range of subjects and ideas that interested us both. She was almost old enough to be my grandmother. Her courteous, aristocratic ways were reflected in her surroundings. Her home, though very modest, was scholarly and booklined, full of memorabilia from pre-revolution Russia which she had managed to get out before the holocaust.

It was she who told me that Subud, as the movement was called was worth investigating. Her son and daughter-in-law, George and Lesbia Kadleigh, were involved in it, having finally parted company with Francis Roles for good. George and Lesbia, together with Reggie Hoare of Hoare's Bank and his wife, and Basil and Hilda Fenwick who had been regulars at Dr. Role's meetings for some years, had decided that the Coombe

Springs set-up was not for them. They had been there, found the spiritual practice, the *Latihan*, to be realistic in some way, but thought a degree of control was needed if it was not to get quite out of hand.

They had succeeded in persuading Bapak, as Pak Subuh was affectionately called, and his wife Ibu, to start an entirely separate branch of Subud under their own auspices. For this purpose they had rented a practice room at the Royal Ballet School premises in Colet Gardens, to the intense annoyance of Dr. Roles, whose own property Colet House was just next door.

Colet House had belong to Ouspensky himself. It had been sold at his death, but after a few years it had come back on the market. Francis Roles had been able to raise sufficient money through the Society to buy it back. As a discipline and exercise in attention and self-awareness, his followers were even now engaged in painting and renovating the colossal mansion in silent, workmanlike teams. It had got into an extremely neglected state.

As it was absolutely forbidden to have any connection with the firm next door, a highly foolish and laughable situation now developed. The approach along Colet Gardens from Barons Court tube—this area is now part of a wide, through carriageway, but was then purely residential—meant that people attending meetings at Colet House and those going to the *Latihan* in the Royal Ballet School were completely unable to avoid encountering one another.

However, the Colet House people were strictly forbidden to converse with or even acknowledge the heretics. They therefore marched straightfaced down the road, glancing neither to left nor right. They even stepped back into doorways to avoid being contaminated by the perfectly harmless people with whom they had previously shared experiences at meetings, but who happened to have developed different opinions on the best method of working on themselves. They were "going a completely different way".

I confess to having been so amused by this absurdity that more than once I spoke directly to Work people whom I had had to my home, or lunched or dined with in the past in amicable friendship. Hot flushes of embarrassment suffused their faces as they shuffled their feet and murmured that they must go. One Mrs. Hick, whose husband ran a 'group activity' based on poetry reading, rushed into my arms with delight at seeing me—once a regular visitor to their flat—only to 'remember herself' in time to push me off with such violence that I stepped back into the gutter. She then went at a gallop through the entrance to Colet House and slammed the door.

I had parted company with Francis Roles without rancour on either side and he had kindly said I should keep in touch with him personally and let him know of any interesting developments in my own life. I was to write to him at his home address, not via his secretary in the Work—a rare privilege, for others were not allowed to communicate except through Helen. But in fact the correspondence between us soon became desultory and then lapsed.

Pak Subuh was a very sexy man. I noticed this as soon as I attended his first lecture. His hands were continually caressing the inside of his thighs, and there was something in his expression and his posture that gave me certain ideas.

His basic theme was that man needs help from a higher level if he is to advance and fulfill his position in the world and his true destiny. His book, *Susila Budhi Dharma*, under his full name, Muhammad Subuh Sumohadiwidjojo, means the *Way of Submission to the Will of God*. It suggests that the intellect and imagination stand in the way of 'submission', and that the complete surrender of the 'self' is necessary. A considerable part of the book is devoted to a discussion of sexual relations as a way to release, and to fulfillment of the divine nature within man.

His personal story, which he told frequently at his lectures, was that he had been chosen to 'open' people to the power of God. As a youth he had sought a master in his own country. Everywhere he went he was refused, with the words "I am not your master. Your master will come to you". One day in his own home, he experienced an hour of enlightenment. He realised that his master had entered him. He could now open the way for his wife and family and for others in due course.

The 'opening' was a very nebulous procedure. At first it seemed as innocuous as 'listening to God', or self-remembering. But the effects were a very different kettle of fish indeed. We were told in advance that it was essential that men and woman should be separated for this practice. They were not to be in the same room, or even in the building at the same time. The men's *Latihan* with Bapak would be at a certain hour: the women's with Ibu, considerably earlier or later, to avoid any chance encounters on the way in or out of the ballet school.

I went along with Madame K. and Lesbia, who was by now also qualified to be one of the 'openers'. However it was Ibu who 'opened' me.

As we went from the cloakroom where we had left our coats, down the corridor to the long room with a barre, for the ballet students, a strong scent of incense assailed my nose. I assumed joss sticks were burning somewhere. But I could see none.

About thirty women were gathered in the empty room. Those to be 'opened' were brought to Ibu. The others moved about freely, or sat on the floor, waiting. On the command 'Begin' the women started concentrating in some way on their inner sensations. This led fairly quickly to swaying movements or perambulation round the room, sometimes with arms raised or outstretched. A low, unorganized chanting began, swelling into a curious, not at all discordant sound that gradually increased in pitch, though no discernible melody could be picked up. It was clearly spontaneous and rather pleasing to the ear. For about ten minutes the wordless chanting continued rising and falling. The students' movements seemed in some cases almost like the Kathakali temple dances: in others more like Greek dance or Russian ballet. Some remained seated, often cross-legged, with closed eyes, moving only shoulders and arms or hands.

Everyone seemed happy, save one middle-aged woman who suddenly broke into wailing and then loud sobs. One of the 'openers' went to her and comforted her, hushing her, avoiding undue disturbance.

Meanwhile I had awaited my turn and now stood in front of the Indonesian lady. She was dressed in oriental garb, a big, slightly coarse-featured woman, whose interest in each individual seemed a bit perfunctory. No instructions were given save to stand facing her, willing and submissive to the power. She began to breathe deeply, her heavy breasts rising and falling.

95

Uncertain what to expect, I remained in readiness. In fact at the end it appeared to me that nothing at all had happened. I sensed no power, no presence, nothing out of the ordinary at all. In a few moments I was told I had been 'opened' and waved to circulate with the rest.

The chanting and dancing was a bit hypnotic in its effect. The only instructions I had been given in advance by Lesbia was that I should watch that I did not get carried away. At Coombe Springs, where no restraint at all was exercised, people had taken to throwing themselves about the room, shrieking and screaming, banging their hands or even their heads against the walls and floor, in an apparent attempt to rid themselves of a thousand devils. Clearly the 'exercise' was some sort of releasing or cleansing process. The violence or otherwise of the reaction would depend upon the nature of the individual.

It was the contention of Basil Fenwick, the Hoares and the Kadleighs, that the 'releasing' effect of the Latihan was enormously beneficial and had a cathartic result almost immediately. But that it could be used to far better advantage by those who had experience of 'self-remembering', and who were already acquiring self-knowledge, than those who came newly to esoteric or spiritual practices and 'let it all hang out'.

I had been warned not to do the *Latihan* alone at first. New initiates were to attend the communal gathering once or twice a week only. This could be increased, and solitary practice could be permitted, when one was properly established in the art. For several weeks the only thing I experienced was a pleasant relaxation, the rather nice feeling of being able to dance and chant, like an uninhibited child without making a fool of myself.

That, and the incense smell. I discovered there was no incense. Though I smelt it strongly on almost every occasion, there was no incense burning there at all.

Discussion with others led to a curious discovery. Some could smell incense one day, not the next, and others could smell it when I could detect nothing myself. In addition, some people smelt other scents. Attar of roses was a common one: also mimosa, lily of the valley and a variety of flower scents. One woman found she always smelt the perfume Coty L'Aimant. An oddity was a large, fat girl who told me she normally smelt bacon and eggs frying! From this I formed the tentative conclusion that people smelt what they wanted to smell. If food for the body was more important than food for the mind, the heart, the spirit, that was what the nostrils appeared to receive.

This curious phenomenon sent me back in thought to Mallory's *Morte D'Arthur*. The Arthurian legends associate the Sangreal with both scents and with food. The maidens would bear the Holy Grail into the hall where the knights were assembled. It would always be accompanied by 'sweet odours'. And in at least one account, each knight found placed before him such food as was most pleasant to his taste.

Later, when I was with the Maharishi Mahesh Yogi, I learnt a good deal more about the so-called 'subtle strata' of the senses. Just as the human ear can detect only a relatively small range of sound—a bat's cry, for instance, or a supersonic dog whistle being inaudible to most people—so, said the Maharishi, are we restricted also in the range of our other senses. Only in meditation were scents, sounds, sights, taste, touch outside the norm of human experience ever encountered. But his teaching stated adamantly that all this was a waste of time—a half way house only, to the transcendental state.

For the moment, though, I found it to be an interesting curiosity. I did some researches into the history and usage of incense. I found in the Old Testament that the Jews had been given exact and detailed instructions about the making of incense for purposes of worship. Was the mixture of these particular ingredients of spices, herbs etc intended originally as a way of opening those inner doors of the mind, tapping the subtle strata for a specific purpose?

Later I encountered the work of Enid Case, an interesting elderly lady living in Devon whose small book *The Odour of Sanctity* contains a varied collection of other people's, and her own, experiences of what she called "scentings". Her conclusion was that scents of flowers, tobacco, incense etc, which are not accounted for by the physical presence of these things, were usually associated with emotional experiences of some kind. People smelt flowers when moved by bereavement and loss. Perhaps that is why Madonna lilies and other heavily scented flowers used to be brought into churches for funerals and mourning.

Tobacco was often described in words like "I smelt Father's pipe, so I knew he was still around". "I got my mother's favourite scent after my little girl died, so I knew she had come to comfort me." Naive though many of the thoughts were, the reality of the experiences seemed beyond doubt.

I thought that, of such a nature as this, may be all apparitions, the feather touch of angels' wings on the pyramid of Teotihuacan: and—voices. They may be real, but could they be any real indication in themselves of spiritual advancement? Very possibly they came from a lower level than I was becoming aware of, inwardly.

It soon became apparent to me why men and women were kept so strictly segregated for the Subud practice. First one friend then another sobbed through the Latihan and confessed afterwards to having fallen in love with someone else's husband. Presently, sexual stimulation rose to such a pitch that young people were breaking up their marriages or their long-term partnerships and linking up with others, and again others like a perpetual version of an old-fashioned 'excuse me' dance.

There was a man in Francis Roles's set-up, quite a lot younger than myself, to whom I had always been rather attracted. I thought the attraction was reciprocated. I had disciplined myself against thinking about him since there was clearly no future in it. Apart from my own now long established marital state, I knew Jim to be charmingly seductive and promiscuous, and my intelligence had long ago told me to be extremely wary of him.

Now, the walk up Colet Gardens became a ridiculous ordeal of "shall I see him? Will he appear at one of the windows? Will he emerge from the door just as I pass it?" My heart thumped like a schoolgirl's and in the night hours I suffered the torments of the damned from sheer sexual desire for him! At the same time, reason and will prevented me from making any move, even when I learnt a little later that he had left Francis Roles and was presumably free to meet whoever he chose, as well as being for the moment unattached. (He had been one of Roles's 'trusties' who had defected after the Subud experiment.)

The big question in my mind was, why are we all, even middle-aged women and well-adjusted, happily married men, getting so sexy? Gurdjieff had described sex energy as the raw

98

stuff from which finer forms of energy could in due course spring. Dividing the human mind into artificial compartments, to make his point, he indicated the need for the transformation or transmutation of the basic energy levels into something that could serve the higher man. Of these, procreative energy turned to artistic output was clearly a comprehensible aim. I set myself to turn the useless stuff in that direction, sitting at my desk to write for hours at a time when I could not sleep. My output of novels was fairly easy still, and they were all well reviewed. I wondered whether my creative ability was improving. I was turning out a lot of philosophical notes in between while, and a mass of poetry. But though more prolific than before, I didn't think it to be in any way likely to set the world on fire. Much of it was too personal in any case, and unsuitable for publication.

One day a rather sharptongued woman, who normally behaved with at least a reasonable degree of good manners, turned on everyone in the cloakroom and subjected them to such virulent and unjustified abuse over some trivial wrong that I was amazed. On the same evening I was struck by the exaggerated behaviour and bizarre clothing of a hitherto not remarkable young professional woman. It occurred to me that what we were tapping in the *Latihan* was a source of raw, but absolutely neutral energy. It would therefore enhance and develop the tendencies or the intentions of the people who were 'open' to it. The creative might become more creative and busy, but the bad-tempered could well become more bad-tempered, the vain more filled with a desire for self-aggrandisement. It was a release all right. But it might well prove in the end to be a version of Pandora's Box.

What the source might be, I could not hazard a guess. Since it brought no higher knowledge with it, it was presumably not of a high order itself. Perhaps it was a discarnate being, desiring to help the world, but not being itself of a level to do anything very useful. Perhaps it was only of the level of the elements. The theory of the existence of elementals, beings associated with the air, the water, fire, and the earth itself, was one I had been looking into recently. Sylphs, undines, salamanders and elves are quite an interesting field of study in themselves!

Madame K. was the only person I could talk to freely on the subject of Subud. Elsie Abercrombie was 'opened', but her health was now failing rapidly and she was unable to proceed, and was in any case not very enamoured of the thing from the start. Almost everyone else was either euphoric about it and determined to stay with Bapak through thick or thin, or had left in disgust when the sexy side or other undesirable manifestations had come uppermost in themselves. Although the process of infiltration into one's being was fairly slow, and non-violent in its first manifestations, it was certainly becoming deeper and less controllable with time.

At first the old Russian lady was able and willing to discuss the process as frankly and coolly as I was myself. But later, she began to trouble me a good deal. She seemed to have become almost perpetually ill since starting the practice, and one ailment after another assailed her. With deep humility she said to me: "It is a catharsis, you see. I must bear all this. The impurities are working their way through me. I shall be better soon".

But she looked drawn and exhausted. Eventually I was struck by the thought that day to day living brought continual 'impurities' into everyone. A moment's temper or dislike, a flash of exasperation at someone's stupidity, any contempt or inner criticism of the life around, might manifest itself in one as an 'impurity'. The illnesses might be psychosomatic in the true sense of that much abused word. Even other people's sins or shortcomings, if observed and taken into herself, were being 'digested' by her own system, instead of falling away from her harmlessly. Everything was being affected by her diligent practice of the *Latihan*. Since no-one is perfect, obviously no-one could possibly avoid the day to day 'impurities' which come of living in the world.

At home, I now practised it privately as instructed. It interested me to find the spontaneous way my body, which though tall and no longer young was still very supple, moved into oriental dancelike postures. Hips, neck, arms, hands and feet took up positions foreign to my previous experience. Sometimes the room seemed to fill with incense as I practised. There seemed to be some connection between the dance movements and the incense, and the spontaneous attempt to assume the lotus posture with Reggie Carroll as a child, and the darkened, incense-filled room I had at that time momentarily perceived. It was also of the same nature as the Tibet experience, when running up the Banbury Road at Oxford, I had felt myself encumbered by heavy padded clothing, and had become briefly so disorientated that I had to turn into the University Parks and sit down while I sorted out my present identity.

Once my daughter, now a teenager, surprised me by commenting that she could smell incense in the cottage at Westerham where we lived. She went around looking and seemed to locate its source as an alcove beneath the stairs. On this occasion I could smell nothing at all. But it interested me that it could be picked up by another human being, unassociated with the Subud practice. I gave her no explanation of the matter and she soon forgot about it.

We women only saw Bapak very occasionally when he came to England to lecture. I always sat well away from him. I found I liked him and Ibu less and less. My distaste was strengthened when a woman friend, who had taken Ibu shopping in Oxford Street, at her request, reported with great embarrassment that the Indonesian woman had stolen costume jewellery, silk scarves and other small items and stowed them in her bag. A courteous protest that in England we normally pay for what we take from shops, brought a casual brush-off. She was Ibu. She was entitled to have what she liked.

Bapak was travelling widely in the United States and other parts of the world, starting centres everywhere. Hollywood took him up in a big way, and various film stars, starting with Eva Bartok, who was 'opened' at Coombe Springs, declared their allegiance to him and expressed their delight with their results. They were more energetic, more alive, better actors now—and no doubt a lot more sexy into the bargain. In fact, they had become somewhat enlarged versions of their former selves.

Meanwhile Coombe Springs was beset by a series of different scandals, and unexplained happenings. A newcomer to the practice, who had been given the usual warning not to do the *Latihan* too frequently, or alone until so instructed, got so carried away that he went into some sort of catatonic trance and eventually died. The press made much of it. They did not want to hear the explanation that the initiate was afterwards discovered to have had a history of mental and physical

101

instability, and could in fact have suffered a heart attack at any time. The episode shocked everyone. Those closest to the scene were thrown vociferously onto the defensive. What was a man with a health history like that doing at Coombe Springs anyway, people asked? They did not know. They thought he was all right. They only found out afterwards, they said.

Suddenly the grotto in the Coombe Springs garden was rocked by a series of completely inexplicable explosions. No cause at all could be found. People living in the house were decidedly frightened. It seemed apparently rather like a poltergeist phenomenon. John Bennett began to wind down the whole Subud experiment a short while after this. Dr. Roles no doubt nodded "I told you so". But Bennett's reason was that he was becoming interested instead in the Sufi master Idries Shah, to whom he gave the Coombe Springs property in entirety in due course. Nevertheless, his *Concerning Subud*, and *Christian Mysticism and Subud* showed that he had valued the practice and thought that it could indeed help to open inner doors of understanding.

Meanwhile the Ballet School group continued, more restrained, more controlled, watched over by people with a good deal more common sense than the screaming bunch Bennett appears to have admitted. It went on for several years after I myself had left.

Though less in the news, the Subud practice continues still, all over the world, though Bapak died, in his eighties, in June 1987, and Ibu before him. At Subud House In Norwich, near my present home, a collection of mildly creative people live with one another in harmony, practising the *Latihan* together daily. They are one of numerous similar small communities. They are happy in their work. But when I asked quite a talented artist and writer in his early forties why he limited himself to the possibilities inherent in the practice, he answered revealingly: "I can't live without it. I've tried once or twice. But when I leave and go away from the others I begin to disintegrate. Everything falls apart. Subud is essential to me, you see."

I looked at him. It was an intelligent, open face. He was a scholarly man. He had sent me some fine poetry. But he was unable to function from his own creative centre without support. In his middle years he had several broken relationships and marriages behind him, and the juvenile commune spirit still ruled him. I thought he had not really found himself. Also he had not earned a regular living for years. He had previously taught English abroad.

For me, two years was enough. I decided to slip away quietly from the Hoares, the Kadleighs and Basil Fenwick and work on my own for a while. The importance of Subud for me had lain in seeing the many levels from which power can be drawn, and in realising how easily one can fall under influences over which one has virtually no control.

But the *Latihan* practice remained in me, as did the 'listening', the self-remembering, and the experiences I had had in Mexico. To relax and calm myself in adversity, I have sometimes let that strange psychic power flow through me, moving and swaying, chanting to myself in the privacy of my bedroom or my study.

But the watchful inner 'I' commanded me now to be more watchful what I did. It is not the psyche but the Spirit that is the Jewel in the Heart of the Lotus. I wanted to go for that.

8

Bill Kadleigh, George and Lesbia's only son, answered the telephone in Madame K's flat one morning when my friend Ailsa Lenney rang up to speak to the old lady. Bill was a medical student and lived with his grandmother at the time. His life was tragically short, for he was killed in an aircrash on his way to a conference a year or two later.

Bill returned to the phone after a moment to say: "She seems to be sleeping soundly. I don't like to wake her." Half an hour later he realised she was dead. She had slipped from life some time in the night hours, her self-imposed catharsis seemingly incomplete.

Around the same time, Elsie Abercrombie also died. She had been in hospital for some weeks, and had proved an unusual patient. Any attempt to deal with problems with electrical apparatus of any kind proved quite dangerous to the nurses and the doctors. She would warn them: "Be very careful. You will get an electric shock." Knowing better, they would apply the electrodes or whatever in a normal way, only to be subjected to a violent jerk. One nurse, trying to stimulate her circulatory system, was thrown back across the room, as soon as the power was switched on. Though completely unable to explain the situation herself, Elsie's sense of humour caused her to chuckle even on her death bed, when her small frame had shrunk almost to nothing but the vital power was still greater than the norm. The nurses were nonplussed and appeared to think her senile. She was not.

I sat beside her during her last hours. Opening her eyes she reached for my hand and whispered: "Better go now. I think I'll just hang on here for a bit." I kissed her forehead and left her. In the morning they told me she had died soon after I had driven away. Standing by the graveside in the country churchyard, I

104

confess I felt rather sad again. I had lost Rodney. And now these two old ladies, both so much wiser than I that they had stood in loco parentis to me, had also moved on their way. I had always tended to be drawn to older people more than to my contemporaries and their going left a gap.

I had decided that nothing much could come of maintaining close contact with the remains of Rodney's group in Mexico. After his death the planetarium project had been abandoned. A long building nearby which he was erecting to use as a spinning and weaving workshop had become a weekend bungalow. And soon a number of the followers, including the Dickins family, had put up holiday residences on Rodney and Janet's land, and moved in for enjoyment and mutual succour and companionship.

The shrubs and trees that Rodney had planted had apparently grown apace in the fertile soil. I am told the whole, once bare hillside, is now so thickly shaded that the residences can scarcely be detected from the air at all.

Mema had taken complete charge of Rodney's few people now, and Janet was her obedient disciple. The Chamber of the Sun and the Chamber of the Moon had been converted, at Mema's command, into two chapels, the one to the Christ, the other to the Madonna. The library had not only been abandoned as a building: the valuable, and in fact quite priceless collection was mouldering away in various people's garages, devoured by ants and rotting with mildew.

Dr. Rouhier in Paris was so upset to hear of this that he wrote letters and sent messages via myself, suggesting that at all costs the remaining books should be put together and housed in dry conditions and a place of safety, pending any decision about their future. His letters were not answered. A verbal reply given to me by a traveller from Mexico was that Mema had vetoed much of the collection as being unsuitable reading for Roman Catholics. The first editions, and the priceless volumes on magic, alchemy and so on had been deliberately destroyed. The other works would just disappear quietly. Nothing could apparently be done about it. Janet who had inherited everything, had a perfect right to destroy them if she wished.

Mema now had a group of young trainee Catholic priests from an ecclesiastical college around her. Her 'voices' were conveying Christian messages to them. In addition, she had developed the stigmata. Her bleeding palms were shown every Friday. I never saw them, of course. I know many people were deeply impressed by the manifestation. But someone who had seen it said to me: "I saw how it was induced," and would not be drawn further except to express contemptuous disapproval. I believe the appearance of stigmata in many cases tends to be associated with hysteria.

After a certain period of time the various phenomena ceased, and in due course the entire clairvoyant faculty faded out of Mema entirely. After Janet's death, no more was heard of it. Mema's son Tony Dickins told me in 1980 that he knew nothing at all about it: "Mother simply won't speak at all of the past".

Chloe had been safely married off to Tony when they were both twenty-one. As Roman Catholics, they quickly started a family, and soon had three little girls, close to one another in age. Tony was training to be a doctor. But he was immature still, prematurely married, and in due course went off to sow a few wild oats in other fields. Chloe was left, plucky and philosophical as ever, to cope with three babies and grass widowhood.

Those who had always been against Mema and held her to blame for all that had 'gone wrong' were full of condemnation of Tony: and even more so when, on Janet's death, he returned quickly to Chloe's side as she claimed her vast inheritance. There seemed to be a general opinion among the Work people in England that Janet had been rendered almost destitute as a result of Rodney's enormous, uncompleted projects, and Mema's financial demands in her later years. In fact her money was all held in trust for her, her Victorian father having believed that women were incapable of handling their own finances. It was the income only that was squandered, or given away in generous gifts to those she loved. The capital remained intact. She herself lived very simply in her widowhood, not from necessity, but from religious conviction and from choice. She spent most of her time teaching Mexican children in an orphanage. She was crippled with arthritis, but always smiling, tranquil and content.

Tony and Chloe embarked on somewhat more profligate

106

spending as soon as she came into her inheritance. Tony liked to enjoy himself. Travel, fast cars, big houses all appealed to him. He had also cultivated the art of hypnosis which he said he found useful as a doctor. Chloe appeared to be a willing subject. He could cure her headaches. He tried once to persuade me to put myself at his mercy, but I laughed him out of it. I had a feeling it was being used to induce forgetfulness in Chloe. When they visit England I find increasingly that Chloe is unable to remember her own past, and the notion that she once promised to "carry on the Work" with Tony has long ago been abandoned.

"We are not in the Work", Tony told me on a recent visit. Now well qualified, he works as an endocrinologist in the United States, and Chloe is glad to help him in a secretarial capacity. The marriage appears to have settled down into a normal relationship, Tony handling the money affairs and setting the tone for living. The three girls have grown up as attractive young Americans, and the household seems entirely materially orientated. In her early forties, Chloe had still not read her father's books and asked me where to begin to study, as she supposed she should familiarize herself with them some-time. But I don't believe she did.

Looking at her contented, middle aged face, seeing her pride in the girls and her acceptance of her husband's dominant role, with trusting affection and forgetfulness, I pondered on the plans which were never realised. But no doubt she has her own destiny to fulfil and it may be a worldly one.

Of the original followers of Rodney Collin in Mexico, only John Grepe, who used to run the Libraria Britannica, and his wife still describe themselves as being "in the Work". John telephoned me recently to berate me about an article—which he had not read but had heard about—in which I mentioned Rodney's name alongside that of James Webb. Apparently he felt that no-one had a right to set out on paper anything about my brother-on-law without his permission. A pleasant, well-intentioned man once, he had grown bossy. He was one of three men who each felt that Rodney's mantle had fallen specifically upon their personal shoulders. The other two have faded out. John demanded: "I want to see that article. Send me a copy please so that I may consider it". I saw no reason to do more than tell him where it had appeared. During the conversation I suggested to him that truth is many-sided—where Rodney and everything else is concerned—and there are many forms of love of him. He didn't take my point, and on the subject of my various articles and my occasional lectures we just had to differ.

After the Subud experiment I entered a fallow period. Ouspensky's ideas about 'starting again' in some way, not simply going on and on repeating old psychological systems, now had much more reality for me than before. I had seen how Francis Roles' people in particular had got stuck in a rut, afraid of anything new. At the same time, those who opened themselves to 'direct methods' of growth clearly went through dangerous phases and often lost their way if they were too willing to be 'taken over' in some manner.

Somewhere, I felt, there might be a master who could hold and teach me and whom I could really trust. But in the mean time, like Eric Kennington in his studio, and Rodney Collin hewing into the rock at the Panetarium in Mexico, it might be better just to 'chip away' at the stuff of life, using what knowledge I might have gained and cultivating any talents I might have as a writer and as a speaker. I therefore withdrew from all group activities for a couple of years and occupied myself with my personal affairs.

One day I was standing at a window of a house in London where I was staying with some friends, when I experienced a strong scent of lilac in the room. There was apple blossom in a tall vase on the piano, but the scent was clearly not from that source. I had not had any 'scentings' for some time, but as lilac was associated in my mind with Chateaubriand and the convent of Notre Dame des Oiseaux, I thought at once of Rodney. Tentatively, looking both round about me and then with closed eyes, enquiring within myself, I whispered: "Rodney?"

The remembered voice, heard occasionally through the years in the ears of my mind said simply: "The crossbow." The word meant nothing to me at all. But so that I shouldn't forget what I had heard, I wrote it on a scrap of paper and put it in my handbag.

108

A few days later, Ailsa Lenney came on the phone.

"Joyce, there's an extraordinary Hindu master who has been lecturing in London recently. Come and hear him. Ernest and I are very much impressed."

Ernest Lenney was a German Jewish antique dealer and a good pianist. He had hovered at the edge of the Work for many years, but never been really inwardly committed. The British had interned him in the Isle of Man as an enemy alien during the first part of the war, and he had never wholly got over the shock of it. All the same he had used the time of enforced idleness to read and study, to his ultimate advantage. He was extremely scholarly.

"I think we have to grow for ourselves", he had told me once. "Outside help isn't really necessary. Its all in us." He and Ailsa lived in Earls Court and I went along to lunch with them. However, just as they had left Rodney, later left Francis Roles, and dabbled in and left Subud after a brief time, they had already lost interest in the "remarkable Hindu master". They seemed to have become wanderers like myself. "I only want peace", Ernest said. "Peace, peace. I want to be left alone."

After lunch, Ernest sat at the piano playing in desultory fashion as we talked, lapsed into silence and talked again. It was summer and the long curtains were blowing lightly at the open windows into one of the Earls Court garden squares. Suddenly I realised he was playing "Für Elise". This rather haunting melody by Beethoven appeared again and again whenever Rodney was in any way involved. It is a curiosity that I have not unravelled. Mema played it on my piano at home in Westerham, and my then schoolgirl daughter took it up and played it continually. It had apparently been played round the bier during the vigil night at Cuzco.

People choosing a disc, apparently at random, for background music during a quiet evening would often, I noticed, pick it out first when I was there, in various different houses. Quite recently in 1986 a strange boy at a party I attended was said to have the "misfortune that the chakras are permanently open, and he can't tell the people in the room from the many others he sees around all the time—its a great difficulty for him". I looked at the rather vulnerable young face at the grandpiano across the room. "Play something for Joyce," my hostess called to him. Without pause or hesitation, not even glancing at me, he went into "Für Elise".

On that afternoon with Ernest and Ailsa I waited. Then I said: "Well, you may as well give me the name of the Hindu master anyway, and perhaps I shall think about it." I took with me a note of the Indian name and an address in Prince Albert Road, Regents Park, where he was then residing. Later I mounted the staircase to attend a small meeting there to which, on telephoning, I had been readily invited.

I climbed in innocence, accompanied by a dozen or so devotees and aspirants, all strangers to me, who were crowding into the hallway. I was entering six years of my apparent destiny. They destroyed me as a novelist and writer. They left me as a shadow of my former self. I swung from the heights of heaven to the depths of inner despair, and escaped eventually barely with my life.

Some traditions say that each soul must go through three big initiations before escape from the thrall of this life can be attained. After the third, a conscious choice can be made, whether to return to help mankind, or to move on. My first initiation was undoubtedly begun in that moment with Hugh Ripman in Mexico and completed on the pyramid when I recognised my brother. The air seemed full of angels then, but all the events of that crowded period of time were part of it. I do not count the Subud initiation as being in the same category at all, though perhaps it was indeed an initiatory experience of a lesser kind.

The second big one was to be by extraordinary stages a pilgrimage into the pit, into the valley of the shadow of death; though it was seen as such only by very slow degrees. The climb out of it has taken me many years.

But little indeed did I realise where I would be going next as I walked up, quite cheerfully and with interest, to enter the lecture room.

The first person I encountered there was Jim, for whom I had yearned so fruitlessly for years. I didn't know whether to be pleased or not to see him—he was a disturbing influence. We greeted each other with some embarrassment. But with him were several of my other old associates from Colet House, and on the whole they were a bunch of people whom I felt to be

110

endowed with common sense: genuine aspirants who were trying to free themselves from the bondage of outdated ways. So I joined them with a certain sense of inevitability. Clearly we were all together on "La Ronde", and our pathways were to cross and re-cross down the years.

In a moment there was a murmur from beyond the doors and we rose to face the master as he entered. His name was the Maharishi Mahesh Yogi.

9

The Maharishi entered the lecture room smiling benevolently. He was wearing white silk robes and holding a sheaf of red gladioli. His long black hair curled down to his shoulders. He was bearded.

After looking round the gathering of familiar faces of those who had come to hear him give his usual evening lecture or to answer questions, he caught my eyes and gave me a long, steady look. Later I found I was the only newcomer that evening. He always noticed a strange face, I learned. The room was dimly lit. The Maharishi did not like bright lights. In daytime his curtains were often half drawn keeping the sunlight out. He had lived many years in the solitude and darkness of caves in the Himalayas.

He looked impressive. I felt almost sure this was a genuine Master, a guru. We all sat down, very crowded on the carpeted floor. There were no chairs. I awaited his words with alert attention.

Instead of beginning a formal talk, his deep, rich voice asked rather surprisingly: "Any questions? Set the ball rolling!" His English was rapid and colloquial, not always easy to under-stand because of the sing-song Indian accent. He talked on various aspects of Hindu philosophy. A young man asked for a definition of Yoga. "It just means union. All One." An elderly German enquired about the different types of Yoga, begining to reel off his knowledge: "Hatha Yoga, Kriya Yoga, Raja Yoga, Karma Yoga, Tantric Yoga, Gnana Yoga —"

"Yes, yes. Ways towards union. Different ways. Hatha Yoga, it is just the body. This belongs to Karma Yoga, this simple system of transcendental meditation I am giving you."

His eyes were huge and luminous. Though I was tucked away in a far corner of the room between Jim and another old friend,

112

my legs bent up under me because of lack of space, my vision restricted by the heads and shoulders of others, I had the curious impression that his eyes were very near, that they saw me.

I began to think of other teachings and techniques and philosophies that I had studied in the past twenty-five years, comparing and weighing them up against his words. A phrase from Ouspensky's teaching came into my mind. It concerned a diagram of a double-headed arrow, indicating 'I' and the object of attention.

"No, the double-headed arrow, that is no good, that is divided attention", said the Maharishi's voice. My body leapt as though convulsed. He said—he actually said—the words that I was thinking. My heart began a rapid banging like a drum tattoo and I seemed not to be breathing. This sentence, thrown out seemingly casually was evidently directed at me. The great eyes were huge and close. I shut mine and breathed deliberately. When I looked again his eyes were ordinary and distant, seen in the half darkness between the heads across the crowded room.

I tried to remain calm. Someone was asking about the crucifixion. "The cross, yes. But Christ did not suffer. It only seemed to those standing by that he suffered. The cross is symbolic." And a moment later:

"To meditate we withdraw inward. It is like pulling an arrow back on a bow. Pull it back to its full extent, then release it. The further we pull it back, the greater the power when we release the arrow. In the meditation we draw back and come out into life with great energy."

"Maharishi, I am a Christian, and —"

"This evening we will talk more about the arrow and the bow instead of the cross. You British always want to suffer! It is not necessary to suffer. With my meditation you can be happy."

The piece of paper in my handbag that had "crossbow" written on it now made sense. When he rose and left, the lights were switched on. I looked round. There were even more familiar faces in the audience than I had realised.

One, an erudite old lady, Beatrice Mayor, once a well known member of the Bloomsbury set and an aunt of Malcolm Muggeridge, came over and seized my hands. I had known her for years. "It's so good that you've come here!" she cried. "You must come into Maharishi's private room and meet him personally. She tugged me gently by the hand and ushered me into a much smaller room, introduced me, retreated and shut the door behind her.

The Maharishi was alone. He was seated cross-legged on a deerskin laid over white silk sheets on a divan bed. The deerskin had belonged to his master and went everywhere with him, I learnt later. The room was full of flowers, heavy scented, and held the lingering perfume of joss sticks. He was holding a red rose. Because of the smallness of the room, I seemed to be very close to him.

"You have come for the first time", he remarked.

"Yes Maharishi." I began to converse with him with great hesitation. There didn't seem to be anything to say. I felt it would have been better to keep silent in the presence of this undoubted guru. He questioned me. In five minutes he said: "I will initiate you tomorrow. You will begin to meditate and be happy. Come at twelve o'clock."

I backed out. There were people waiting to go into the room. Someone took me aside and gave me instructions and information about the initiation. One must bring flowers and fruit. One should not have eaten food immediately beforehand. I went slowly downstairs to the front door. I felt that I needed more time, that there were a great many questions to be answered. After the Subud experiment I wanted to be careful. But when I tried to formulate the questions I could not produce any coherent ideas. I just knew I had come across something very important indeed.

When I opened the door I found the group of old acquaintances sitting outside on the steps: Elizabeth Jane Howard the novelist, Jim, now a television reporter, a young doctor called John Allison and his wife Susan. They were all smoking, which was against the custom of the house, for Maharishi did not like the smell of tobacco. So they had come out into the air. Were they all initiates? I asked.

"Yes, its wonderful!" Jim said eagerly. "You'll have a marvellous experience tomorrow". And "yes", the others echoed, they were very happy with what had happened to them. Soon we were joined by Stephen Andrews, a bearded Canadian artist in whose South Kensington studio I had spent pleasant hours of

114

conversation in the past. Cyril Frankl the film producer was also there.

Although I was very uncertain where I was heading, I felt fortified by the presence of old friends. If the Maharishi himself advised getting on with it, why should I hesitate? I asked myself.

In the morning I went early to London. Mindful of the instructions, I ate no breakfast. I took with me flowers from my own garden, fruit bought at Victoria Station, the new white handkerchief which was a symbol of purity and innocence of intent, like the white scarves given and received in greeting in Tibet. And the equivalent of what would have been a week's salary if I had still been working as a journalist in Fleet Street. This donation was required from all candidates for initiation.

At the house was great bustle, noise and laughter. Tremendous, vigorous life seemed to surge through it all the time. People ran up and down stairs, called to one another from room to room, and slammed doors with impunity. There was nothing monastic about the atmosphere that surrounded the holy man.

Johnson Bates, a middle-aged businessman who had previously lived temporarily with Maharishi in a flat in Pont Street, was nominally in charge of the new residence. But he seemed a bit out of his depth. Maharishi had appointed him 'leader' of the initiates and he felt the need to take firm control of the household.

He had gone round putting up notices, SILENCE, PRIVATE, and REMOVE YOUR SHOES, while Maharishi had been away for a few days. On his return, Maharishi had said: "What is this?" and had all the notices quickly taken down. He did not want rules, regulations and restrictions. Happy with their Master, the household quickly adopted boisterous ways. The domestic work and the general running of Maharishi's affairs was carried on haphazardly by various people who had, uninvited, taken up residence there.

Most of the occupants of 2 Prince Albert Road had full-time jobs, and worked for Maharishi in the evenings. The mainstays of the household were Nina, who was secretary to a spiritualist association, and Ulla, a German divorcee who worked as an art teacher in a technical college, and had previously been with Francis Roles.

The door of Maharishi's room was closed when I arrived for

115

my initiation. Outside it were a number of pairs of shoes. I realised that the previous evening I had entered his presence still shod, and felt clumsy for not having observed the Indian custom at once. I removed my shoes, and waited.

There was a lot of laughter and talk inside the room. From time to time the door opened and smiling people came out. Others took off their shoes on arrival and went in ahead of me. I was not called. The hours passed. It was long after the time set for my initiation. I grew hungry and longed for coffee, but dared not go away in case I missed my appointment.

Ulla came running down the stairs from the upper floor of the tall house, in stockinged feet. She stopped to talk. "You'll have to be patient. He has no idea of time. Some don't wait. Others do. It depends how much one wants to learn to meditate."

At that time hardly anyone had heard of the Maharishi Mahesh Yogi. His presence in London had attracted little notice in the press, and such comment as did appear was mostly caustic and fun-poking, or loftily superior. Reporters found his activities good for a laugh in the 'silly season' of August. But mostly they ignored him. It was the summer of 1960 and his travels round the world building up his Spiritual Regeneration Movement and all the allied organizations he later founded, had in fact only very recently begun to get under way.

It was a period of formation, and led into a turning point for him and his Movement, in which I was myself later involved. It is this early time that I remember with some happiness: the days of innocence that blended one into the next. And after my long period on my own, it was so good to be back with others who were united in working towards higher development.

Some time in the afternoon Maharishi emerged and beckoned me to follow him. We entered the long room where he had sat answering questions the evening before. The tall windows were now open to the afternoon sun. It was carpeted in green. Bright cushions were scattered about the floor where people had been sitting. At one end was a simple altar on which stood a portrait of Maharishi's master, the late Sri Bramananda Sarasvati Shankaracharya Jagad Guru of Yotir Math in the Himalayas, one of the guardians of the spiritual tradition of Shankara, which stems from ninth century India. It is one of the Saivate traditions: that is, it springs from Siva the destroyer or breaker-down, while other traditions spring from Vishnu the maintainer or preserver. The Hindu Trinity is of course Brahma the Creator, Vishnu and Siva. Later when I came to know a little more of the 'holy tradition' to which Maharishi belonged, the fact that it was a Saivate tradition seemed of great significance.

Beyond indicating the portrait of Guru Dev, the Holy Master, Maharishi told me little at this stage. I laid my gifts on the altar in front of the picture, as he indicated. Candles and incense were burning there. Standing in readiness were bowls of water, rice and coconut.

Maharishi requested that I "hold the mind in devotion". I looked at him in silent query. Devotion to him? To God? To the Hindu gods? He answered the unspoken question: "We invoke the masters of my tradition. There is great meaning in invoking the masters of the tradition."

Western writers who discuss the practice of Transcendental Meditation have laid great stress on the fact that the practice consists of the repetition of a Sanskrit word or mantra which each initiate is given for his private use during the initiation ceremony. The *method* of repeating the mantra is the secret of the meditation. Mantras can be found in books, but they do not generally work for those who just read about them, and try to use them without help. Many mantras are ancient and obsolete words, having no actual meaning now. The effect seems to lie in the vibrations of the word, which is repeated silently, inwardly.

The ritual actions and Sanskrit words of the initiation ceremony were not explained or translated, but they appeared to be mainly invocations of the Hindu gods, who are offered token food and drink and called upon to aid the aspirant, whose intent—shown by the white handkerchief—is innocent and unsullied by worldly purposes or sin. Some such invocations must have been at the core of many pre-Christian traditions and embodied in the rituals of the Mysteries, as well as being the basis of primitive Shamanistic initiations. However, I attached much importance at a later date to the realisation that we were apparently invoking the elemental kingdom. I did not know this at the time.

The little ceremony was not long, and it was impossible for me to know why it made such an impact. It was very different from the Subud 'opening' where it appeared to me that nothing at all had happened at the time, and results came afterwards by undetectable degrees. After being told exactly how to repeat my mantra, I found it running in my mind with great rapidity, almost automatically, as though some power other than my own was operating the mechanism of my brain. Maharishi told me to "remain in meditation", and added that he would return later, "to check how you are getting on".

Two, three hours passed. The time did not seem long and indeed I was mostly quite unaware of its passage. It did not occur to me that he had failed to return. I did not think of anything else but sat, relaxed and happy, crosslegged on my cushion, feeling a curious enjoyment and content.

Rush hour traffic started to pass the house. The working day was over. People coming from their office day began to enter the room where I sat in meditation. I heard them sit down on the floors in ones and twos as they quietly entered. I did not stir or open my eyes at all. I knew that they were meditating too.

At last, I became fully aware of my surroundings again. I opened my eyes and looked at my watch. I glanced at the tranquil faces all around me, their eyes closed, their features still and relaxed. I got up quietly and went downstairs to the hall. Though I had eaten nothing all day, I had no hunger or thirst. A feeling of pleasure, lightness and satisfaction filled me. It crossed my mind that I felt as I remembered to have felt during a happy love affair of long ago: contented and carefree as one rose from bed, and full of simple and innocent enjoyment of all the things of the day and of the night. I felt as though I had been made love to with great skill and tenderness, and had slept and rested and wakened up again. As though I had been cleansed and renewed, like a child. As though I were completely innocent.

Before starting for home, I spoke briefly to Johnson Bates, who told me that Maharishi would want to check my experiences the following day. "He has gone out now. He has forgotten all about you. Come in the morning."

I had been told to meditate for half an hour morning and evening. In the morning I took my bath, then sat down and began. The mantra ran easily and naturally in my mind, and again the happy, clean feeling assailed me. Vivid pictures began to appear in my mind, mostly of laughing children. The familiar loved face of Rodney came smilingly forward out of the mists of memory and his voice sounded within me. We seemed to be again together on top of the pyramid, in happy and trusting friendship. That had a been a happy year ..... Gradually I realised that I was thinking instead of meditating. I was no longer repeating the mantra. I began to repeat it again.

Then the half hour was over, though it seemed to be only minutes since I had sat down and begun. I dressed, did a few essential household tasks, snatched toast and coffee and set out through the early morning traffic for London.

In those days when his organization was not large, Maharishi would frequently take a new initiate under his close observation and supervision, instructing him or her while using his or her services in many ways. Over the years this changed, and thousands were initiated without ever meeting the master at all. It seemed I was fortunate at coming in the early stage. Finding I was a writer he soon had me composing leaflets, arranging the layout of posters for meetings he was to hold at the Caxton and Conway Halls, and beginning to draft out other documents.

I soon discovered that he had a highly intelligent mind, a retentive memory, and that he held a dozen projects in his mind at once and was continually mentally on the move. As I read aloud what I had written he would interrupt to tell me to ring Stockholm and book a hotel for him to stay in, to telephone somebody in Athens with regard to a proposed visit, to send a message to Baroness So and So in Hamburg. Or to ask: "What is the biggest hall in London?"

"The Albert Hall, Maharishi."

"How much does it cost? How many people will it hold? call them up! Tell them we will take it for a world congress soon." Though he worked and thought with great rapidity, his method was to get half a dozen people engaged on outline plans, then scrap them all in favour of more clearly evolved ideas as they occurred to him. He was essentially oriental in his approach to his work and to his followers — gregarious, talkative, unpunctual and with a smiling charm and a happy laugh that won forgiveness again and again for work done, and put aside and redone by someone else, and then thrown away all together after hours and days of effort.

People came and went all day. He liked to have people round

119

him, pressing in on him, sitting at his feet, as pupils crowd in on the master by tradition at home in India. We wrote sitting crosslegged on the floor, interrupted by the perpetually ringing telephone, the arrival of newcomers, or to go and stir the vegetable curry simmering in the kitchen. Once a day he would eat, and all who were at the house at the time would eat with him. He was a complete vegetarian and lived mostly on the curries that the Indian devotees cooked, and fruit, yogurt or milk.

On the first day I worked with him for eighteen hours. I was not conscious of the time. He himself seemed tireless. When he said: "Telephone Lady X. She will give me some money for a lecture tour", someone answered: "She will be in bed, Maharishi. Its the middle of the night." It was about 3 am.

"The middle of the night? Everybody should go home then", he said, looking round enquiringly. "You don't want to go home?" We shook our heads and nobody moved. At once the work and planning began again, for clearly he himself had no wish for sleep.

I dossed down on a few cushions in the downstairs room for a few hours. Thereafter I came and went most days, turning my hand to whatever task needed doing: from vacuuming carpets and washing the dishes, to writing drafts of booklets which urged the need for meditation in the Western world. Everything that I wrote in straightforward journalistic style was altered back into flowery oriental language before publication.

When there was time, we sat and repeated our mantras in meditation. Most of us were at first fascinated and held by visions, voices and subtle sensory perceptions which were pleasing, interesting or an inexplicable curiosity. This was not new to me, of course. But it had never been wholly understood before.

Maharishi said these experiences belonged to the 'half-world' in which spiritualists and clairvoyants commonly dabble. I would describe it now perhaps as the psychic rather than the spiritual level.

"That is no value. Leave all that. We go beyond all that."

Maharishi's simple theory was that the mind wil' turn naturally towards the source of its own being if it is shown an easy technique. This is the "kingdom of God within", and the source of all existence. "Great happiness, energy, creativity, love can be tapped by this simple means", he said, "for the mind easily transcends this world and enters the field of the Being." So the initiate finds all tensions, world-weariness and all negative emotions falling away from him. He goes deep within and emerges renewed and refreshed.

So completely convinced was he of his simple system of Transcendental Meditation that he spoke confidently of completing his work within three years. After this he would return to the Himalayas and to a life of solitude and meditation in the mountain caves in the Valley of the Saints at Uttar Kashi where his spiritual brothers lived. The work he was going to complete was "the regeneration of the world".

Maharishi had lived in the ordinary secular world of India as a boy, and had taken a degree in physics at Allahabad University. Some time before his university education was completed, he encountered the Shankaracharya of Yotir Math, who was being borne ceremonially through the streets of Allahabad on a holy day.

The young student abandoned his worldly career and followed the holy man, living thereafter among recluses and monks, engaged entirely upon spiritual advancement. He emerged again about the age of forty-five, after the death of his master. He preferred the phrase "after Guru Dev left the body". He felt that Guru Dev required him to help the world.

From his early, worldly experiences, the man now known as the Maharishi Mahesh Yogi, drew his ideas of how to get things moving in a secular community. He had had no experience of life outside the enclosed community since he was a very young man. He began in a matter of fact and logical way, by considering the size of the population of the world, and calculating how many must begin to meditate per day, per month and per year: how many would need to be empowered to initiate others. How many candidates the new initiators would need to handle per week, per month and per year; and what percentage of these must in turn be made initiators. Yes, yes, the whole world could learn to meditate in three years! Regenerated, the world would experience no more wars. All men would live in happiness and peaceful brotherhood.

He sat smiling, his huge brown eyes shining, whiteclad upon

his master's deerskin, his arms full of flowers. We looked at him and loved him. We treasured his innocence. In his presence who could dare to voice the *Weldschmerz* that moved in our dark minds, shadowed with knowledge of banishment from Eden, and dim understanding of the place of a skull called Golgotha?

We closed our eyes and taking the traditional mantric words that "cause all good vibrations" as he told us, we felt our minds turn inwards through subtle and subtler strata of experience. Beyond the visions of the half-worlds, we found something infinitely delicate, infinitely precious and sweet: the water of the well of eternal life, for sure. We returned not knowing where we had been or what we had encountered there. We thirsted and entered the place again. Joy filled us and our whole lives seemed fresh and new, like the morning and the evening of the first day of the world.

Now it seemed I had found a way to do, by intention, that which had come so spontaneously on the evening with Hugh Ripman long ago. But it began to make sense that I should have felt then that I knew something—but didn't know what I knew! "The conscious mind cannot perceive the nature of the Being," Maharishi said. For this reason it was difficult to bring anything lucid back from the transcendental state. Nevertheless, one grew continually more hungry for the practice.

After a few weeks I was chauffeuring Maharishi about London in my car. When he said he wanted to go and speak to the undergraduates at Oxford, I offered to go with him. Though my parents were now dead, I took especial pleasure in the idea of going back to my childhood home. He normally travelled with a small entourage, but at the last moment he decided to be driven down alone by Henry Nyberg, a retired Dutch Jewish antique dealer who had recently joined the Movement and who later became its leader. I was to go ahead to the Randolph Hotel and prepare for his coming.

I already knew enough of the routine of his lectures to know that really several people were always needed to cope with the influx of candidates for initiation who would follow his talk. I therefore telephoned Stephen Andrews, the Canadian artist, who had already travelled about with Maharishi and knew the drill, and whom I regarded as quite a trustworthy friend. I hoped he would come down and help. The message was taken by Dr. John Allison who said he would pass it on. They had adjoining flats.

From London we had booked a large double bedroom for Maharishi, and another for myself, and had hired the hotel ballroom which was to be turned into a lecture hall for the evening. There were a great many things to be done before Maharishi's arrival. I was kept busy arranging flowers in the hall, putting out leaflets, seeing that seating arrangements were right. He always sat cross legged to speak, and so that he could be seen, the hotel staff arranged a table for him to sit on, on the platform. I covered it with one of Maharishi's thin brown blankets and banked it with flowers, the way he liked it done. On top of the blanket would go his deerskin when he arrived.

At his request, I had invited the press, and the Oxford Mail and Times sent a young reporter and a girl photographer. I had been able to pull strings to get the paper's attention because of my old association with it before the war. Between arranging the hall, seeing to Maharishi's food, re-arranging his bedroom in the way he would like it, using a tallboy as an altar, and dealing with many early enquirers, I ran up and down stairs and along the corridors at superhuman speed. I needed help, but there was no sign of Stephen.

When Maharishi arrived with Henry Nyberg, I mentioned the absence of helpers with some dismay, for they had brought no-one else with them. Henry made it clear that he was just dropping the Master off here, and he himself was en route to his Wiltshire country house. Maharishi said cheerfully: "You will manage very well by yourself."

When he was settled in his room, I brought the reporter upstairs to him. I asked the young man if he would mind removing his shoes, as was the custom, and he did so in an amiable and friendly fashion. When he entered Maharishi's presence he paused, and bowed before sitting down. This was a great change from the national press, whose representatives rarely showed courtesy towards the Maharishi and were often rude, sarcastic and unkind.

Maharishi gave the customary Indian greeting, palms of his hands together, mumuring "Jai Guru Dev", (Hail, Holy

123

Master.) I watched Maharishi's shining face as he spoke in his simple, childlike way of his hopes and aspirations for the world. It was clear that at this time he had not considered that it might not be only the absence of 'methods', 'practices' and 'ways' to higher consciousness that kept the world in its present unhappy state. Someone repeated to him the cliché "Christianity has not been tried and found wanting: it has been found difficult and not tried". "My way is not difficult", he answered, missing the point and entirely sure of his success, no matter what had been the fate of other teachings.

The young reporter listened politely to all that Maharishi said. He asked questions, made notes, closed his book and courteously left. Maharishi looked pleased and confident. "This one will really write all about me? He will only write what I have said, and not infer things that I did not say?" This had happened a good deal with the London papers—the deliberate distortion or exaggeration of his simple words.

"I think he will write truthfully and without adverse comment", I told him.

The girl photographer came in. She was a different type all together. She refused contemptuously to remove her high-heeled shoes. Her little tough face took in the setting and the background, the incense and the flowers banked behind him. She ordered him peremptorily to move to another position where the background was less cluttered. Looking puzzled he said: "No, no," and did not do so.

With an expression of annoyance, she thrust her powerful lamp into my hand saying: "Well, hold that. Stand there and shine it on his face." And to Maharishi: "Look this way. Turn your head. Raise your eyes. Hold it. Right." A flashlight exploded suddenly with a bang. She swore, and began to fumble to replace it, banging her things about in an exaggerated show of disdain for him.

Maharishi, himself so gentle and polite in manner, looked in astonishment at the hard, bold young face. Then he turned and looked at me with an expression of bewilderment, uncertainty, almost fright. Holding the lamp steady to highlight his features to advantage as the girl told me to, I smiled reassuringly. He smiled, then laughed as the camera flashed and clicked a couple of times. She left disagreeably and without a word to him, as though she had been photographing an animal or an inanimate object. He looked at me. "It will be all right?"

"I think the photographs will be all right, Maharishi."

"It is very important to get publicity," he said for the hundredth time.

"But you need good publicity, Maharishi. Some that you have had has been detrimental to you."

"All publicity is good publicity. There is no such thing as bad publicity", he answered blandly. I was touched. How very little he knew of the western world as yet. Although it was already some time since he left India, he had been mostly in the Orient until recently, moving from his own land to Malaya, Burma, Hongkong and Honolulu, and very briefly to the USA before arriving in London. I grasped suddenly the aloneness, the courage, the enormity of the ordeals that he was undergoing in his self-imposed exile. And the urgency of his idealistic dream.

At the last moment John Allison turned up instead of Stephen Andrews. He had a vague excuse for his own presence, and I saw by the evasive expression when I questioned him that he had not delivered the message, but had found it a good opportunity to get nearer to Maharishi for his own private purposes. Trailing along with him was Elizabeth Jane Howard. Hoping for practical help, I asked Jane to complete the flower arrangement and John to cope with the tape-recorder which was in position, but not plugged in or loaded. I rushed off to attend to phone calls, and ten minutes later returned to find both of them sitting with Maharishi, talking philosophy, oblivious of time. This surprised me, for they had always been competent people before. It began to dawn on me that a certain vagueness, an unwillingness for action, an avoidance of responsibility pervaded certain sections of the Spiritual Regeneration Movement.

Maharishi usually talked at great length during these early lecture tours. He knew that those who stayed were more seriously interested than those who soon got bored and went away. He maintained always that the meditation was for everyone, not only for those with knowledge and understanding of religious teachings and philosophical thought. All the same he had to catch his applicants by theoretical discourse at first.

He taught mainly in terms of the Hindu philosophy in which

125

he was so well instructed. He told people that the practice of meditation did not mean abandoning their own religions. Their understanding of the dogma and rituals of their own church, and the practices and customs of their own land, would deepen with the deepening meditation. No-one was to imagine that he must abandon western ways.

All the same, some of his followers soon took to Indian robes, incense in their homes and the carrying and giving of gifts of flowers. Many took to Indian food and professed vegetarianism. It was the beginning of the era of Flower Power, and the Flower Children with their bare feet and sandals, long hair, trailing skirts, seemed to be multiplying throughout society like little echoes of the Indian masters whom some encountered and others had heard about. "Love and peace" they crooned, embracing one another.

One day, having to go on to the platform with a French woman who drifted round Europe in a sari as a member of his entourage, Maharishi said glumly to an intimate: "I wish I had not to be introduced on the platform by Madame B. The people will think we are both crackpots together." The rapid way he picked up slang and idiomatic phrases caused everyone affectionate amusement.

After the lecture at the Randolph Hotel people milled round me and I began to try to make appointments at fifteen minute intervals throughout the next day and the following one. They pressed in on me, questioning, demanding, anxious and eager for attention. I knew too little. I was not qualified to answer their urgent, personal questions. I played the part of secretary, noted names on a pad, and at last flew upstairs again. Hotel porters, a little bemused but very friendly, plodded after me at my request carrying the many vases of flowers. I took them into Maharishi's room.

Jane was crouched in an armchair, huge-eyed and silent. John was talking about Ouspensky, running on and on. Maharishi was clearly not listening. He was lost in thought. I moved about the room, putting flowers by the small altar that I had set up with Guru Dev's portrait, and the candles and incense sticks ready.

I asked him if he would eat now? I had arranged for a

vegetarian curry to be sent up earlier, but he declined it. He said he would like yogurt, but it was late and the kitchen was closed. He settled for fruit and some biscuits from my picnic basket, and drank milk and was quite satisfied.

We began to talk of the evening's events. John and Jane were still bent on personal philosophising, and at about 1 am he suddenly cut across their words with seeming impatience and said: "You should go. Go home now. Go back to London." They had been of no practical use, had merely cashed in on my cry for assistance, and by the glance he gave me as the door closed behind them, I realised that I should not have taken this initiative. I was left alone with him. After a moment I said a bit diffidently:

"Maharishi, tomorrow I do think it will be really necessary to have two or three others to help with all the people. There may be forty or fifty people to initiate in two days. How can I look after them all? May I not telephone to London for some helpers to come in the morning?"

"No, you will manage by yourself. It is not necessary to have anyone else."

I sat with him another hour while we made notes for other plans and projects. A World Congress at the Albert Hall was still in his mind. It should be held soon, he thought. And then a large conference for the initiates who had already been meditating for some months. After that he would set out again on his travels to Germany, Scandinavia, Italy, Greece, Paris. And in a few months out of Europe again and to South Africa, he thought. Then perhaps back to the United States, over to New Zealand and Australia, and back to rest in silence in India the following January.

He was looking for a suitable place in India for the building of an Academy of Meditation. When it came into being it would be the world training centre for initiators and advanced initiates in TM. Here they would come to meditate with him for long periods of time, to be instructed in the Hindu philosophy in which his theory was rooted and in the esoteric knowledge he intended to impart bit by bit. But at that time he stressed that any further tuition or knowledge of secret practices would be reserved only for those who seriously desired it. For the

127

majority, the simple system of TM would be enough to enhance the possibilities of their personal lives and ultimately to 'regenerate the world'.

When eventually he had finished work for the night, he lay down on the white silk sheets which I had spread over his bed, turned on his side and supported his head on his hand. I took his thin brown blanket and spread it over him. It seemed a very inadequate covering, but I knew he was very rarely inconvenienced by changes in temperature. He would never use the blankets and eiderdown that were provided in hotels.

He asked to have the window open. The air seemed chilly, but he said he was not cold. "The amount of clothing worn is just a matter of custom", he had answered, walking through Regents Park in his thin silk dhoti and bare sandalled feet on a raw and windy evening. Fresh air was always important to him. When people came and went he would frequently have the window flung wide. I supposed that his sensual perceptions were finely developed and that he was uncomfortably aware of the impure odours of western meat-eating humanity.

I returned to my bedroom, bathed and sat down to meditate. But this time my mind could not be held steady. A dozen thoughts, considerations and anxieties for the next day thronged through it. I had seen that it was no use to persist in the plea for helpers. For some reason I was to be obliged to go through the next two days alone with him. I lay down. All night the familiar chimes of Great Tom, the bells of St. Mary the Virgin and the many city and college bells that I had known all my childhood and youth, announced the passing of the hours.

In deep strata of the mind dim thoughts were forming about this strange, impressive man, of whose profound knowledge I had absolutely no doubt. In his presence I often fell silent because of the insignificance of my own self, my questions, my aspirations, by comparison with the motives and purposes that I sensed in him.

But the aim? To regenerate the world? The impossibility of the task seemed at variance with the apparent wisdom of this sage. The lectures and teaching bore out the essence of many books of philosophical and religious thought that I had studied in the past. In his private tuition there were continual hints of esoteric knowledge. He gave me the impression of being 'a man

128

who knows'. People such as Francis Roles were only men who had been taught something and believed it—a very different thing. This was more like Rodney in his prime. But perhaps stronger and steadier, for he came from an old and well established discipline, and had, it would seem, developed slowly over many years of work.

There seemed absolute honesty of intent. But there was something very unrealistic in the aim and his complete belief in it as a real possibility was strange. It seemed inevitable that the world would sully him.

10

In the morning when I went to Maharishi's room there was already a crowd queuing along the corridor. I asked them to take their shoes off and large undergraduate toes were revealed sticking out of undarned socks. Some of them, giggling, took off their socks as well and went barefoot.

He began to see them, not individually as he normally did with newcomers in those days, but in little bunches. Then he sent them out to me. I instructed them about the gifts of fruit and flowers. By midday there were people all down the corridor and stairs, chattering and laughing as they waited. He was running late already.

An elderly hotel resident began complaining loudly: "What are all these shoes doing all down the corridor? What do all these young men want? Undergraduates everywhere! Disgusting".

I quickly reorganized things. My own large bedroom became a waiting room, and I engaged an adjoining room for meditation purposes. I was in and out, conducting, instructing, trying to keep an eye on newcomers, to get people to keep their voices low, to keep the corridors clear, to prevent the new initiates and the non-initiates from getting mixed up, to see that the candidates for initiation did not burst in on those who were already meditating. The elderly resident pottered past and looked through my open bedroom door.

"Well really, Madam! Twenty young men in your bedroom. I shall speak to the manageress".

In the adjoining room new initiates sat on the two beds, the chairs or on the floor with eyes closed. The laughing, chattering students had become still and silent. Their faces looked washed clean, tranquil and at peace, like a dozen young Buddhas cast in bronze as the afternoon sunlight filtered through the half-drawn curtains on to their quiet faces. I looked at them for a long moment before going out to instruct and attend to others.

All day the people came and went. Most were students, but there was a sprinkling of older men and women: two Indians: and a girl who was evidently a mental case. This one suddenly began to cry wildly in the corridor and had to be hushed and led gently away from the rest.

"Good gracious, this is a positive madhouse!" the old lady cried, popping out indignantly once more to find out what was going on. The manageress came up, and apologetically asked that her old established and respected resident Lady So and So should be humoured. Could we perhaps move to rooms on the floor above? she asked.

Maharishi looked glum. "No," he said. "We will not move." He was silent for a few moments. "There will be no more trouble," he said, with a curious expression on his face. "Now, we will continue." I went to fetch the next candidate.

To my surprise the old lady had disappeared. Her door was firmly closed and no further complaints of any sort were ever made. In fact I never saw her again. It was as though she had been bidden to sleep, to forget, to disappear from our circles and not to impede us even to the extent of being conscious of our presence any more.

It struck me, as I pondered on it later, that Maharishi might have the full and conscious use of the kind of power of thought transference that Elsie Abercrombie had used for mischievous purposes as a child. A knack or a naughtiness on Elsie's part was a disciplined art in Maharishi's case.

Maharishi talked to the mental girl, instructing me to remain in the room. To my surprise he then initiated her. In a few minutes she was sitting quietly with the others, all devils apparently cast out, repeating the mantra peacefully.

New initiates were normally brought out of meditation for 'checking' of their experiences after thirty minutes. I appointed a sensible young German called Volkurt Knudsen to note the names and times that each began to meditate, so that they were brought out to sit on the queue on time. When Maharishi had seen each, he sent them home, or to meditate again, according to how they had fared. I was of course too inexperienced at this

131

time to check anyone's experiences myself. I scarcely even understood my own.

I was supposed to take money from them all. It soon became clear that little was forthcoming. A week's income meant a week's university grant for most of them, and what were they to live on if they gave it? I consulted Maharishi. "Let them pay what they can", he said. One boy declared he had only a few pence and got away with it.

In stockinged feet, to save taking my shoes on and off, I flew up and down, back and forth, and by some miracle seemed to keep everything moving smoothly and with reasonable speed. At about half past four in the afternoon I asked him if he would like to eat something, for neither of us had paused since breakfast time.

"No", he said. "We will talk about the World Congress now. Telephone the Albert Hall and get the date arranged."

"Yes, Maharishi. But the young men? Many are still waiting."

The glum look returned. "I am tired of the young men. They ask questions for the sake of asking questions. Bring them all in together and we will make an end of it."

I hesitated, wondering how best to sort the matter out. There was an opportune diversion. One of the porters arrived with a copy of the "Oxford Mail" which he had got for us, unasked. A large, attractive photograph of Maharishi in half profile and smiling, graced the front page. There was a long and well written story with it. "Read it to me", he said.

Trying not to feel anxiety about the comings and goings and queues outside the room, I sat and read to him. The reporter had been faithful and honest in his account. All was well until I reached the last sentence. Touchingly, he had ended the story of his interview with this extraordinary Indian master who was going to "regenerate the world in three years" with the words: "For my part, I shall meditate on the strange innocence of the Maharishi."

"What does that mean?" said Maharishi, making his eyes enormous. There was a clamour outside, a vigorous knocking at the door. I got up and peered out into the corridor. The students pressed close, talking all at once. "When will he see us?" "I have to dine in college." "I have a lecture to attend."

132

"My tutor is expecting me and I'm late now." "We have waited hours."

"Very well", Maharishi said, "let us continue them."

It was about 11 pm before he had finished the initiations, and all the checkings and further instructions for the first day were completed.

All, that is, except for two boys who had come for their first appointment after the shops were closed, and so were unable to buy their gifts of fruit and flowers. I asked if they could share someone else's gifts, or have some that had already been used, for all the rooms were now overflowing with fruit and flowers.

"No, no. They must bring their own. Those that have already been offered on the altar we do not offer again."

I told the young candidates to go and try and get hold of something somehow, from their colleges or from one of the other hotels perhaps. They returned seeming almost distraught saying they could get absolutely nothing save two apples. they were determined to be initiated. They pleaded with me. I conveyed their pleas to Maharishi. He was adamant.

"If they do not bring gifts according to the tradition, I do not initiate them." I told him they had tried. "Let them come tomorrow then." They had said they had exams all day tomorrow. Would he not stretch a point for them? He remained silent, looking straight in front of him.

The young men waited half the night, unspeaking, side by side on a sofa in the corridor. In the morning they were gone.

At 11.30 pm he asked if I had eaten. I had not paused a moment since first thing that morning and of course neither had he.

"Shall I get something for you first, Maharishi?" He had again refused curry earlier. He would have yogurt, he said. Although I had made arrangements with the night porter, something had gone wrong in the kitchen and there was no yogurt available.

"Doesn't matter," he said, and at once lay down, turned on his side and propped his head on his hand. "Go and eat", he said.

Although I knew how very little nourishment he needed, I still felt anxious that he should go all day with nothing and should not have what he asked for. I left the hotel, drove round the city to all the restaurants that I knew, and at last found an Indian restaurant open in Walton Street although it was almost midnight. I had a quick meal myself, then persuaded them to give me two cartons of yogurt, and bore them proudly back to the Randolph.

I entered his room quietly in case he was asleep. His huge dark eyes turned towards me. He saw the yogurt, sat up shining and happy, and I placed a dish before him.

"I have been lying here thinking that if the body needed food, there would be food", he said. He laughed as he ate. "You have eaten too?"

"Yes, thank you, I have eaten."

When he had finished I brought him water in a dish and a towel, in the manner he was accustomed to. I stooped over him and he dipped his fingers and dried them. Then he said:

"What did he mean? 'The strange innocence of the Maharishi'?"

I didn't answer. I took away the dish, washed it, hung up the towel and began to clear up the rice, dead incense dust and fallen flowers round the alter. To my back he repeated: "What did he mean? Hm? Hm?"

I could not think of anything appropriate to say. When he still persisted I remarked that our Bible says unless you become as a little child you cannot enter the kingdon of Heaven. "He thinks you are like that little child, Maharishi. It's a nice thing to say really."

Maharishi watched me. I did not want to meet his eyes because I knew this was only a half truth. I felt unable to say anything that might seem harsh or cruel, or a judgment on him in any way at all. I glanced at him and away again as I moved about the room.

"He thinks I can't regenerate the world?" said Maharishi's voice behind my back. I agreed reluctantly.

"He thinks you can't regenerate the world, Maharishi."

There was a long silence.

"Will you sleep now, Maharishi?" He looked suddenly older. He confessed that he was a little tired. He lay down. He did not seem to know whether he was cold or not. I placed the brown blanket gently over him, in case. Then I opened the window a little. He did not glance at me, but stared into the distance. As I

134

left the room he said to my retreating back:

"I shall meditate on those words, 'the strange innocence of the Maharishi.'"

There was trouble with the mentally disturbed girl first thing next day. I was surprised that he had not realised there might be repercussions there, but it was part of the 'strange innocence'. She came lolloping along, crying and looking wild. She was almost incoherent and attracting a lot of attention. I let her jump the queue and get quickly into Maharishi's presence. I marvelled at the way she quietened, the rapidity with which normality and calm returned. Clear-eyed and happy, she left the hotel seeming healthy and whole in mind and body. I felt in my bones that this was a miracle that would not last. But for the moment I was concerned only to get her out of the way of the others.

When I went into his room Maharishi said: "We should appoint a leader to look after this new meditation centre at Oxford. Who can lead them?"

I suggested one of the Indians, because he had been helping me ably and sensibly. He dismissed the idea at once. Two or three other possibilities occurred to me—older people who had seemed responsible and of sound judgment as far as I could tell. None was acceptable to him. He thought for a while and then said: "I will appoint that German boy. He is here?"

Volkurt Knudsen had indeed returned first thing, although the previous day we had told him he had made a good start and need not come back. Nevertheless he had appeared very early, with a gift of three huge chrysanthemums for Maharishi. He was sitting quietly waiting with the flowers in his arms, although I had warned him there might well be no further opportunity for him to see Maharishi. Maharishi had evidently sensed that the boy was there, for I had not told him. I ran to fetch him.

Twenty minutes later Maharishi said to me: "Here is the leader of the Oxford Centre. Tell them."

Volkurt was led back to the others. He spoke very inadequate English. He was at the beginning of his first term at the university. His father was an industrialist in Hanover. I had

135

heard him tell Maharishi that morning that he had been accustomed to pray and meditate on the Cross, remaining kneeling for an hour at a time. His earnest young face was filled with light as he spoke to Maharishi. Clearly he was far more spiritually conscious than the others, as Maharishi had been quick to perceive. In the presence of the other initiates he looked very young. He struggled gamely to make himself understood, and continued to help me all morning.

At about mid-day Maharishi suddenly said: "I think we will go back to London now". I reminded him he still had many appointments to keep. He looked downcast. "They talk so much", he said. "Well, we will stay one more hour."

I went into the rooms where people were waiting and twenty faces were turned hopefully towards me. It was impossible to choose who should see him and who not, so I took them in apparently at random, hoping my choice would be in some way directed rightly. So some were initiated and checked, some not checked, some given appointments and never initiated at all.

I sent down for the bill. I took the money from the initiations and added the cash from the tin box in Maharishi's room. There was not enough. I got out my own cheque book. The telephone rang. The manageress, sounding apologetic, said there had been an error. The bill was too high. "But the extra rooms?" I asked. "We feel the Indian gentleman was disturbed and inconvenienced by a certain lady. In the circumstances there will be no charge for the use of the two extra rooms." It seemed astonishing, and yet I had begun to feel that nothing was astonishing any more, with the Master!

I tumbled my things into my overnight case, put his few belongings in the tin box, gathered up the best of the flowers and fruit. Willing people came forward to help, and someone fetched my car round. We went down in slow procession. The hotel staff, who had looked coolly on the little white-robed Indian on his arrival, pressed forward, smiling. He gave flowers to anyone who caught his eye in the corridor and the foyer.

Volkurt piled the luggage in the car himself instead of leaving it to the porters. At the last moment he said: "Could I perhaps come to London? Please ask the Maharishi for me, in case he has to say no." The young German always showed good taste.

136

Maharishi smiled at him. "Yes, yes, get in, there is plenty of room."

Volkurt leapt into the back seat among the fruit and flowers. We drove away from the smiling, waving group. Volkurt asked a number of carefully formulated questions as we drove. Then he leaned back, remarking that he had had his share of Maharishi's attention and would now be silent. In my driving mirror I could see his eyes were closed. Maharishi's head drooped forward and I thought he was briefly sleeping too, but in half an hour he was wide awake again.

I brought out a matter that had been uppermost in my mind for some time now.

"Maharishi, not all the initiates returned for checking as instructed, this morning. If often happens new initiates don't go on meditating, I think."

"Yes, yes, they will go on. They all want to be happy. They will meditate and be happy."

"Maharishi, although the meditation seems so easy by comparison with practices that need austerities and disciplines, I too sometimes find I can't do it."

"How is that? You can't meditate? Only sit and close the eyes and begin."

I began to try to explain that when tired or anxious as I had been these last three nights, I could not hold my mind steady. I had kept worrying about my responsibilities, what I had to do, making plans and so on. "Something in one resists the meditation in such circumstances. It seems like contracting out of life, turning one's attention in quite a different direction". I thought of John and Jane, lounging there while I ran around doing everything. I had also noticed other previously busy people growing more lethargic and withdrawn. Yet it seemed obviously important to meditate. "What is the impediment?" I asked at length.

He thought about it for a while, as though he had not faced this problem in anyone before. "It is your sins", he said at length. He seemed to go on thinking about it. For myself, a line of thought started up as to what the word 'sin' may actually mean in the last resort.

In fact, only a small percentage of those initiated in these

137

early days did carry on. The majority faded away quite soon. This was to be his first pointer to the need for a change of tactics later on, in his dealings with the busy western world.

In the late evenings at Prince Albert Road we would sit in Maharishi's room having coffee and sandwiches while he drank milk, and there would sometimes be time for conversation. Often extremely interesting things were heard. He told us about his beloved Master, of whose continuing presence he was at all times conscious. There would be questions on Hinduism, and sometimes laughter and chatter about current topics and the western world as seen through Maharishi's eyes.

He told us that democracy was in its essence bad, since the whole of creation works in a hierarchy. "Therefore a kingdom and princes is better than an electoral system of government", he said. He seemed to know everything that was going on in the world and laughed at the absurdity of tactics and policies of governments. But in between the lighthearted hours, one noticed a deepening gravity in him. Later, he would have no conversation at all on current affairs or household trivialities. "I am not here to teach politics, or economics—or cooking", he would say. "I have only one thing to sell: meditation, meditation, meditation."

There were considerable changes going on in the household. Johnson Bates had decided to leave. There was no one in charge now. Though some businesslike and sensible people came, most did not stay long. The most faithful devotees were a rag, tag and bobtail of society, many quite impractical, impecunious and belonging to the slightly lunatic fringe.

"How can the Movement grow unless important people come?" he asked. "How can I manage unless more money comes? How to get more publicity?"

Later of course be became established in the press and the public's imagination and through television his face became well known. Probably no oriental master of the Flower Power era was so familiar. There was a considerable influx of teachers from India at the time, but few had his charisma—or his flair for catching attention.

By string-pulling I gathered representatives from most of the national dailies. They harangued and mocked him, still convinced that meditation was only good for a passing laugh. They accused him of being a charlatan, asked him to "stand on your head or something, to make a good picture", and enquired why he didn't get married and raise a family?

He looked surprised. "No, no, we do not marry."

"How do you travel about, Mr. Maharishi?"

"By car and by train and by aeroplane."

"Have you a car?"

"I have devotees who drive me in their cars."

"Who pays your air fares?"

"I have devotees who pay the fares."

"You must be making a lot of money?"

"No, no."

"What's that you're drinking, Mr. Maharishi?"

"Cow's milk."

"I suppose you thought there was a yak tethered in the back garden", I snapped, suddenly fed up with all this. They sniggered.

"You must have very rich friends. Who looks after your financial affairs?"

"The money is in that tin box." They roared with laughter.

He was quiet that evening and very thoughtful. He seemed to be falling into despondency. Eventually he told us he would see no-one outside the household. He would 'go into the silence' for a while.

For most of the next three days his door was locked. He neither ate nor drank. We tiptoed about and muffled the telephones. We supposed him to be meditating for many hours in his own possibly much more advanced way. We realised what his problems were. He could not see the world through our own western eyes. It was obvious to us why his flowery oriental manner was not attracting many sound people. The approach was wrong. In addition, he could not see why the sound people were not immediately grounded and held by the meditation as he expected. All the people at Oxford in fact fell away, except Volkurt, who remained loyal for several years. He was also attracting far too many neurotic or mentally abnormal people, who took up a great deal of his time, but could not remain in a balanced state unless he continually yanked them back there.

139

Many of them had extraordinary experiences and insights of the type described by Jung in connection with his patients. They could not adapt their inner lives to their outer lives and live a normal day to day existence in society. They hoped to get from him the help that the medical profession had not been able to give them. But they were exhausting him, and as they became increasingly agitated and distraught, it was sometimes a case of confusion worse confounded in the end.

He had told us that the meditation worked by way of the central nervous system. If this was impaired, meditation was not possible. Electric shock treatment left the central nervous system damaged, he said, and was therefore a completely evil thing. It destroyed all possibilities of higher development. Many of the mental cases had in fact been subjected to ECT and in the end he began to send them all away.

When he emerged from his days of silence a strong and purposeful look was on his face. He had shifted his stance a little. If the world would not go his way easily, he would adapt himself to what was possible. He would look with a more wary eye on those who came to see him. He would weed out the crackpots and concentrate on those who might make a real impact on the state of the world as they advanced in meditation. Although he did not like organizations and rules, he would have to make a few. He found that people liked to meditate together, and would sometimes go on longer and show some signs of becoming established in the practice if encouraged to be together in a group. He couldn't see why they needed this sort of encouragement and mutual support, but if they did need it, he would get an organization together and provide it.

The childlike belief in the regeneration of the world in three short years was beginning to fade. He began tentatively to restrict and bind his followers and make rules for them. As his innocence began to go, imperceptibly, his first vision began to fade with it.

Maharishi's principal assistant was a tall young Anglo-Indian named Philip Williams, who was almost always at his side. He had just embarked on a career in the law when he met Maharishi and abandoned everything for him. Later he went to

India and became a Brahmachari or novice monk, wearing the Eastern robes and long hair and beard that the tradition demanded. Maharishi named him at this stage as his own successor, though this decision was destined to be thwarted later on.

Philip Devendra as he was later called, was much more worldly wise than Maharishi himself. But he believed in "breathing the Master's breath", bending to his will in all things, and even in trying to carry out the most impossible requests. Maharishi told us in his charmingly naive way to "go and see the Queen and ask permission to build meditation cells at Buckingham Palace. We could have them underground, under the gardens. She will be very pleased with the idea", he said hopefully. Or: "Go to 10 Downing Street and ask for an interview with the Prime Minister. He can order meditation cells to be built in all the towns." We laughed affectionately and said we would do our best. Philip worried continually about how to contact the highest in the land and put Maharishi's case to the western world.

Struggling valiantly to get everything on a more business-like and acceptable footing, Maharishi called a few people together and appointed them as 'trustees' to get the Movement on its feet. But though devoted to the SRM, they were people who had no organizing ability, drive, or money of their own, and soon he grew exasperated by their dilitoriness.

Off his own bat, he had some flowery-looking writing paper printed with the heading *His Divinity Sri Bramananda Saraswati Jagad Guru*, and a picture of Guru Dev and himself at the top. He described himself as *His Holiness the Maharishi Mahesh Yogi*. Obviously to the public at large the suggestion of godlike status would seem absurd if not actually blasphemous, but rather than argue with him we simply typed everything on simple residential paper. When he found out, he was puzzled and increasingly exasperated. Eventually, after a somewhat heated meeting with the trustees, he announced:

"I sack you all off. Go! Go!" Defeated, they went their way. He announced that henceforth Nina would be leader of the Movement and the household. She was devoted and had a good deal of insight. "It's like being the spearhead of an army", she said. "We are forging on into difficult country. All the supplies

141

and equipment and administrative staff are lacking, but this is much less important than people think. We'll catch up on everything in due course."

This vision seemed fine; but Nina had no business head, was always borrowing money or in debt; dabbled in the occult; went to see clairvoyants and healers, and told fortunes with cards. It was clearly not within her power to do anything much of a practical nature to foster his long term aims, and eventually he realised this.

Among the people who frequented the house were about eight or nine former members of the Society for the Study of Normal Man; and several others who had one foot still in Colet House and the other in Prince Albert Road. Maharishi's teaching appealed deeply to those who had been taught according to the Ouspensky system, that Man is a self-evolving, self-creating being, and that to realise their full potential they needed a 'direct method' to open the higher centres of the mind. Anything involving ways of meditation or prayer seemed worth examining, especially to those who had also had passing contact with Rodney Collin, and knew that he had taken profoundly to the idea of prayer in his latter days.

Francis Roles himself had met the Maharishi through Beatrice Mayor. He apparently felt that TM bore all the signs of springing from the same sources as the Fourth Way. He thought that, unlike Subud, it seemed perfectly safe. He therefore introduced his followers to Maharishi at a big meeting at Colet House. But after being kept on a very tight rein, they were profoundly shaken by this departure from the norm, and they divided at once into two camps: those who fell for Maharishi's strong personality and those who wanted to 'keep the system pure' and would have nothing to do with flowers and incense and Sanskrit invocations. Because of the furore that had been caused, Dr. Roles quickly clamped down on free contact between the two households.

For a considerable time Maharishi treated the Ouspensky followers coolly. He was not interested in their 'system' which he thought was a hotchpotch of bits and pieces of old teachings and quite valueless. All the same, he accepted money from Roles and used it to hire the Albert Hall. But the so-called World Congress was a disaster. For the first time he

142

encountered hostile heckling; and the press, previously so mocking, turned nasty and published articles ranging from "Where does the Maharishi's money come from?" and "Is the laughing yogi a charlatan?" to "Is TM a dangerous practice?" In addition, the lack of proper follow-up and 'checking' facilities meant that the potentially large intake of new initiates soon faded away to nothing.

Looking at Nina with large, sad eyes he said: "The gods are angry with me. I am not going fast enough. I shall go into the silence again."

When I was discussing this period with Colin Wilson years later I commented that step by step Maharishi had come to terms with the world, losing his cleanness of intent in the process. The story was not exactly Faustian—he had never deliberately traded with the Devil. But he had sought a compromise solution to his situation. Colin drew my attention to Camus' words in *The Rebel*: "Innocence, the moment it begins to act, commits murder."

Wagner symbolised this in the figure of Wotan. He is the archetypal representative of pure inspiration. But he can't put his inspiration into practice unless he has some kind of power. In order to gain this power he is forced to trade one of his eyes in exchange for the "force of the law". The whole tragedy of *The Ring* springs out of this dubious bargain.

So Maharishi too had to make his bargain. He was not enamoured with Dr. Roles, who was only seeking a method to supplement the Ouspensky system rather than a practice that would supersede it. But he had seen at Colet House a body of businesslike, well-organized excessively disciplined and efficient people, with money and useful contacts in life. He needed their help. They would have to do. He sent for Francis Roles.

I heard him turn Francis Roles's will to his own, by the skill of his tongue, on several occasions, and I am certain that, intelligent though he was, Dr. Roles did not realise what was happening. He was flattered. He was given the power to initiate others. He felt himself to be on equal terms with the guru. He would keep the esoteric core of the Ouspensky teaching and the esoteric core of Maharishi's tradition, and blend them nicely for serving up to the Society for the Study of Normal Man: the

143

former for the growth of "the line of knowledge", the latter for the growth of the "line of being".

Almost overnight, a great change came over No. 2 Prince Albert Road, as Dr. Roles proceeded to take charge there in a big way to "get the Movement on its feet" as Maharishi requested. He looked with jaundiced eye at the odd collection of 'devotees' and the motley crew of followers who camped out there and ate in the kitchen without payment.

"There are a good many people here whom we don't want to see any longer", he said briskly to the inhabitants. Rapidly the house was swept clean of all who did not fit into the Ouspensky concept of right living. The office and business arrangements were smartly taken in hand. The oriental style booklets and leaflets were swept away without a second glance. Professional journalists in the Roles organization set to, to produce modern, up to date literature. A bank account was opened, accountants employed and legal help obtained. And soon the name Spiritual Regeneration Movement of Great Britain was put before the Charity Commissioners and accepted, thus giving the Maharishi's work a proper status in the country and a mantle of respectability at last.

11

For personal reasons, I was absent from Prince Albert Road for some months. When I returned, there was an unnatural hush in the house. I looked in the main reception room. It was full of new initiates, sitting in a row of upright chairs, hands folded in their laps, waiting in silence for 'checking.' A few timid and nervous faces turned to look at me. In the adjoining office my old acquaintances from Colet House were now in charge in a big way. There were no smiles, no laughter. They were obviously bossy, yet curiously on the defensive, too.

I went down to the kitchen where there had always been cheerful noise and chatter. There was silence. About a dozen people seated round the long table jumped guiltily and looked over their shoulders. These were the old inhabitants of the house. Ousted from the upper rooms, deprived of their previous duties, I found they sat and chewed the fat down here in the basement like trolls in the underworld while the Ouspenskyites functioned upstairs.

There were almost two households now under one roof. The unofficial 'checkers' and 'guides' lived below, and people who knew the drill crept down to them by the outside basement steps. If they were seen by the officials upstairs they were stopped and turned away. The ridiculous cloak and dagger business was to protect the simple system of TM from getting adulterated by 'all that psychological stuff' upstairs. And the upstairs was 'keeping the system pure' from the 'crackpot, lunatic fringe' in the basement. Nina had taken to her bed in a state of nervous exhaustion. All the warmth and naturalness had gone from the Movement, and even the position of Philip Williams, the master's appointed successor, seemed to have been undermined.

In one of the now empty rooms Philip and I discussed the

situation, then looked at one another in silence. He was a tall, good-looking man with great dignity of bearing, even in Western clothes, and with hair cut short like a European. In India with long hair falling to his shoulders and his beard almost to his waist, he became an imposing figure indeed in the white robes of the Brahmachari monk. His gentle eyes shone with love for his guru, physically so much smaller than himself. "He's like a Biblical figure, like John the Baptist, tremendously impressive", somebody told me then. "We must just continue to meditate," he said now, when we had remained quiet for a while.

Maharishi had always maintained that meditation could change outer circumstances for the better, as well as altering inner attitudes. I went to Maharishi's room, which had always previously been open for initiates to meditate in in his absence. Now the door was locked.

I went into the big meditation room where I had heard him speak that first evening and listened or meditated many times since, sitting with crowds of others. It was empty. No candles or incense burned on the little altar. No profusion of blooms was massed beside it or on it as Maharishi liked. A single delicate orchid in a cut glass vase stood near the picture of Guru Dev.

I sat on the floor crosslegged and closed my eyes. The room was silent. It was deathly cold.

When Maharishi returned from his travels, the grave and brooding look he was beginning to wear habitually filled me with a growing sense of unease. I felt there was enormous strength in him, but that he was beginning to be rather ruthless in using it. I began to see that he was holding his devotees in thrall in a manner that was growing more and more alarming. He seemed now to have definite hypnotic power. Most of us could be summoned at a distance and would come at the inner command. I once walked out of a committee meeting in my home village, impelled to go at once to Prince Albert Road. He handed me a document. "I need you to edit this," he said. I realised later that we always saw only what he wanted us to see, heard what he wanted us to hear, neither more nor less.

I observed many things about Ouspensky's teaching when I

146

saw my former fellows in full sail among the defenceless devotees of Maharishi. Its value and its dangers were at once apparent. They were much more reliable than the former checkers and guides. They kept a proper duty roster, were punctual, kept promises, kept records, kept tabs on everything. But they were much less able to express themselves clearly and simply on the subject of the meditation, and frequently added buttons and bows of their own invention during checking sessions. Everything that occurred was interpreted in terms of the teaching they had followed at Colet House. They had not read much or any philosophy or comparative religion because of the way Roles 'blacked' most other books and studies. They were like obedient children, limited in their ideas as a result of their schooling, and had not reached the potential of their intelligence.

Maharishi eventually achieved his aim of securing an ashram in the foothills of the Himalayas at Rishikesh and invited selected people to join him there. At the opportune moment I received a legacy which would have paid the fare for me. But in spite of my long-held wish to see India, I decided not to go. I was becoming too nervous of the outcome.

Dr. Roles and a number of others went with him. But soon, becoming disenchanted in various ways, Francis Roles went off on his own and visited Sivananda, an elderly guru who had been established in the same area for years and had an ashram frequented by many westerners. He had let it be known that he did not approve of Maharishi's mission. For this reason, Maharishi's devotees had been actively discouraged from wandering off to see what spiritual goodies the other guru might have to offer.

Francis Roles eventually collected his luggage and departed prematurely for England. Here he announced that he had forged a link with a much greater master than Maharishi, and that henceforth his followers would have a link with Sivananda himself. There would no longer be any connection between the Society for the Study of Normal Man and the Spiritual Regeneration Movement.

Roles had an old link with an organization called the School of Economic Science, which had a part financial interest in Colet House. They were one of the many offshoots of the

147

Gurdjieff/Ouspensky heritage. Leon MacLaren, a barrister who ran this school and Francis Roles together now started the London School of Meditation. The financial resources and practical help of the Study Society were therefore withdrawn from the household at Prince Albert Road as abruptly as they had previously been given.

A tremendous burst of publicity followed the formation of the School of Meditation. Posters appeared in the London tube stations, public meetings were advertised in the "Times" and the "Telegraph". People who applied to the School were initiated according to Maharishi's formula, but without hearing anything about the Maharishi himself.

During all this time Roles was having a good deal of trouble with his own people. The separation from SRM was fine, as far as people who had never liked the little Indian master anyway, were concerned. But certain people had formed deep personal attachments to Maharishi and felt that their lifelines were being peremptorily cut away. Dr. Roles offered them by way of compensation a distant link with the "greater master" who was now sending them letters and spiritual instructions from Rishikesh. But this was not the same thing at all. Most of them were never going to have the chance to go to India and sit at the feet of Sivananda as they had once sat at the feet of Maharishi in the meditation room at Prince Albert Road or the lecture room at Colet House. A big meeting over the matter became rowdy, and a lot of people walked out or were banished from Colet House for good.

Maharishi faced Dr. Roles on one final occasion, in which he made a vigorous attempt to turn the powerful Englishman with all the resources and money, back his way. For all his skill, his undoubted hypnotic and telepathic power, he could not do so. Those who were there reported seeing an expression of naked anger on the face of Maharishi when he finally realised he had failed to impose his will on a man whom he clearly regarded as being in all ways his inferior. "He looked frighteningly human, not like a Holy Man at all", someone told me.

It had already occurred to me that, in spite of the claims on the flowery writing paper, Maharishi could not be called a fully-realised man. Nevertheless, he might well do very useful work in the troubled world of the times—and he did have

148

'higher knowledge.' I was far from being ready to abandon him.

After the parting from Roles, Maharishi summoned the Ouspensky throwouts and appointed new leaders from among them. Under his hypnotic will, all those who had been appointed, now dug into their own resources with gifts and subscriptions and covenants to fill the gap left by the departing benefactor. These were ploughed into the new Foundation: but in conditions of considerable secrecy, like buying shares in a business which may prove profitable later and from the sale of which it is deemed prudent to keep all but your best friends.

At this point Nina was dispensed with all together. "She's not the sort of person we want at all—completely unsuitable. She must go," the new masters declared loftily. To get her off their backs, one of the leaders installed her in an attic flat in Welbeck Street. Soon the 'trolls' from the basement at Prince Albert Road began to find their way there. Swung from the pit to the gods—puffing up three long liftless stairways and emerging into the sunny top floor rooms—they regained their breath, sat on the floor and dropped easily into meditation.

Afterwards they would discuss the good past and the sad present and uncertain future like a band of ragamuffin political refugees. They were goodhearted honest people some with considerable depth to their thought, and conversation there was often a lot more interesting than among the rigidly narrow Ouspenskyites who reigned supreme now in Prince Albert Road. I thought Maharishi had shown a ruthless disregard of the human heart in accepting so indifferently their exile from the fold.

Maharishi decided to hold a summer course in a sports hotel in the mountains at Hochgurgl in Austria. The price for attending it was to be high. It was becoming clear that only people who had a fair amount of money could keep up with him now. For some time he had been adamant that candidates for initiation should pay a week's income. This he described as the Indian tradition between master and pupil. But now he began to ask big fees for certain additions to the basic technique. Many people thought that they should not be asked to pay for 'spiritual benefits'. They would refuse the techniques that in their hearts they wanted, preferring to spend their money on material benefits instead.

Personally I had no objection at all to paying for knowledge. I would pay to learn some specialist subject. Why not then, for ancient knowledge, which might well be of more value than all the rest put together? Nevertheless I am inclined to think that there is a legitimate question as to the *status* of a teacher who asks for money. Krishnamurti, Ramana Maharshi and other spiritual leaders of repute always refused payment. In some way the belief that 'the Lord will provide' supports such people, who always seem to receive enough. But Maharishi was beginning to have ambitious plans.

Once when I had been alone with Maharishi at Prince Albert Road, taking dictation, he had suddenly digressed to say: "If they tell you you may not enter my room, take no notice. Enter. Always enter".

I looked up from my notes not knowing what he meant. His eyes had their far-away look.

"There is no-one to prevent me entering, Maharishi. I always just walk in as you told me to before".

He laughed. "Yes, yes. Always do that".

At Hochgurgl, having dumped my luggage I went to Maharishi's room. A long queue of people stretched down the corridor. Most were strangers to me and of many nationalities. After an hour Vincent Snell, an orthopedic surgeon who was now the English leader, came out and said: "He isn't seeing any more people tonight. He's going to sleep". The queue broke up and people drifted off. I started downstairs myself, but changed my mind as I suddenly remembered Maharishi's words to me. Going back, I tried the door. Vincent looked out and said in the brusque Ouspensky manner: "I told you all to go away".

"I think perhaps he will see me"?

"I said no".

I moved away, hesitated at the top of the stairs, and eventually turned back with a strong feeling of being called to the room where the master sat. This time the door opened and I went in.

Maharishi rarely slept for more than two or three hours a night, and then only lightly. He had little use for people who were proud to have 'slept like a log'. Sleep should be so light that even when sleeping one should be aware that one was asleep, he told us. Most of us had learnt to experience this strangely light but refreshing sleep under his tuition. At other times when he needed rest, he went into deep meditation, sitting upright in the lotus posture. When not sleeping or meditating during the night he was invariably reading or writing.

He looked up from his work. "Ah", he said when he saw me, "here is Joyce! She will carry on. Vincent can go." Snell went with a very bad grace. I settled down and took up a pen, like old times. But when his eyes looked into mine, it seemed to me that the expression in them had quite changed. The frank and trusting look had now entirely gone. A shrewd, worldly wisdom was becoming visible in the little lines about both eyes and mouth. When the smile went his face was dark and purposeful.

Throughout the course, a small team of Ouspenskyites guarded him, sitting with him as he worked on his new translation and commentary on the *Bhagavad Gita*, and preventing others entering his presence. The remaining 'trolls' had christened the newcomers the Chosen People, because of their arrogant ways, and the inner circle was now known to them as the First Eleven. As I was becoming more and more disenchanted with the situation, I soon gave up trying to re-enter the inner circle, and began to do some inner pondering out on the mountainside, often in company with one or two of the 'trolls' who could now not gain access to the master at all.

The peaks round us were snowcapped and running with streams and waterfalls. A light breeze moved continually among the bushes and the clumps of deep pink alpenrosen, and fanned limbs already beginning to burn in the midday sun. We were very high up, and the rarified atmosphere might have been partially responsible for making every one's experiences somewhat exaggerated. I realised that at 7,000 feet up in the Valley of Mexico with Rodney I had experienced curious thoughts and even illusions, and had not been able to exercise proper balanced judgment. Certainly there was a good deal of bickering and quarreling, excitability and even almost hysterical distress among the many factions on this course. The emotional 'trolls' and the intellectual Chosen People had their counterparts also in the other nationalities.

151

Each day Maharishi came down to the big dance hall to lecture and answer questions. There were 200 initiates, most of whom had been grounded and established in the meditation by rules and regulations and disciplines which were quite foreign to his original ideas: but at least—unlike the first intake—they had kept going. He spoke in English, with German, Scandinavian, French and Italian interpreters taking up his words in different quarters of the hall.

He spoke mostly of the Vedic teachings of India, allying the ancient theories with his own ideas, and explaining the depths of the Transcendental Meditation technique. On Hindu philosophy he was extremely erudite, and he was also reasonably familiar with the Christian gospels and liked to quote from them. But he persisted in his theme: "Man's birthright is to be happy. No more about suffering. Meditate and you will be happy". This refusal to accept suffering as being an essential part of evolutionary growth was a big stumbling block to many, especially those whose beliefs were rooted in Christianity.

It had begun to seem to me that Maharishi's teaching was an attempt to turn the world back to the innocence of its own beginnings, to Eden before the coming of the serpent. It was Pantheistic in conception, and in his Christian interpretation he was nearer to Pelagius than to the saints, with his belief that man was not born in sin and therefore had no need of redemption.

It seemed to me to be *possible* that a return to a First Cause could be achieved by a simple and childlike trust that God is good. But in my heart I believed that the way forward for man was not by returning to first beginnings, but by pressing onward in some way. In this I was subscribing once again to the idea of man as a self-creating being, as Gurdjieff described him, and thinking of an evolving system of some kind, and of the growth of consciousness. I did not think one could actually contract out of the suffering that seemed to be a part of life in a developing world.

If there had been something missing from the Ouspensky system, which necessitated seeking a 'direct method', there was also something missing in this teaching of the Maharishi, I now thought.

After a few days, Maharishi sent for me and said:

152

"Why don't you come and help me each day with the Gita commentary? I have been waiting for you."

So for the remaining time, I went in and sat with the First Eleven on the floor, joining in the work. Maharishi was making a translation of the Sanskrit text, comparing it with various other translations and dictating a commentary on each verse. *The Bhagavad Gita*, literally the Song of God, is "the cream of all the cows of the Vedantas", Maharishi said. Basically it is the story of an encounter on the battlefield of life. Arjuna faces the lord Krishna and seeks understanding of the human predicament, in which to do battle and not to do battle both seem to be equally indefensible lines of conduct. There have been as many commentaries on the Gita as there are commentaries on the Christian gospels. Maharishi's version was dedicated to proving that there are hidden references in almost every verse which are related to transcendental meditation, and the use of mantras.

He digressed to say that the mantraic tradition was fundamental spiritual knowledge running through all religious practices. There is of course a tradition that the name of Jesus can be used mantraically. Some of the monks on the monasteries on Mount Athos are said to use the practice. And the idea of creative sound is found in the mysterious opening to the Gospel of St. John: "In the beginning was the Word, and the Word was with God, and the Word was God...And the Word was made flesh....."

This sense of the magical or holy power of words is undoubtedly very ancient, and the energy that can be aroused by verbal ritual has obviously long been recognised. The repetition of prayer and chanting in the Christian church was certainly intended originally to trigger off in the partaker inner and subtle vibrations, arousing ecstasy or rapture, in the act of worship. The mantraic tradition of the Hindu and Buddhist disciplines is of the same nature.

As a young girl, still obsessed with Tibet, I had at one time begun repeating the mantra 'Om Mani Padme Hum,' 'Hail to the Jewel in the Lotus'. The magic syllable OM, which is said to be the primordial sound underlying all creation, had a curious effect, making me almost lightheaded.

But Maharishi warned us: "Never repeat the mantra OM. It belongs to a tradition of recluses. It causes withdrawal from the

153

world. It is a very dangerous mantra for 'householders' to get hold of. It has been wrongly used in India for generations. That is why my people are so passive, so unwilling to help themselves. They would rather starve than make efforts to grow food and develop the country."

When instructing candidates for initiation nowadays, Maharishi would tell them: "We take some words which by our tradition we know to have only good and harmonious effects, and we begin to experience the vibrational aspects of them in subtle and subtler states. The mind eventually experiences 'point' state of thought, and slides off from that subtlest state of thinking into the field of the Being. Mind is out of the field of relativity, and reaches the source of all creation, all power: of Absolute Being. Ultimately, by use of the mantras of my tradition, the cells of the brain will be changed. We shall see changes in the metabolism. We shall be able to prove it. We shall have fully-realised, cosmically-conscious men."

One evening, alone with Maharishi, I asked him what he felt now about the progress of his work.

"Your three years are nearly complete."

"I think now it will take nine years", he said. "In these first three years I have moved very fast, scattering the seed. Some died, some has grown slowly, some has grown well. Next three years we will build meditation centres everywhere, get some good buildings in all the cities, where all the people can meditate in separate cells."

They should meditate in silence and preferably in darkness, he had recently indicated. He yearned still for the silence and darkness of the Himalayan caves, he said, where the mind could turn inwards on itself and plumb the depths of its own being and reach the kingdom of God within. Clearly there is much precedent for his strong leanings towards monastic solitude and silence as a road to self-realisation. But I did not much like the idea of darkness and caves myself, being more inclined by nature to turn my face to the sun.

"And what will you do in the third three years, Maharishi"?

"We will consolidate the position", he said with a determined look, as though challenging and over-ruling any possible opposition or doubt.

154

12

The human mind is subject to its ebbs and flows of consciousness and understanding. Although I had begun to feel that an alien influence was impinging on mine, I continued for a considerable time on an indecisive path.

Ouspensky and Rodney Collin had fostered as a matter of course the growth of individual freedom and dignity, never subjecting other people's wills to their own. Maharishi *wanted* our wills to be subject to his. He was His Holiness. He was the Master. We were to remove our shoes when we entered the presence. We were his devotees. That was now increasingly clear.

I could not feel entirely happy about total commitment to a powerful and ambitious master. But I could not make up my mind to leave such a remarkable man, whose avowed aim was to help the world at this time of accelerating descent into chaos and conflict everywhere.

I was also influenced at the time by the fact that several of us had at times seen a halo of light around his head. Someone told me that in the half-darkness of a hotel room in Rome he had seen a clear gold nimbus suddenly shine out from him. "Maharishi, you seem to have got a halo!" he had exclaimed in astonishment. "Very likely", he had answered indifferently, scarcely glancing up from his work. "It comes from the hair".

This is a known phenomenon, of course. Similar experiences are recounted by Paul Brunton in his *In Search of Secret India*, Arthur Osborne's *Ramana Maharshi* and Yogananda's Autobiography. In addition, the SRM's new secretary once observed "a green light like a jewel" shining out of the centre of his forehead, the third eye position. These things could not be explained by any rational means, but a number of rational people, myself included, saw something. I felt they must be a sign of higher development of some kind.

I still thought the practice of TM was quite separate from the Master. Through it, I had experiences of inner light, or irrational happiness, and of knowing something about the nature of life, but in a way which I could not formulate in words. One seemed to go to the fount of knowledge, to know that all was well, that everything is much simpler than it usually appears to be, and that at the source of all is joy and peace. One need not *do* anything at all. One had only to *be*.

I often thought of the words of St. John of the Cross:

"I entered in I know not where
And I remained though knowing naught
Transcending knowledge with my thought."

Soon after the international courses began, the new trustees in England—the First Eleven—put No. 2 Prince Albert Road on the market. This was certainly one way to deal with its intractable inhabitants! There was now no headquarters for the Movement and no common meeting place. A few initiations took place in various private houses, but otherwise little happened. Maharishi sent messages from abroad urging them to be more active, to hold big meetings.

The first public meetings in this new stage were addressed by J.M.Cohen, the author and translator. He was an experienced speaker, who enjoyed the sound of his own strong voice. But of course it was very soon painfully obvious that neither Jack Cohen nor any of the First Eleven for that matter, had a fraction of the pulling power of the Maharishi himself. He, white-robed and bearded, was a very charismatic figure indeed.

Cohen could give a rattling good talk on Mexico, where he had recently visited the remnants of Rodney's group, or on Spain on which he was an authority. But he tackled TM with a boisterous and hearty enthusiasm that cut very little ice with his audiences. "It brings more energy, more creative power, more ability in your job, more harmony in the home!" he cried enthusiastically. "Above all it is a way of relieving all tensions and strains. Meditate and you will relax!" he breathed earnestly, unaware that his gesticulating hands, his continual foot movements, his habit of tangling his fingers in his hair and tugging as he spoke, gave the very opposite impression to relaxation. He had never had the patience to sit through Maharishi's lectures on the courses and to learn the subtleties of the teaching, so he had very little depth to draw on.

After the frantic rush of a series of not very remarkable or successful meetings, the whole thing seemed to collapse. The Ouspensky people talked a lot, but it was all hot air when you got down to it. It now seemed that they were proving themselves far less sensible, less long-sighted and less resourceful than those who had remained with Dr. Roles.

I kept away from the Movement. However I began to notice a very odd phenomenon, which seemed to be directly connected with the meditation, which I was still practising. Wherever I might be, I found myself continually drawn into conversations with people in search of help. I gradually accepted that I must be an involuntary carrier of Maharishi's influence, whether I liked it or not.

My husband and I moved from our house in Kent, and took a flat on the seafront in Brighton, not far from the house where he and his brother Rodney had been born. Just before we were due to move, I got a letter from my old friend Patric Kirtlan, a professional astrologer who lived in Brighton. He wrote: "Joyce, was it you who told me about a year ago of an Indian Master who teaches transcendental meditation? I find I keep on thinking about it recently. I want to know more".

With a marked lack of enthusiasm, I looked out some of the little modern booklets that had been prepared by the Chosen People for publicity purposes. I put them in an envelope and addressed it to Pat, hoping to hear no more of it. But the following morning he was on the telephone first thing, saying: "When can I see you? These booklets are most interesting. I want to hear much more".

Pat was a scholarly man in his mid-fifties, knowledgeable on many religious and philosophical studies and also well versed in the occult tradition. I felt decidedly glum and I answered that I really had nothing to do with SRM now. But we could meet in Brighton, I told him, explaining our plans. He reacted with pleasure.

When I went down to see the decorators in the flat I dropped

157

in on Pat and his wife Vicki as arranged. He had studied all the literature carefully. "We will gather some people here, and you had better come and talk to us about it", he said. "You don't seem to have any good reason for abandoning it. Perhaps you're just lazy."

Within a few months of the move to Brighton, I had a group of thirty, then forty, then sixty-five, stemming from Pat's first initiative. I realised by now that there is so great a hunger for spiritual teaching in this country, that people will cling to and sit at the feet of almost anybody who appears to know something that they don't know. However, I was not at all happy about my situation, and for this reason I was decidedly reluctant to hold meetings. Pat Kirtlan, a volatile and eager man by nature, continually pushed me. But when eventually he was able to hear the Maharishi himself, at a meeting at the Conway Hall on one of his now rare visits to England, he and his wife returned quiet and subdued.

"He is spiritually ambitious", Pat said. "At first we thought from his writings that we might eventually attain cosmic consciousness through his teaching. Now we see we were mistaken". They ceased to join the group of meditators that still tended to gather uninvited round my fireside.

One day I was invited to visit Colet House to attend a performance of Dervish dancing. Francis Roles had been introduced to a master of the Mukabeleh, the Dervish whirling dance that springs from Jelalludin Rumi and the Sufi school at Konya in Turkey. Francis had now taken this, in addition to his version of TM, and the Gurdjieff dance 'movements'—complex physical exercises—using them all as practices to help in increasing the consciousness of his people. They therefore continually used a variety of different disciplines towards the same ends.

The ritual impressed me, not only because it was extraordinarily beautiful to watch, requiring a very high level of attention to perform correctly: but also, because exactly the same innocent, unlined, childlike freshness and cleanness was seen on the familiar faces of the dancers as one always saw with people in deep meditation.

I had no doubt that the whirling dervishes and their English followers attained exactly the same state as the transcendental meditators—and that this state could possibly also be reached by other means. But this realisation didn't in itself help me to know what that strange state, that seemed like waking sleep, could actually be. A major point about it seemed to be that it was associated in some way with a state of no thought. Maharishi's teaching frequently dwelt on the importance of not having continual trains of thought running on and on, "like skating on the surface of a pond". "Hold the mind steady", he would say. "We dive deep into the pond of our own being. We come to the source of Being."

In his *Experiment with Time* J.W.Dunne speaks of this same idea of holding the mind steady, as a way of entering other dimensions of time. But his theme is that we experience only the three dimensions of ordinary living because our minds are conditioned to this continual running on and on of associated thoughts and ideas. Everything we see, hear or experience with the senses triggers off a little thought which triggers off a series of other associated little thoughts, one of which we follow, into yet another network of thought, through all our waking hours. In sleep, he felt, this compulsion to remain 'on the surface of the pond' was in some way loosed, hence the strangeness and wildness of our dream life.

He began the experiment of holding his mind steady but lightly on any object or idea and not allowing it to pick up associative thoughts. Eventually he began to have experiences of diving into the depths of time, of seeing sometimes into the future, plunging with better understanding into the past, observing himself and his life as from a fourth, even a fifth dimension of time. And suspecting other dimensions existed, that his mind could not reach without lapsing into a state not only of no thought, but of no experience.

I began to think that Maharishi's meditation, and possibly all forms of mantraic meditation, had something of a similar nature behind them. But in the case of Maharishi, the great boost that was given at the beginning, by the power he seemed to be able to call upon through the tradition of Shankara, was almost like a tail of a rocket launcher, that gets the missile off the ground at a great rate, then drops back as soon as it is under

159

way on its own power. Hence the ease and delight with which people meditated at their initiation and for a few days afterwards. But later they had got to do it themselves, and then it was not so easy. It was for this reason that Maharishi had gradually found disciplines, rules, regulations, gatherings, courses, were necessary to hold people to their own intention to meditate.

At one course I met a young Norwegian, Kjell Kolflaath, who was an interpreter for the Scandinavian contingent. We exchanged letters, and co-operated over the preparation of a long poem which Maharishi had written and sent over with requests that it be "edited into proper English". Kjell edited it into proper Scandinavian English and I dealt with it in proof, but when it appeared eventually in book form it was mostly back in the flowery Victorian style the Master preferred!

One day I received from Kjell a tape recording made in Norway when Maharishi was talking with a few devotees one evening. It concerned his early travels, after he had left his spiritual brothers at Uttar Kashi, when his guru had 'left the body'. The more I pondered on this tape, the more troubled I felt. And judging by the newspaper and magazine articles which were now appearing with increasing frequency, I was not the only one who was beginning to feel certain doubts about his origins and his true purpose.

He had always given us to understand that he was an especially beloved and favoured pupil of Guru Dev, the former Shankaracharya of Yotir Math. Yet it was apparent to us that, favoured or not, when Guru Dev disappeared it was not he who became the next Shankaracharya. He had suggested by implication that this was because he had already been assigned a greater task.

The long, informal talk I had now received was probably not intended to be recorded at all. In it he said that he had gone out from the Himalayan Valley of Uttar Kashi after the appointment of Guru Dev's successor, and travelled to Madras, in South India, where he visited monasteries and temples with no clear aim in view. He was not at that time on a mission. He had had no instructions. It seemed he had simply wanted to get

160

away from the valley. The implication behind the words at this point was that he was in very low spirits.

He had already told a few of us that he had had spiritual experiences in Madras, at the shrine of the goddess Lila Lakshmi, who is in fact the Hindu goddess of wealth. From the Norwegian tape it became clear that the idea of 'regenerating the world' had originated there, and not before.

"I thought", said the familiar voice on the tape, "why not give some of the divine glory to these poor people of South India? Then later I thought, why not regenerate the whole world?"

It was impossible not to read into this narrative the impression that he had left Uttar Kashi in disappointment or anger because he had not succeeded to his master's seat. The experience of being guided by Lakshmi had put in motion the whole train of events that followed. If he was not going to be Shankarachaya, why not go one better? Why not make a name for himself that the whole outside world would get to know?

He began to teach in the villages of Madras. People would always come to hear a holy man. Like people of all times, they wanted to know how to attain the 'divine glories' of which he spoke? He thought about this, and told them he could give them a simple technique of meditation which would be suitable for them. He chose mantras of the 'householder' tradition. These are said to be weaker in their effect than the more frequently used mantras which are really meant for recluses. The term householder covers all those who have commitments in life, who must till the soil, grow the food, procreate. The tape made it clear that his giving of the householder mantras was at first a simple experiment. It appeared to work. The villagers liked his meditation and became happier. Both the technique, and the particular mantras which were later the basis of the TM practice, were evolved, over a period of weeks, down there in Madras. The variation between this tale and his normal version was quite marked in places—though it was clear that he had convinced himself that Guru Dev had guided and directed the course of events in some way from beyond the grave. But it was very apparent indeed that his Master had not given him this task in person, as he had previously implied. It must have been a short step from the experience at the shrine of Lakshmi, to the conviction that Guru Dev had work for him to do beside

161

which the covetted office of Shankaracharya would pale into insignificance. This deepened my growing conviction that Maharishi had in him a considerable lust for power.

The experimental nature of the techniques became more and more apparent to me. Many people besides myself were by now feeling very unsure where the meditation was leading them. A desire to withdraw from life, and to be committed to no-one and to nothing, seemed to be growing in them. They were no longer as active or interested in the world as they had been. Of course, many did not continue to meditate deeply, and therefore got no very marked results. But a large section of initiates now took to the meditation with a profound emotional satisfaction, and could not be prevented from remaining in it almost continually. From time to time Maharishi gave advice to try and counteract this tendency to remain all the time "in the treasury counting the gold, instead of spending it the market place". He was dealing with people who were becoming recluselike, householder mantras notwithstanding.

A few had alarming experiences, not unlike a cataleptic trance. This sometimes took the form of being unable to open the eyes or to move. This experience is associated with Kundalini Yoga, and is certainly no part of a householder way of development, for it has obvious dangers. It is said to be caused by the sudden rising of the fine nerve energy which, Indian tradition says, springs from the source of life itself. It is conveyed in the human body by the spinal cord. There are various ways of 'raising the Kundalini' and various results may ensue, including sexual excitement and arousal.

Some who had these experiences drew nearer to Maharishi in the process. They became close devotees who had in fact renounced the world. The new paid secretary of the SRM entered many curious states. During one of Maharishi's lectures I saw her go involuntarily into trance. She was unable to stand up at the end. The leader of the German delegation, who happened to be nearby, lifted her chin sharply, calling her name. Later she said: "I could hear you all talking to me but I couldn't respond". Afterwards we 'guides' were told to arouse such people gently, passing a hand in a circular motion over their heads and calling them softly. This seemed common sense to me, but it was not the Teutonic way. The Germans habitually yanked their people out of it, regardless of the shock to the nervous system.

Such strong reactions were rare, but those of us who experienced the deeper states became familiar with various responses of the nervous system, such as tingling, trembling, quivering of the spine and occasionally sexual stimulation or erotic visions. But we had been taught to 'go beyond all that' and usually we could control it. However young people were sometimes unable to exercise control. They seemed to lose all desire for a normal sex life. They found full satisfaction in the meditation, and drifted around unwilling to work or do anything in the world. I began to notice that professional people also seemed to be affected by the curious lethargy which came over serious, regular practitioners of TM. The householder traditionally experiences the joys of the flesh and all the sensual pleasures of life. It is the recluse who does not look for the satisfaction of the senses in worldly pursuits, who expects to withdraw from this need into a state of 'non-attachment'. But everyone was becoming increasingly idle. And now I found I myself could no longer pursue my career as a novelist.

Maharishi seemed quite unaware that the meditation he had given us was counterproductive—if he wanted us to make a really big impact on the world! Those who could at first have moved mountains by their energy and efficiency, now had not the will to do anything much, and would not put their hearts even into propagating his work. There was slowness and vagueness everywhere. The Movement seemed to grow almost entirely as a result of Maharishi's *own* will and determination, and his conscious manipulation of the people and the situations he encountered. Nobody seemed to have any will but his. They wanted to sit at his feet and just be happy.

It now occurred to me that Saivism—the tradition that springs from Siva the destroyer or breaker down, (as does Shankara's teaching,) may always tend to turn life *back* in some way. If one wanted to go on, to reach full self-realisation, something quite different might be required. As Herman Hesse wrote in *Steppenwolf*—and Colin Wilson quoted this in *The Outsider*: "No, back to nature is a false track that leads nowhere but to suffering and despair. ... The way to innocence, to the uncreated and to God, leads on, not back, not back to the

163

wolf or the child, but even further into guilt, even deeper into human life ... Instead of narrowing your world and simplifying your soul, you will have at the last to take the whole world into your soul, cost what it may......."

This had reality for me, and seemed more in keeping with my natural, inherent attitude to life than anything which ultimately led to contracting out in any way.

At the Flower Power time, there arrived in England a Guru belonging to the Vaishnavist path, that which stems from Vishnu, the preserver or maintainer of life, the second person of the Hindu Trinity. Swami Vishnu Devanunda took up the cause of the Hippies and dropouts who had drifted far on the Saivist way, and tried to discipline them into some sort of acceptance of the needs of the world, bring them back into this age. Though both paths may only be other attributes of Brahma the Creator, the First Person, the clear distinction between these two attitudes to man's evolutionary needs became increasingly important in my thoughts.

Maharishi had often spoken of the Three Gunas, the forces which Hindu teaching recognises as penetrating all creation: Sattva, the light-giving force; Rajas, the force of activity; and Tamas, the force of darkness. All life is said to rest on the interplay of the Gunas, the one eternally blending into the next in a great cosmic dance. In our times, he said, the forces of darkness and destruction were dominant. The light must therefore come again or the world would annihilate itself.

"Nature is always balancing. When life moves on to one extremity, nature gives it a push towards the other." Through "messengers of wisdom" the light giving force would be injected into the world again, he said. Clearly he felt himself to be such a messenger.

But what of those who come, by chance or luck, into *too close contact* with such a 'messenger'. Would it not follow that they might become inactive worshippers, under the power of Sattva which just wants to 'be' and not to 'do,' and therefore individually contributing nothing to the age? At the mercy of such great impersonal forces of nature it would be very easy indeed to be lulled into sleep and fall into the trap of believing nothing more was required of man but just to be: that nothing else was any use at all.

164

By contrast with Maharishi's spellbound followers, Francis Roles' people at Colet House were now getting a great intake of newcomers, who were almost without exception of a calibre that SRM leaders a were rarely having the opportunity to encounter. Sivananda, I learned, had given Dr. Roles a different slant on things. He was keeping his people alert and alive with exercises, disciplines, practices and intellectual stimulation while restricting their meditation to brief and regulated periods in which to dive into the 'treasury' before coming out and busying themselves vigorously in the 'market' of life.

Maharishi now announced his intention of giving us advanced techniques on a course in the Dolomites. He was determined that all guides and well-established leaders should be there. He had already given certain additional techniques, saying they would add to the meditation and speed its progress, as the work was not going fast enough. He had handpicked those who should be given the advanced techniques, and most of us paid a fairly hefty sum for the privilege. He now proceeded to handpick others, again including me in the bunch. I no longer went regularly to the courses, though I was always given groups to lead when I did. I felt myself highjacked into this, the last course I attended.

At Lago di Braes in the Dolomites he took the selected thirty out of the three hundred or so 'advanced initiates' and for the first time referred to the extra techniques by their correct name: they were the *siddhis*—magical practices bringing powers that are familiar to Yogis and holy men, but not generally thought to be either very safe or very desirable for westerners. He had previously referred to them jocularly as 'fertilisers'. "Plants need fertilizing."

The *siddhis* were to be kept secret from all except those to whom he gave them personally. He explained there was a direct connection between the practices and the spiritual or psychic experience he had had at the shrine of Lakshmi in Madras.

He seemed decidedly nervous of what he proposed to do. He seated us in a special way, gave great thought to exact numbers and to the way that we were to face, and abjured us on no account to practice this technique alone at home. It was to be performed always by an odd number of people, but not by three—there should be five, seven etc gathered together. It was quite clearly an attempt to invoke the Hindu goddess, and everything about it smacked of magic. Almost at once some of us became alarmed. The atmosphere in the room changed and seemed to be charged with electricity, as though it were a seance. Power of some sort flooded into us. It reminded me very strongly indeed of the Subud Latihan, in which the room had also seemed strangely charged at times.

Maharishi had previously suggested that the practice of Pak Subuh the Indonesian was undesirable, and had explained: "It comes from some spirit, some strong spirit or entity. It may wish to help the world. But it can't lead you to self-realisation". Now he was giving instructions, making rules and taking precautions in exactly the same way as Pak Subuh had done, and he was clearly more than willing to invoke whatever spirit might come to his aid.

It was very clear that these new practices, of which there were, as he put it, "plenty more in the bag," were far removed from the original simple technique of TM. They were a conscious attempt to enlist help from principalities and powers outside, and many people besides myself smelt danger.

Payment for the special techniques grew higher and higher. By now even the basic courses were very costly, and the additional teaching meant expenditure amounting now to several hundred pounds for each initiate. By 1982 he was asking some people for £1,000 each for further instruction on special courses and this has risen steadily ever since. While the humble and the impecunious gradually withdrew, others scrimped and saved and denied themselves and their families. By 1985 they were paying very large sums to become clairvoyant, to manipulate the powers of nature, to levitate. As far as I know, nobody ever actually acquired these powers to any marked degree. He continued to experiment, however. But it seemed to me he was now passing on esoteric knowledge that was inappropriate for bringing out into the world. He was becoming a very dangerous man indeed.

On the whole few initiates seemed to have improved in any definite way as a result of the practices. They had simply become more self-absorbed and withdrawn. There were a few temporary exceptions: people who seemed in some way marvelously rejuvenated for a while, although this usually did not seem to last. One of these was a German woman pediatrician, Dr. Badoglio, who had seemed suddenly young for her years and very enthusiastic, lively and fit when I had last seen her.

But at the Lago di Braeis in the Dolomites she was seen to have fallen from grace as far as Maharishi was concerned. She had a distaste for taking money. She initiated without payment. She also imposed her own ideas and judgement on people in opposition to his expressed wishes.

He took Dr. Badoglio to task on a number of points and she apparently held her ground against him. When it was clear that she was no longer biddable, he lost his temper and dismissed her from his presence. Henceforth, he ordered, she was not to be admitted to the hotel. She was not to see him. She was on her own: an outcast.

Having found lodgings in a nearby village, Dr. Badoglio turned up at Lago di Braes every day, pleading to be admitted to Maharishi's room. He refused to see her. With two women friends whom she herself had initiated, she made the bus journey up the valley each morning and they wandered around talking to people outside. Maharishi, told of this by the First Eleven, sent a message out that they were not to be aided and abetted or even conversed with. Hour after hour, day after day the three middle-aged women sat by themselves on one of the seats by the mountain lake staring at the hotel in silence. Initiates taking their morning constitutional before the lecture, or a breather before the evening session of meditation, passed by hurriedly with embarrassed faces. Less easily coerced, the 'trolls' and I all stopped at one time or another to talk to the poor outcasts.

When I looked closely into the face that had seemed so clear-skinned, shining-eyed and young-looking two years ago, I was horrified. The smooth, unlined countenance and eager, happy look had quite faded out of existence. The skin was deeply grooved and sagged in heavy jowls. The neat grey hair that had fallen in becoming waves was dragged back in a tight 'bun'. The eyes were haunted, like the eyes of an inmate of a concentration camp. The doctor had become, in the last weeks, an old woman. She seemed as though possessed, under a

167

spell. Unable to gain admission to Maharishi's presence, she was equally unable to cut her losses and go away from this place.

From my bedroom balcony overlooking the peaceful lake and the pineclad mountains slopes I watched the silent vigil. He is completely without compassion, I thought. These decent, well-intentioned, spiritually-minded women had become like subjects of a magician's sorcery. A hopeless, fruitless love for their Master and a growing, dull malevolence seemed to issue from their silent forms.

Maharishi was no great lover of the open air, but on the courses he would emerge from his room for an hour or two, to see and be seen in the neighbourhood. Occasionally he would organize an expedition to some vantage point, to sit and talk and work, or meditate with any who came along.

In Austria we once drove with him to a high pass above the snowline, where the road ended at the Italian border. Here he had his blanket and his deerskin laid out on a rock, and sat and dictated his commentary on the Bhagavad Gita in the cold and brilliant mountain air. We wrapped our coats and sweaters round ourselves and shivered. In his thin silk garment, he himself seemed completely unaware of the low temperature at this enormous height. He didn't react at all to the bitter chill.

The frontier guards at that lonely mountain outpost leaned on their rifles and looked on in wonderment at the strange gathering. He called them down and gave them each a long-stalked flower. They laughed as they accepted them. Then one of them, grown grave, suddenly and unexpectedly knelt down in the snow before him and bowed his head. Maharishi gave him some sort of brief acknowledgment or blessing and he rose and backed away. I suppose he would remember the strange encounter all his remaining years—for who could expect to find an Indian holy man clad all in white seated among the snows on a mountain peak and handing flowers to the lookers on?

In the last week in the Dolomites, Maharishi announced that a time of spiritual significance was approaching. It would coincide with the last day of the course when the moon would be full. There should be a *puja* or festival and an invocation of the gods in celebration.

The Italian initiates decked the trees with candlelit lanterns, and strung smaller ones out along the waterfront. The small boats that plied for hire at the end of the lake were brought down, and a lantern was hung at the bow of each. Other candles were placed in waxed paper cups and set afloat on the water.

Maharishi came downstairs at midnight as the great moon was rising over the huge black peaks and touching the darkened water with iridescent rays. He got into one of the small boats, which had been decked with flowers for him as well as hung with lights. Those with him took the oars and pulled away from the shore. About a dozen other boats had been lined up in readiness and there should have been enough for most of those who wanted to embark and go out into the centre of the lake with Maharishi. But while people were watching Maharishi's progress down the lakeside path to the water, one of the ever-jealous Chosen People, evidently feeling the need to keep all but a few away, had run down the path, loosed them all, and pushed them off from the quay to float to the other shore. At the quay heading there was a furious argument and fierce recriminations from the many who had had no choice but to walk behind Maharishi in procession and see their vessels being cast off and got rid of before they could get to them. The act had the kind of mean-spiritedness that was all too common among the ex-Ouspenskyites, causing deep hurt and disappointment to people for whom this little episode would have been a once in a lifetime experience.

Some of us, older and tireder perhaps, had simply settled down to lean on the railings and watch the proceedings from the shore. There was no sound but the wind in the trees and the light splashing of oars in the darkness, and our quiet talk. The two boats in which the First Eleven were safely ensconced converged on Maharishi's boat in the centre of the dark lake. Lights could be seen dancing in a close group out there, but they were too far away for anything to be heard. We learned later that he had said Sanskrit prayers and invoked the Hindu deities, and thrown flowers from the boat onto the surface of the waters.

I walked with a few others to the landing stage as they returned. As I looked down, the slight, bearded, white-clad figure looked up at me from the little boat rising and dipping

169

below us. His huge eyes shone in the flickering lantern light. I could never come close to him and meet his eyes nowadays without a deep disquiet. He seemed at times so godlike: and so demonic—both combined. Full of dark powers and readiness to compromise with the evils of this world in his determination to achieve his ambitious aim. He might have power to create. But he had more power to destroy, and in this he shared the lot of common man.

He started back along the lakeside path. The candles were burning low and many had already died in pools of wax. Seeing me by the railings, he beckoned, but I did not follow him. I glanced towards the fir trees and the wooden seat. In front of it, like three grey spectres, Dr. Badoglio and her friends rose slowly to their feet awaiting his approach. In a silent, almost lifeless little group they yearned towards their master. He seemed to see nothing there as he passed by.

13

The Beatles arrived on the scene, and descended, full of joyful exuberance, on the cloistered ranks of a course at Bangor University in Wales. Maharishi had tried repeatedly during the previous six or seven years to attract well-known and influential people into the Movement, and had been crestfallen when he realised his followers had very little influence in high places. It was a matter of surprise and displeasure to him to find that if anyone famous was brought along, there would often be a request for discretion and privacy. But Mick Jagger and Mia Farrow, as soon as they met him, started eagerly on the meditation, and brought the others with them, frank and open in their declared allegiance.

The arrival of all the young pop and show business people had an absolutely explosive effect on the SRM. Almost to a man, the Chosen People closed ranks against them. If they had hated the 'lunatic fringe' and the 'unsuitable people' at Prince Albert Road, who were predominantly weak or ineffectual in life, they hated with much greater vigour the boys from the Merseyside who were so extremely successful in life! The idea that they should aspire to the same spiritual benefits as their better-educated fellows caused hackles to rise at once. "How can they possibly understand these things?" one elderly lady demanded with extreme disdain.

In fact, the quick, bright brains of the Beatles grasped everything in no time at all, and their easy-going and frank attitude to Maharishi was like a spring wind through the pinched winter of the Movement. Their eager discussion and willing chatter meant that word of the meditation spread like wildfire through the younger generation. They flocked in from all quarters. It was impossible to keep up with the requests for initiation. Those who were on drugs were required to dry out first. They were seeking through canabis an experience which could be attained as easily and less harmfully through TM, they were told. Hard drugs were of course not quite so prevalent as the less damaging soft drugs at that time, and people could be weaned off if they had a mind to be.

The phenomenon of the great influx of youngsters chanting "Love and peace" and handing each others flowers, so changed the face of the Movement that many people left and were seen no more.

The Beatles had come to Bangor against the expressed wishes of Brian Epstein, their mentor, and to all intents and purposes their creator as a group. They were deeply devoted to Epstein, who managed all their affairs, and normally they were obedient to his will. But this time they went their own way, and Epstein departed for a day or two in Sussex with friends.

At the university, Maharishi was closetted with the four of them for hours at a time. They yearned towards their new-found Master with earnest attention. But he wanted more of them than quiet acquiescence and obedience. He wanted to use their fame: four sprats to catch the mackerel still in the great sea of contemporary western life. They did not mind people knowing that they meditated. But their actions in the world were dictated by Brian Epstein, and their careers were obviously of great importance to them. Very clearly they could be very useful to him—if only they were free.

One night, while they still sat with him at Bangor, Epstein left a party at the house in Sussex, and quite late—and without any explanation or apparent reason—drove back to his flat in London. He had been expected to stay in the country overnight. In his flat he took a vast overdose of sleeping pills, went to bed and did not wake again. No-one knew that he was in the flat, and forty-eight hours or so passed before the door was opened with a pass key and his body was found.

The Beatles were utterly distraught. They were also bewildered, for there seemed absolutely no reason for him to take his own life at a time when everything was going very well indeed. He was a poor sleeper and did at times take barbiturates. But there seemed no doubt that he had died of far too large a dose to have been taken accidentally. In shock and grief, unable to take their loss philosophically, the four boys turned to

172

Maharishi for solace and comfort. It seemed he already knew what had happened, although he could not have heard by normal means. He said no words of sorrow.

"Now you will be able to come to India with me", was all he said.

A cold hand seemed to clutch at my heart as I heard this news. I reflected on all that I had observed of Maharishi's power and his ruthless will. Other reasons might have precipitated this unexpected suicide, and clearly no-one can ever know for sure. But there was no avoidance of the thought that continually came uppermost: Epstein's existence had been a decided nuisance to Maharishi. His departure from the scene removed the major obstacle to his plans to use the Beatles to bring the entire pop generation into the SRM fold.

In a few weeks he set off again with his entourage to India, with the four boys, subdued and sad, tagging along with the new father-figure who had replaced their old friend and mentor. The great days of the Beatles as a united and well-managed group, effectively ended with Epstein's death, and the slow decline and division into less effective factions started then.

They were to remain in the new ashram with Maharishi, to "deepen their experiences of the meditation" until he felt they could be loosed upon the world as his emissaries in a big way. In fact after only a few weeks there, they left, quite suddenly and precipitately, and three travelled home to Britain, while George Harrison remained in India and became for a while a pupil of Ravi Shankar who taught the sitar. John Lennon took up with Yoko Ono, whose presence seemed to be of a disruptive nature, Paul McCartney found Linda and Ringo also had other fish to fry. Stormy times ensued before the slow decline.

Individually and as a group they were asked by the press on several occasions why they had deserted the Maharishi so quickly. They were tactful and careful. "Well, he is human after all. For a while we thought he was not", they said. "But we shall go on meditating."

When Maharishi himself was asked about their departure he answered: "They were too unstable. They would not renounce their Beatledom. But as long as they go on meditating they will be mine", he added with a dark laugh.

But by now his numbers were growing apace, and although

he lost Jagger and Mia Farrow and a number of the other 'big names' fairly quickly, his movement was gathering momentum in an extraordinary way.

"Get them in the net! They can't escape", he said to his intimates on many occasions as the numbers increased and the money flowed in. Lila Lakshmi, goddess of wealth, was working for him now in a big way. By the early 1980's he had money and property all over the world, cars, a helicopter, and a university in his name at Freshfield, Iowa. Seven thousand people gathered round him there in 1984, and thousands attended his courses in Europe and the United States. I watched all this from the sidelines, hearing news from a few old friends, but no longer participating in the activities at all.

I learnt that the rules were growing more rigid. In 1986 a friend complained that her husband had been held virtually *incommunicado* at a course in Yorkshire, and her attempts to contact him by telephone during a family emergency were fruitless. "Students may not be interrupted during courses for any reason whatsoever, unless it is a life or death matter", a secretary told her.

"Its very urgent".

"Nothing is as urgent as the work we are doing here".

"I will write then, by first class post".

"As you wish".

The letter was not handed to him until he was leaving three or four days later. It had been date-stamped on receipt the day after posting but withheld.

In 1987 the USA courts were faced with a case brought by three erstwhile devotees and teachers of TM at the Maharishi University of Iowa. They claimed £64 million for damages, saying they had paid thousands of dollars to the Maharishi and into the University coffers for lessons that would turn them into "masters of creation". They had been led step by step to pay more for further techniques to "gain power over natural laws", and had given their teaching services free. After years of study they ended up, not in Nirvana, but "beset with anxiety, rage, guilt and loss of memory". They had "lost a crucial period of life when they would otherwise have been obtaining university degrees, developing a career and establishing family and social relationships". All they had got from the levitation exercise,

174

(which was done from the crosslegged seated position), was "a rude return to earth and chronic arthritis"! Fearing reprisals, the plaintiffs filed the court papers under the names John Doe, James Doe and Mary Doe.*

Few in England complained so vociferously. Stoically, they took their cushions along to the main centre, now at Mentmore Towers, to ease any possible "rude descent" if they should indeed take off! If dissatisfied, like me they mostly cut their losses and faded out.

I often thought about Philip Devendra, who was supposed to be Maharishi's successor when he should eventually retire from the world, and who had seemed to me to be one of the few who had grown in spiritual stature during the years. We corresponded, and he would enclose a few pressed blossoms from some Indian garden or hillside, which I kept in a little scented wooden box. But after some years I ceased to hear from him.

Then one day, over twenty years later, Philip arrived unexpectedly in London. He was completely exhausted. He was also penniless and so distraught that he did not know which way to turn for help. He went to Nina's flat in Welbeck Street and she took him in. He did not want to see anyone, and practically no-one knew of his arrival. He was nearly 60 now, had no income, no means of resuming his career in the law, and had to borrow money to support himself, while he looked for work.

He explained that he had become more and more deeply troubled by the effect of the meditation. Maharishi was keeping him to long periods of fasting and meditating in darkness in the caves, and this had continued unabated for several years.

"In the end I thought I was going mad, alone in the caves", he said. "Maharishi gave me no assistance, no guidance. He just laughed and told me to go on." Terrifying experiences had come to him as he sought to obey the will of his once beloved and now indomitable Master, as he had always done, without complaint.

Eventually in desperation, he came out and went to see the Shankaracharya, who had followed the activities of his erstwhile spiritual brother with interest for some time. The Shankaracharya apparently advised him that he should

* See article in *The Sunday Times*, 30 Nov. 1986, Mark Hosenball.

175

leave—just "slip away quietly" without letting Maharishi know that he was going until it was too late to stop his departure from the ashram.

Nina good-heartedly supported him during the trauma of his re-adaptation to western life. Eventually, unable to find anything better, he got employment as a waiter in a Japanese restaurant in London. By living frugally and saving most of his wages, he accumulated enough to pay his debts and get a ticket to take him to the Phillipines, where he had a sister. He told Nina that he would write, but he never did so. He appeared to have been a completely broken man.

Around this same time something came out in the news that was completely astonishing to me. Lennon suddenly denounced Maharishi at a press conference in the USA, partly on the grounds that he apparently had a considerable sex life.

"There was a big hullaballoo about him trying to rape Mia Farrow and a few other women, and things like that", he said. "We stayed up all night discussing, was it true or not? We went to see Maharishi, the whole gang of us, the next day. I was the spokesman. I said: "We're leaving." He gave me a look like: 'I'll kill you, you bastard'. I knew then, because he gave me such a look, I had called his bluff."

Although there is a tradition of religious eroticism in India, Maharishi came from a celibate line of spiritual brothers, who deny the body and have few physical needs. When we first knew him he ate little, slept little, wore little clothing against the cold, had few possessions. He seemed all Spirit, all Light. I don't think any of us who were around him then and looked after him, ever associated him in our minds with sexuality. He did not touch us, we did not touch him. He was as unsexy as a young child.

Yet, once the gossip began, some of us started to cast our minds back, and to see for the first time the significance of a period when he had first begun locking his door in the afternoons, closetted alone with one young woman or another. Although the hypnotic influence seemed to have kept us unaware of what was going on at the time—we thought him to be giving 'special tuition' to chosen devotees—we now realised something different. There was a certain wide-eyed, fair-skinned type of girl to whom the dark-skinned Indian is

176

frequently attracted. We saw now something that he had intended to conceal. He had departed from the Holy Tradition of his Masters as worldy needs had gradually got a hold on him.

John Lennon was the only one of the Beatles who frankly and openly spoke out about these things, though not until many years had passed, after they had parted from him. The others always used tact, discretion and forebearance in parrying questions about their Laughing Guru. They live still. But Lennon, facing a mad, mysterious assassin who apparently believed himself to be the true John Lennon, died, like Brian Epstein, a premature and inexplicable death. Perhaps his lifespan had come to its natural termination. But remembering the naked anger and hatred that could blaze out of Maharishi's eyes, I shiver when I think of it to this day.

"There are some men whom one offends at one's peril", as Eliphas Levi said. I cross myself, remembering the power of the arrow on the bow.

14

After leaving Lago di Braies, I was never in Maharishi's presence again. But slowly a sinister aftermath began to make itself felt.

At first, I simply experienced a sense of freedom. Suddenly the stream of candidates for initiation faded out. No longer apparently was I carrying a pack of saleable spiritual goodies that attracted the attention of the hungry everywhere I went. No longer did people come to my house. We had moved out of central Brighton into the countryside and were far less accessible to the car-less. The Brighton group was taken over by a newcomer from London. I went back to my desk, intending to resume my career as a writer.

I seemed not to have had the time, not to have had the driving urge for quite a while. Now I was determined. But it seemed extraordinarily difficult to get going again. I had previously thought that creativity, and all forms of artistic or creative work were very important for mankind, and were in some sense the justification for man's existence. Through art, one glorified God, and in some way one even partook of the act of creation, tapping the same powerful stream from which all 'creatures' of the Almighty originally issue forth.

Now, it was all a labour instead of a delight. The more I struggled to write my fifth novel, the more I was overcome by a feeling of the fruitlessness and vanity of all human endeavour. A sense of futility filled me as I considered the interplay of characters, relationships and situations. All themes seemed worthless. Every premise, every concept appeared false or valueless. When eventually it was finished, my publishers rejected it and my literary agent had no success in placing it elsewhere.

Gradually depression began to overwhelm me. Everything in

life seemed purposeless, meaningless and arid. I was sliding into a complete nervous breakdown. I had been given access to some very deep strata of the mind, and I was now no longer able to enjoy any of the outer experiences of living, or any normal level of rational thought. Inwardly I called perpetually to Rodney, but there was no sense of his presence any more. Derry, although he was Rodney's brother, had no interest in philosophy, psychological development or the spiritual life, and though kind, was totally unable to understand my misery. He suggested I see a doctor. There was no assistance there, save advice to take tranquilizers and sleeping pills and try to relax and not drive myself so hard.

Then slowly everything began to turn, not just depressing and heavy, but completely sinister. I found I couldn't hold my mind steady at all. I perceived what the intellect had always known but the experience had not as yet appreciated: that everything in life is in a perpetual state of flux; that there is no stability anywhere; that the only constant is continual unrelenting change.

Looking at my hands, I saw them dissolving from the competent, ringclad hands of a middleaged woman, to the slim, smooth young hands of a girl, the little fists of a small child, the tiny curled buds of the baby in the womb. And at the same time they were old and gnarled with the knuckles of an aged crone, and finally the skeleton hands crossed on a body in a grave.

This then was 'Joyce': the changing frame from embryo to skeleton, repeating and repeating in an endless wheel of turning and rebirth. At the same time my eyes became unable to hold steady on any object without seeing it as it had been and as it would be in a time to come: the table was not just a piece of furniture alone: it was also a pile of timber planks; it was a tree in a wood; it was a sapling; a seedling; a flowered seed from an earlier tree dropped on the soil to propagate itself. At the same time the table was an old and worn out thing that someone, somewhere would throw out, consign to rubbish, chop or break or burn. And by its ashes scattered on the wind the earth would be fertilized for other trees to grow.

The sheer terror of living with this normally mere intellectual concept is exceedingly difficult to convey to anyone who has not actually experienced it. The eye perceives the flux so continually

179

that even the effort to place a cup and saucer—china clay, the potter's wheel, the cup, the broken shards it will eventually become—on a table which is dissolving into pieces of timber the very cellular structure of which is visible, is a matter needing almost superhuman efforts of concentration.

The ever-changing faces of the people around me terrified me into a state of almost incoherent imbecility. While speaking to my neighbour or my daily help, I found myself viewing the child behind the ageing face, the skull beneath the skin, and a developing kaleidoscope of other faces too.

I have a certain natural self-discipline and self-control under ordinary circumstances. Using this I struggled to maintain an air of normality so that my collapsing state should not be too apparent. However I ceased to be able to lead a social life of any kind. I shut myself in with my thoughts. At times I went out of doors, and avoiding human contact, walked the Sussex Downs, trying vainly to get a sense of normality or reality again.

One night I lay out on a downland hillside all through the hours of darkness, curled in the foetal position, beset by the belief that I was descending into Dante's Inferno. I saw the horrors of it with appalling clarity. A vision of the everlasting helplessness and suffering of mankind, the sheer awfulness of the recurrent theme of birth, struggle and death, caused me to curl tighter and tighter, wet with dew and with the morning rain. I knew now the sort of experiences that Philip Devendra must have endured in the solitude of the Himalayan caves.

My husband's recollection of this period is quite dim. He had recently changed his Fleet Street job and was much under pressure, leaving home at an early hour and not returning until late. He has memories of no supper on the table, his breakfast things not washed up, my presence or my absence not explained, my face abstracted and my eyes bleak with despair whenever he attempted to look into them. It was the menopause, he supposed, and paid me scant attention, fending for himself as best he could.

For a period of some months I teetered on the brink of what may well have been certifiable madness. Some instinct kept me out of psychiatric hands, for I was quite certain I was floundering in waters far too deep for that sort of intervention or attempt at help. Somehow I must find a way to help myself. But eventually even the inner struggle to do this seemed to die.

There was an oak tree that stood aslant a bank with an overhanging branch across a path I used to gain access to the Downs. I found a length of rope and took it there. I sat beneath the tree and considered how to sling the rope, knot it, make a noose and hang myself. I had always previously thought that suicide was no way out of anybody's problems. It seemed likely that Gurdjieff's theory was right—one would find no escape but would return to deal again with whatever had beset one until the difficulty had been overcome.

I sat with the rope at my feet, repeating and repeating the action in my imagination, but not doing it. I saw my body hanging there, head askew, my torso swinging in the wind. At the worst I would perhaps find myself "asleep, perchance to dream", and go on repeating the action until some sense came of it.

I had actually stood up and taken the rope in my hands again when I noticed suddenly that everything seemed to be changing. In my recent state the rope would have been dissolving into strands, into hemp, into flax growing in a field, flowering and seeding, being gathered, soaked and plaited: and at the same time fraying and disintegrating, rotting into uselessness at the end of its life span.

Now I saw that my deep concentration on the moment, on the rope as it was at that time—not what it had been or what it would become—had caused it to hold steady in its present moment of time. I could perceive it as a piece of rope. Its immediate purpose: to hang myself from an oak tree by a path. The tree also had remained steady, neither dying nor becoming a sapling or a seed. And the path was as it was in that moment—bare of leaves for winter, with branches stretched like hands against the sky. It was like the television technique of stopping characters and situations in mid-action, leaving everything poised and immobile while the viewer contemplates it before it moves on again.

The secret of recovering 'normality' then, must lie somehow in holding attention steady in the present moment: not allowing any slippage in the mind.

It had occurred to me long ago that to all intents and purposes the 'present' is normally a non-existent experience.

Even the words that you are reading in this line are already in the past for you as you read each one. The rest of the sentence is still in the future. Where then is the present? As soon as one has spoken, or listened, the experience is past. The next bit, even the next second, is in the future. Man lives in this perpetual extraordinary state—blind to the future even a second away, aware at least temporarily of the past, but unable to experience anything that can rightly be called the 'present'.

The intense concentration and narrowing down of my mind as I contemplated my own intention with the rope had apparently suddenly triggered off a mechanism that in a normal state enables one to function in the world. It was evidently an automatic function, operated in some way by attention, or perhaps by *intention*, but normally completely unobserved.

Directed attention then must somehow be the key to getting back my sanity. Standing with the rope beneath the tree I had reached the turning point in my breakdown. I felt as though someone, somewhere—Rodney, Ouspensky or who knows who—had witnessed my hour of desperation, and had mercy on me. I had been thrown a lifeline instead of given a noose with which to make an end of living.

Eventually I turned for home. I put conscious attention on each tree trunk, each dead leaf, each pebble on the path, saying to myself there *is* a 'now', and I can and will hold to that.

I had re-acquired the art of getting the moment 'into focus'. For months I had been looking at life as though through an unfocussed microscope, seeing far too much, far more than I could use profitably in any way at all. I had been viewing great patterns, ever-changing designs, as I tried fruitlessly to manipulate the instrument of observation and 'bring it down' in some way. Quite suddenly I had got the knack of focussing on what I wanted to observe in that moment. I had become 'normal.'

As I worked slowly towards recovery I began to be convinced that too easy, too frequent experience of the transcendental or 'bliss consciousness' state had been directly responsible for the appalling situation I had been in. In deep meditation one plunges into timeless experience. A zone of unchanging, absolute perfection is recognised. But in this world, time and circumstances must be focussed on, understood and rightly used if one is to live normally. The attempt to struggle back to this had left me stranded in a fearful half way house, perceiving both too much, and yet not enough, of man's position in the world.

The mantraic tradition of Shankara seems to gradually destroy any interest in the evolutionary process, until, as Maharishi had once said of recluses, "even if they want to take action in the world they cannot do it". Even his modified and adapted version of the tradition had had that effect in the end. I had been seeing the eternal cogwheels on which life rotates, like someone who watches the hands of the clock going round, but who has forgotten how to tell the time.

It took me at least two years of inner, private struggle, to return to a mode of living where I could think lucidly, read books again, converse and enjoy the company of friends. I had continually to bring myself, by acts of conscious attention, back to 'now'. I must have escaped a spell in a mental establishment by the skin of my teeth! I must have struck my friends and neighbours as rather odd for a long, long time. Fortunately the menopausal syndrome can be used to cover a multitude of eccentricities and idiosyncracies, and I was able to fall back on that. However, my power as a novelist had gone. By going beyond all that sustains the creative imagination and continually entering the 'still centre' I had robbed myself of my God-given talents, intended for usage in this world. As though brain-damaged, I lived stoically from moment to moment for a very long time indeed.

Eventually my reading brought me to the realisation that the transcendental or bliss consciousness state is a perfectly well-known phenomenon, and there are plenty of ways of inducing it other than through TM. In his *Altered States*, for instance. Paddy Chayefsky describes experiences in an isolation tank, where "thinking, normally linear and logical, becomes holistic and patterned". Experiments at the Harvard Medical School in the 1960s included inducing a subject into altering his normal state of consciousness through hypnosis, self-induced trance or by a pharmacological agent such as dimethyltryptamine. Even a "giggling, shuffling madman" under this drug treatment will sit still as if in a trance and when questioned will say things that "indicate he feels a communion with great and powerful metaphysical forces". By the time I left the SRM I was pretty well convinced that we had been inducing a trance state, in TM.

In *The Relevance of Bliss*, Fritjof Capra, Rupert Sheldrake, David Bohm and others describe a considerable number of different ways in which the same experiences can, and have been known to occur, either spontaneously or by deliberately inducing it. These include prolonged chanting or intoning, withholding breath or extreme ascetic disciplines such as protracted fasting and the deprivation of sleep. Apart from modern drugs such as LSD, there are hallucinogenic mushrooms and other consciousness-altering plants which have long been known to the shamanistic tradition and the witchdoctors.

When the Maharishi began to make an impact on America, in 1970 R.K. Wallace and Herbert Benson at the Harvard School conducted studies that showed the "physiological correlates of TM". The controlled tests indicated changes in the pattern of brain electrical activity identical with those induced by chemical and other experimental means.

In the USA meanwhile, a woman doctor researching the subject of transcendental experience in a small priory so appalled the monks by proving that the exalted states they reached after long and arduous efforts of discipline, could be induced in a few moments by a jab in the arm that they renounced their vows and abandoned the religious life altogether!

Nina Coxhead, who compiled *The Relevance of Bliss*, faced the question of whether she "wanted or could handle this kind of experience, this Bliss-Shock". Her considerable researches had led her to realise the cases for and against attempting to enter the bliss state are equally strong. The risks had become apparent to her. In the end she decided "yes, let's pursue it, let's induce it, let's take a chance, let's live in the world with gusto.....but in full awareness of that from which we are created". She had not actually succeeded in inducing the state at the time of writing, however, notwithstanding various efforts.

In spite of my timid and tentative childhood, I suppose I have always lived vigorously and 'with gusto'. But my adventures have got me into some dangerous places. I had set the seal on my own life in that moment in the sixth form common room long ago, when I heard myself say spontaneously "there are two ways of doing it. One is like the nuns here, heads down, not looking, not touching, always seeking God inside themselves, and the other is looking and getting involved and wanting to be part of the world—because that is God too". By recognising both ways I had made it inevitable that I would dabble in both.

The most important thing at this stage, however, seemed to be to get myself grounded in life again. The early childhood 'urgent thing forgotten' was clearly something to do with the evolutionary process, and not with contracting out of it and asking to be relieved too soon of the task of man on planet earth.

I pondered on my own origins in this world. As a child I was always drawing, painting, writing poetry, inventing things. It occurred to me very young that if you make things, do anything creative, the creative energy of the Godhead can flow through you. You become a channel. Sometimes the things that were made by my hand or written with my pencil, seemed to be done 'through me' rather than 'by me'. In the act of being an instrument of creation I found happiness. It had been, during childhood, the only true happiness I found in an apparently alien world. For this reason I retreated into it constantly, in the hermitage—the window sill, behind the velour curtains—or in a corner somewhere unobserved.

My mother, turning cakes out of baking tins in the kitchen, or embroidering with her quick, fine needle in the firelight glow, spreading the cloth and inspecting her work, in the way that I too stood away from my work and looked at what I had done, seemed to share the same silent knowledge of the creative act. She rarely talked to me, though with my father I would often have long, grave conversations and exchanges of ideas. But mother was always busy with her own affairs and we did not function on the same wavelength. However we had a common and unvoiced bond in making things.

"Creative people are always happier than destructive ones", she would say, advising some grumbler or idler to get and set hand to the plough. "That's nice", she would say of something I had made—quick and casual praise thrown out in passing.

Sometimes, as I grew older, I would garden with her. Each flower, each plant amazed me with its complexity, its colour, its scent, its every-changing nature. I would kneel on the grass in a reverie, examining the veins of a petal or leaf, considering its life, its function with awe and delight. I thought of growth, procreation and death with a simple innocence, and felt, without the assistance of 'technique's, something of what Maharishi called "the divine glories".

Every insect, every ladybird crawling up a stalk, struck me as equally remarkable and beautiful: so tiny, yet so perfect and full of purpose. Its minute internal organs and its senses fitted it for its little life on earth, and for its place in the great scheme of things. Everything is part of the same thing, I thought. It occurred to me in those young days that God manifests at all levels. Wherever the observer is though, he tends to see the manifestation from his own level only, his own viewpoint. I saw that to the small insects a bird might be God, because it was big and powerful, terrible to the smaller creatures. I wasn't God to them because I was too big to be seen. They couldn't possibly be aware of me at all, even though I had power to move them about, to do whatever I pleased with them. A ladybird crawling across my palm must be as hopelessly unable to see what I was, as I was unable to see the whole of the Milky Way. To my dog and cat I might be God though: a benevolent God, provider of food, shelter and love. So perhaps if you provided food of some kind, and loving gifts you would be safely embarked on the line that led to a much higher God; and yet in a sense *you* would be God too because you were God to the littler ones. Perhaps the things I made were in the end going to be a kind of food, food for people's mind and hearts, not particularly their bodies..........

"That's nice". Mother, passing by, paused briefly to inspect the way my annual seeds had grown in a riot of colour beneath an old stone wall. "You have grown those very well".

"God grew them", I said tentatively, meaning the Big God, the Creator.

"He couldn't have grown them if you hadn't planted them there and watered and looked after them", she answered in her brisk manner, beginning to snip away with her secateurs, deadheading the roses.

It was true, of course. The Big God could make wild countryside or woodlands, but he couldn't make a garden. He couldn't paint a picture or write a story—except by using people

186

as instruments, willing instruments through whom he could channel His powers. In that sense he *needed* me and everyone, every creature to fulfill its own function. I suddenly realised that creature and Creator and creativity were inter-related words. I looked about me, at the trees and lawns, the tabby cat watching from the wall, the young dog bounding across the grass from the terrace, with a sense of sudden revelation. This is what it means in the prayer book by *Creation*, I thought. I began to sing to myself softly: "I too will something make........"*

"Nearly time for tea", said Mother, drawing off her gardening gloves, stooping to restrain the puppy. "Get on dear, do, if you want to finish weeding that flower bed today". Thus with her practical common sense she would bring me down to earth and back to 'now'.

I seemed to have come full circle, forty years on. I could not believe that man is a deviant species, destined to go on despoiling the earth by sprawling across its surface like a growing cancer, as has been suggested by Peter Russell in *The Awakening Earth* and others in recent years. In spite of my low state, I remained convinced that humanity has a role to play in the evolutionary spiral. Like Laurens van der Post in *A Walk with a White Buskman*, I felt in my bones that the Creator may Himself still be evolving and that we have to help the process in our own way, at our own level.

There is almost always a sense of good and positive purpose in any creative individual. Even the cook who prepares a meal with pride, the householder who paints and decorates his home, the people who grow their own vegetables, tap that source of happiness, it seems. But it is alien to the sad dwellers in blocks of flats with no gardens, beset by planners and officials telling them what to do, lacking the freedom even to paint their front door the colour of their choice. Deprived of a patch of earth in which to dig and plant, carrying their convenience foods home

---

* I too will something make
And joy in the making;
Altho' tomorrow it seem
Like the empty words of a dream
Remembered on waking'.
                    Robert Bridges.
                    I love all Beauteous Things.

from the supermarket, hearing canned music all the time, they never sing and whistle as people used to do when I was young. Obstructiveness and an uncooperative attitude seems to me to spring largely from the denial of freedom to *create*; from being supervised and organized and pressed into uniformity and conformity by councils and governing bodies. Families with garden gnomes, prefab ponds and brightly painted doors may not by remarkable members of the human species! But they are generally much more cheerful, optimistic and filled with humour than the tenants of controlled, gardenless, petless elevated flats. And a bit higher up the creative ladder, at the level of the arts, I knew that there was joy. Left to their own devices, people will always make something.

The enormous problem that I had to face following the nervous breakdown was the knowledge that the stream of creative energy, once so vigorous and prolific in me, had been dammed, diverted or even destroyed all together. I therefore had no source of happiness and satisfaction. Judging by the conversations I had with various artists, writers, musicians and a ballet dancer, this experience of the meditation effects was shared with them. "The ballet used to be my life. Now its just the way I earn my living". "I don't seem to want to paint any more. I'd rather just sit in the sun". "I can't get on with writing my book. I don't seem to feel much interest in anything but TM", were some of the comments I heard.

Realising that a vital part of me was now non-functioning, I set myself, *faute de mieux*, to live without it, adjusting as best I could as though I had a paralyzed limb. Who could tell how long it might be before the life force could flow through it again? It was in fact ten years.

15

I had only the intellect to work with. Emotion could not be aroused. All the artistic fields were therefore cut off, and I could enjoy only craftmanship, with its small and modest pleasures. Being inveterate movers, we pulled up our roots again and bought an old flint house at the foot of the South Downs. Here I scrubbed, cleaned and polished, with vigour and determination, and once again set myself to tend a garden. I was not creating. I was carrying on other people's work. The land was fertile but neglected. Each day I laboured, clearing and digging, planting and sowing and going to my bed at night exhausted.

A young lecturer from Sussex University who had rather a sharp tongue, dropped in to see us. I came indoors with earthy hands and windblown hair, apologising.

"Come and see how I am progressing", I invited. "These shrubs were out of hand and I've pruned them. I've weeded all this area. I'm replacing old stock".

He glanced about without interest. "Gardening is the last resort of those who can't form relationships with others or do anything worthwhile in life", he said.

I was appalled. It was true I rarely went anywhere or saw anybody but my intimate circle nowadays. Was I perhaps contracting out of life? I went on thinking about his caustic words after he had gone. What then should I be doing?

That evening, for the first time for ages I heard a voice that seemed as though it might be Rodney's. In the same way that it had once uttered the mysterious message 'the crossbow', it now just said 'the place of the birds'. The words meant nothing. I paused in my small domestic tasks and looked about me, listening inwardly, in hope. My eyes fell on a deep blue flowering plant that a neighbour had brought me and which I had placed on a side table. It crossed my mind that once, years ago in Paris, I had bought a similar plant in the *marché des fleurs* near Notre Dame and given it to Dr. Rouhier and his daughter, Odette. They exclaimed with pleasure. "The beautiful blue! It is the colour of the glass in the Sainte Chapelle—the colour that the glaziers forgot how to make and could never afterwards repeat. What is the flower called"?

"En anglais, 'cineraria'."

"Ah, cinéraire"!

The memory of the little incident was suddenly as clear as yesterday, and with it came the almost immediate recollection of the convent where I had visited Chloe to tell her of her father's death: Once the home of the Fourth Way School man, Chateaubriand, now the convent of Notre Dame des Oiseaux. That was surely the place of the birds'. Perhaps then, something would happen if I went back there? But almost at once I felt that it was to Dr. Rouhier, not to the convent that I should make my way. I telegraphed, and Odette booked me a room at the Hotel Jacob where I had previously stayed.

In the morning I walked up the Rue des Saints Pères and turned into the Boulevard St. Germain. At the Librairie Vega the old man and his daughter greeted me lovingly. I had always called him 'Mon Père', as Dr. Rouhier sounded too formal and Albert too intimate for so erudite a man, much older than myself. He held me in a comforting, bearlike embrace, my head against his shoulder. We had not seen each other for a long time.

"You will stay a few days?" he asked.

"Perhaps a week. Today, I will go and light a candle in Notre Dame for Rodney and perhaps revisit some of his favourite haunts, and then come back, if I may?"

I soon settled into a routine and stayed on longer than I had said. I would potter and read in the shop during the busy morning hours. Then if business was slack he would take me out to one of the pavement cafés for a *cassis* or a *citron pressé*, and we would sit talking in a leisurely way as we watched the world go by. His big stomach bulged over his trousers, his blue beret was always over one ear, his long beard covering his shirt front. He looked exceedingly Parisien.

Dr. Rouhier was not only learned in esotericism. He was full of unusual ideas of his own, and much more interesting than

190

those whose ideas had crystalized in some system. He spoke of the design of Notre Dame as reflecting the perfect man—an idea often put forward in relation to the designs of gothic cathedrals. Sometimes they are said, like King's College Chapel at Cambridge, to reflect the design of the Cabalistic Tree of Life, certain parts of the church corresponding to the sephiroth of the Tree. But as the Tree also reflects the nature of man, there is basically no difference in the idea. Dr. Rouhier, warming to his own ideas, drew on a restaurant menu an open-mouthed gargoyle that took the rainwater from the roof of Notre Dame. "This is to carry away the sins of the Perfect Man", he said. "Les péchés de l'Homme Parfait."

"Les Péchés? Mais l'Homme Parfait n'a pas des péchés!"

"Mais si. They do not touch him though. They pass over him like rain and feed the earth beneath."

One day we walked through sidestreets to a café belonging to the Guild of Carpenters. "They have esoteric knowledge, Les Charpentiers", he said. He introduced me in turn to everyone eating there, and I shook hands with each one. In a corner, stretching from floor to ceiling, was an intricate and beautiful replica in wood of a cathedral spire, carved in meticulous detail. "C'est le chef d'oeuvre ds Charpentiers", he laughed as I examined it. I realised all eyes were turned to me as I considered it. I realised there was significance in the design, the mathematical exactitude, the numerical arrangements. For "everything is based on Number", as Pythagoras is believed to have said. Therefore the interplay, the inter-relationships of numbers, sequences and measurements can have deep significance. From this knowledge springs the occult science of numerology, and all the complexities of the Jewish Gematria. Here also lie the secrets of the building of the pyramids, which are clearly power points: and the exact measurements, given in cubits, for the building of the Temple of Jerusalem. They all began to laugh as they saw me examining and pondering. "Yes", they indicated one to another. "Madame observes something". There was certainly esoteric knowledge in some of them, I saw, and that was why they were his friends.

At weekends Dr. Rouhier and Odette returned to Madame Rouhier who was an invalid in their country home. But during the week they lived in an apartment consisting of part of an old house not far from the shop. The entrance was through wrought iron gates into a flower-filled garden, thence through glass doors direct into a large, high ceilinged living room.

Here stood an ebony Buddha. As he passed through the garden, "Mon Père" would pluck a flower—a golden marigold perhaps—and drop it into the upturned palms of the Buddha as he passed. It rested there, vivid against the shiny black wood, until it withered and was replaced with something else next day. We would settle to supper, to books, to conversation under the quiet, Buddhistic gaze.

Dr. Rouhier made several attempts to turn my mind to various forms of Yoga, including Tantric Yoga. He had certain knowledge that he wanted to impart to me I thought, but I would have to ask for it. I was nervous, after my previous experiences. I tended to get into long, intellectual discussions, nothing going deep, nothing coming really from the heart.

"Ah, now your brother has gone and you have had certain adventures of your own you have become too timid", he said with disappointment in his voice. He walked me back to my hotel late each evening, bidding me come to the Librairie again tomorrow.

In the shop stood an extraordinary Tibetan gong. It was colossal, and being handwrought, it had certain imperfections in its surface. I often looked at it. "It was once in a lamasery in Lhasa," he told me, but I never knew how he had come by it.

One afternoon we had walked to the church of St. Germain des Prés together, and back slowly along the Rive Gauche, examining the book and picture stalls. We paused, leaning on the embankment wall, looking together at the Bateaux Mouches filled with tourists, gliding along the river below us. Nothing much was happening to me, but I felt quite content in his companionship. I realised I had been getting increasingly lonely.

"But you are not really happy, dear friend," he said suddenly in French, as though reading my deeper thoughts. And then: "Tonight we will shut the shop early and sound the gong."

"Oh, Papa", Odette protested when we got back. "You know they hear it all the way down the Boulevard, even with the shutters up! You really should not".

He shrugged and laughed. They closed the shutters. In the

half darkness we sat down and contemplated the great, dimly shining disc. I think it may have been bronze, but its dark colour made it difficult to identify. Then, slowly and softly he began to tap around the surface with the padded hammer, making everything vibrate on a curious, reverberating note, until at last he found the one tiny perfect point. It was slightly off-centre. "Ecoutez", he whispered. Then gently, slightly louder, loud, very, very loud he struck it. Everything around us shook and trembled. Octave within octave within octave of sound poured forth. The amazing sequence of notes echoed through one's entire being, in a joyous but almost terrifying way. We seemed to be touching the very chords that underlie all life, the primordial chords struck at the first creation. Emotion started up, as though a great orchestra was playing and the bookshop was filled with the very music of the spheres.

World within world, life within life, time within time seemed to open up in a great, swirling vision—everything moving, vibrating, ever-changing, alive, interlinked with tenuous spirals and threads, travelling inwards as though into a great cone-shaped shell, to a marvellous still centre beyond all movement and all sound. "This is the sound of God creating the universe, creating Himself", I thought, trembling in every nerve. For the first time in several years I wept.

The notes died away at last in a long, echoing silence. It had grown dark outside. The street lights, glimpsed through the shutters, threw glancing beams on the shelves of old, leather-bound volumes which jostled for pride of place with up to date paperback books. The dark mahogany desk and chairs gleamed in the half light, and as the normal senses made themselves felt again, the familiar smell of books and papers and printers' ink assailed the nostrils.

Odette got up and switched on the lights. To her relief, no-one had come to bang on the doors and complain. We looked at one another. Tears were in the old man's eyes and on my cheeks.

"I feel as though it opens all the chakras", I said at length. "Perhaps it is quite dangerous."

"Everything is dangerous", he answered. "There is nothing worth doing that is not dangerous. Life is a dangerous game. La vie, c'est un jeu tout à fait dangereux!"

He was not smiling, but now that he had dried his tears his eyes were twinkling, as though at any moment he would begin to laugh.

Well, yes of course! I had played safe for far too long, and now that I had tasted the salt of my own tears and laughter again, I was perhaps ready to be on the move. A sense of adventure mounted in me. I found that I was trembling, full of expectancy that he would reveal new and profound truths to me, if I began to ask. At the same time, previous experience caused my scalp to prickle with fear. I pulled myself together.

"Mon Père", I cried, as though making a dramatic decision to place myself before a firing squad or be led unresisting to the torture chamber, "I am ready to continue to play this dangerous game of life! Only teach me, je vous en prie."

With French gallantry he bent his great bulk towards me, took my hand and raised it to his lips.

"Chère amie, there is only one thing I can teach you", he said. "It is the hard lesson that there are no more teachers for you. Only seek the master who dwells within."

"The Dweller in the Innermost?" I said, repeating a Buddhist phrase that he had used once before. "But I need more knowledge. Give me your knowledge."

He laughed, and with a sweeping gesture indicated all the books around us.

"Everything is there", he said, "in books, in libraries. You have only to take it and make it your own." Then taking a pen, he wrote firmly on a clean white sheet of paper in English: "Call no man Master". He bowed and turned away.

I took a while to digest what had occurred. The sense of disappointment and letdown lingered, though he laughed and hugged me and we continued in our conversations for some days. However I browsed round the bookshop most mornings, gradually realising that my choice of reading was more under his direction than before. It was like a return to the young days at Oxford when I had searched the college library shelves for a clue to the meaning of life. But this time I was not without assistance. Looking back, I see how subtly and carefully he guided my mind to a greater width of learning, drawing my

194

attention to possible different lines of thought and to comparative ways of contemplating the eternal truths. He spoke to me always, not as a teacher, but as a learned friend, attempting to bring me to a balanced point where I could function in some way in my own right. It had long ago occurred to me that there is truth in the old tale of the fairy gold: if you try to pass it on as currency it turns to pebbles in your hands. So it is with one's private understanding of the basic truths of life. One has to get at them and hold them in one's own way, reading between the lines of books, hearing the subtle innuendos of speech, viewing them as conveyed through art. But beyond a certain point one cannot pass one's knowledge in direct words to one's friends, however much one may sometimes long to do so.

Eventually I began to feel that I had arrived where I started and had begun to "know the place for the first time".*

Some sort of framework of thought and work seemed to me to be needed, though, if I was to move forward and no longer vegetate at home. But something in which I would be responsible for myself, and only I would decide which way to go.

Apart from the random reading which I had always done, even in the days when Dr. Roles was 'blacking' anything remotely interesting to his loyal and faithful troops, I thought I should perhaps study something that could be put to good and practical purpose in possibly helping other people a little in the years still ahead. Sometimes you can learn by teaching in some way, I thought.

I had long been interested in astrology. Feeling the need for companionship again now, and for the intellectual stimulation that comes with study, I set myself to do the two year course leading to a Diploma of the Faculty of Astrological Studies—which I gained at fifty. In the course of learning to set up and analyse a horoscope chart, I made a discovery which gave me considerable pause for thought. The chart for the date and time of Rodney's death had every indication of being a

---

* We shall not cease from exploration
  And the end of all our exploring
  Will be to arrive where we started
  And know the place for the first time.
        T.S.Eliot "Little Gidding".

'death chart'. Anyone looking ahead from his natal chart to the progressions and transits prevailing at that time could have seen that something major and traumatic was about to happen, and that it might well mean the ending of his life.

Rodney had taught himself astrology. He had charts for his family and for all those closest to him, and clearly he must have known what was in his own chart that day and hour. It put quite a different slant on Janet's comment that he had put everything in order, saying "something new is about to happen, but I don't know what it is". If he had suspected that he would in fact die in some form of final and traumatic initiation, he might well have resolved to die 'consciously'. Ouspensky had always held that the manner of death was extremely important.

For better or worse, it seemed that Rodney had taken responsibility for himself at the end. "The way towards unity lies in escape from time", he had written once. And his ending could have been his way of going for that.

Astrology is, of course, a study of the qualities inherent in any moment of time. It is a study of cogwheels, the cosmic clocks that tick away our lives. It deals with the apparent correlation between the movements of the heavenly bodies and life on earth, implying that the same laws apply throughout creation: from the galaxies, to the neutrons and protons at the basis of organic life, the same formulae and rhythms seem to hold good. For this reason it held my interest and I became an active member of the Astrological Association and also of the Astrological Lodge of the Theosophical Society.

"We are all people who have taken responsibility for ourselves", I said to Warren Kenton, the Cabalist, sitting opposite him in the Hall at St. John's College, Cambridge, during an Astrological Association conference at which he was a speaker. Warren, who writes under the Hebrew name of Z'ev ben Shimon Halevi, was to become a much respected friend. He looked at me now and answered: "That was worth saying."

In recent times it had been slowly borne in on me that the means to develop and evolve lie somewhere within one's self, and that this should never for a moment be forgotten. There might indeed be masters who know much more, and who may be doing valuable work in the world at any time. But each had his price. And any price that involved selling part of one's freedom to grow naturally, and to open up one's own centres was going to prove in the long run to be too high. I therefore became a kind of freelance, moving as I thought best, learning and occasionally giving talks, in the spheres with which I had made myself familiar.

I was soon on the Council of the Astrological Association, contributing articles to various fairly scholarly astrological journals, and beginning to be in some demand as a speaker. I also built up a clientele as an astrological consultant, and so kept myself continually quietly busy.

One evening, twelve years after I had left the SRM, I was talking at a meeting of the Astrological Association in the National Liberal Club in London. My subject was the Life and Work of Rodney Collin, with an astrological analysis of the natal horoscope and the progressed chart at the time of his death.

As I stood talking to John Addey, the President, waiting to begin, a tall, red-haired young man entered the hall and stopped by the reception table to pay his admission fee. My heart leapt, then plummetted at the sight of him. There was instant recognition. This was one of the people I had known in my childhood memories, for he had returned again and again in a frightening, nightmarish sort of dream that I had had from about the age of nine to twelve or so.

In my dream I was at the convent school I then in fact attended. The nuns used to take us for a picnic on Ascension Day. But in my dream we were in the charge, not of a nun, but of a tall, red-haired young schoolmaster: and this was he. We were grouped round him. He was pouring lemonade or something from one of the tall enamel jugs that were then used. The children were holding out their mugs to be filled.

When he came to me he asked: "Where is your mug?" I realised I hadn't got it in my hand. "I left it at the top of the tower", I said. The tower was behind him. It was a sort of folly, ivy-covered and with a door like a church. In my mind's eye I could see my enamel mug lying at the top on a stone seat or low wall.

"Go and fetch it then," the schoolmaster commanded.

"Alone?" I asked. I felt reluctant to enter the low arched door.

"Yes, of course, alone."

Slowly I went into the tower and started up the spiral staircase. Half way up was an empty room where leaves were blowing about the floor. The stairs continued from the other side of the room. As I emerged into it I heard footsteps running down helter-skelter from the floor above. They were accompanied by a terrible sound: wild, maniacal laughter. As I waited in terror, the schoolmaster came reeling out into the room. He was completely mad. He came hurtling across towards me. He couldn't descend further because I was blocking the way down. In my dream I always stood my ground and screamed. I doubt if I screamed aloud, for nobody ever came to my bedroom. I would wake myself up, sweating and with thumping heart. In a moment I would slide down to the end of the familiar bed, sit cross-legged and hold the two brass knobs in my hands for comfort and security. Just as I had dreamed of my brother and of certain other characters too, I had dreamed of the schoolmaster, but always in this identical sequence of events. However I had not thought of this dream for years.

I was so disconcerted by the sudden appearance of a face so well recollected, the long, thick, rather untidy hair, the remembered eyes, that I followed him visually to a seat in the back row and virtually addressed my whole talk to him. I knew that something would happen afterwards. When the lecture was over he came up, hovering uncertainly on the edge of the small group of people who had gathered round to make comments and ask questions. I knew by now quite certainly that something important was about to begin.

When at length he got to me, I was surprised to find his manner was shy and diffident. I had expected the authoritative schoolmaster's voice. Instead he seemed to regard me with deference. He was writing a book about Gurdjieff and the Fourth Way School, he said. Could he come and visit me at home and talk a little further with me about Rodney Collin? He had already published other works.

His name was James Webb.

Jamie's life was so tragically short that it is remarkable he made so much impact on the literary world, and in particular on those who study esotericism. He published *Flight from Reason* (Macdonald), *The Occult Establishment*, and his

198

magnum opus, *The Harmonious Circle* (Thames and Hudson and Putnam USA). He contributed to *Encounter*, to *Man, Myth and Magic*, and *The Encyclopedia of the Unexplained*, as well as doing a television series on the occult.

He visited me first at my Sussex home, and we talked over a wide field of ideas. He tape recorded hours of the conversations he had with me, and made copious notes for *Harmonious Circle* at my house. He called himself a "historian of ideas". His interest was in the semi-esoteric movements that sprouted in Europe in the 19th and early 20th centuries, and the development of the ideas underlying the outward trends of life. Although only twenty four at that time, he was extremely erudite.

He was a Scot, with some Irish blood in him, and would have inherited a considerable estate at Blair Drummond in Perthshire if he had lived. But he was estranged from his mother and step-father, due to an association with a girl who did not fit into the family background, and whom he later married much against their wishes. He seemed to welcome the naturalness with which he fitted into our household, now that he had virtually cut himself off from his own family and home.

I soon came to feel as affectionate towards Jamie as if he had been an adopted son. Astrologically our birth charts dovetailed to an extraordinary degree. We were both Capricornians with Leo at the Ascendant, and the number of contacts between the horoscopes was such that he could indeed have been a child of mine. I almost forgot about the mad schoolmaster aspect.

He had been at Harrow where he had taken every conceivable prize, including the coveted Winston Churchill award in two consecutive years. He had gone up to Trinity, Cambridge, and had again made such an impact that a biennial James Webb Memorial Prize is now established there in his honour. Later he took up a research grant into the paranormal, and began to write and broadcast and open up a whole lot of different avenues for the future.

"You are more scholarly than I", I told him, when he quoted from obscure and learned sources.

"But you've got the experience. That's what I value", he answered me.

The quickfire exchange of ideas between us was stimulating

and pleasing to me. I had never met anyone but Rodney with whom I felt so completely at home, as with Jamie. We were both rapid speakers, usually rattling on in a verbal shorthand that made explanation and elaboration of one's thought totally unnecessary. Each knew the purport of the other's argument before the sentence was even finished!

One summer day we were having tea under an old apple tree in my garden and talking philosophy as usual. Jamie stretched out his hand towards the tea trolley and broke off his own discourse in mid-sentence to interject: "Another piece of cherry cake, please."

The trivial incident had an extraordinary effect on me. Like a camera shutter suddenly and briefly opening, I saw again the Tibetan scenes, myself as a thickly-clad child carrying cherries to my 'brother'. Now as I cut the cherry cake for my 'son' I stopped and looked at him in bewilderment.

"What is it"? he asked.

"The cherries. They have a significance. This moment reminded me of something".

"Well, cherries *do* mean something", he said. "The opposite to apples. You know, 'comfort me with apples for I am sick of love' and that sort of thing."

"The earthly desires and something to do with the Spirit? Apples are perhaps the earthly commitment".

As we gazed at one another in a silent communion far beyond the reach of logic, I realised how dearly I had grown to love him. The depth of trust and confidence between us was such that we faced one another without guard, without guile or pretence of any kind: we seemed to be two beings who had incarnated within reach of each other many times in different roles. This time it was a kind of mother/son relationship. The doors of my heart, so long closed, opened a little more at each encounter, and laughter and sheer happiness on both sides leavened our most serious conversations.

Sometimes Jamie came down with other people at my invitation. Charles Harvey, President of the Astrological Association, Warren Kenton, Jill Purce whose work *The Mystic Spiral* is to some extent based on material gleaned from my lectures to the Astrological Association on the *Spiral of Life in Astrology*—and a number of other interesting youngsters all

200

gathered at my home for the occasional Sunday lunch.

It was an extraordinary change of scene for me. I had become hostess and friend to a group of people considerably junior to myself. The one thing they all had in common was that they had taken responsibility for their own development—writing, researching, lecturing, contributing in some way to the knowledge that will be the legacy of this particular age.

I was, I suppose, living vicariously through these people. I lectured and wrote quite a lot of articles, but mainly I enjoyed their youthful company, being now well into my fifties.

My interests gradually widened as my contacts grew. At the Theosophical Society I made friends of my own generation, attended talks on the *Secret Doctrine*, Madame Blavatsky's six volume major work, and enjoyed the feeling of widening my field of study. But the members were not advancing much themselves, I thought. Staying in the flat at their London headquarters, in Gloucester Place, before giving a seminar and lecture there, I had the curious feeling that the beautiful old house with its sweeping spiral staircase was full of ghosts. At night there were presences everywhere—in the library, the lecture room, the members' room, on the stairs and even in the basement schoolroom area. The ones down there seemed a bit malevolent to me! But mainly they were benign, though dedicated, as it seemed, to keeping the status quo. The inspiration of an earlier age had crystalized, I thought, within these walls.

In addition, I visited the remnants of the Rudolf Steiner groups in London, but found them weakly disintegrating as the adherents aged and not enough new young blood was entering the seat of learning. The same thing seemed to be happening there as I had observed with the Theosophical Society and with Gurdjieff and Ouspensky groups—notwithstanding the enormous treasure houses of knowledge that had been inherited in all these places. It was like the libraries at Oxford once again: one respected and revered the heritage, but many of the trustees seemed scarcely worthy of the trust. Somehow one had got to make a new approach, acquire fresh knowledge, and probably the younger people held the key to it.

Warren Kenton made it difficult for me to enter his group. We had met at two of his lectures on the Cabala, and he seemed familiar to me from the very beginning. We had friends in common and he knew Rodney's work. A Sephardic Jew, he learnt much from his grandfather and was well versed in the Judaic tradition from an early age. What appealed to me was that almost as soon as he began to publish, he launched out into his own line, presenting the Cabalistic Tree of Life in a form appropriate to this day and age and showing it to be adaptable for almost any work on one's self and one's situation.

The old Rabbis distrusted and disliked him. He had quite a hard time of it. He was disseminating their private knowledge to the masses. It was the old cry: "Keep the system pure". "Keep out those who are not worthy of it." Quietly confident he persisted in his own convictions, using the Tree as a simple framework on which to build ideas. Now well established as an author and a Wrekin Trust lecturer, speaking widely, from the United States to Israel, he is a household name to those who study systems of psychological development.

My recollection is that I persisted each time I encountered him in asking if he had a group with whom I could study. He prevaricated. Eventually he said: "Of course. Come tomorrow".

"Why didn't you invite me before, if there is a group?"

"By my tradition, you are supposed to ask three times," he said. But later I realised that he had made it hard for me because he saw I already had a line of my own to follow.

At his early meetings Warren drove his followers very hard. The demands put upon us in the way of disciplines and 'homework' were far greater than Francis Roles' people would have sustained. I liked this very much. They were of all ages, some, not all, Jewish. They readily took Cabala as a climbing frame on which to set their own thought and mount upon the ladder of the Way. They asked questions, made alert comments, came always with fresh ideas. This I felt was an excellent example of what Gurdjieff and Ouspensky's work should be today. Each man or woman doing his or her own thing! Very different from the crystalized versions I had encountered in other places. They were almost all hard-pressed, with demanding jobs to do in life. They arrived tired and went quietly into silent, undirected meditation. They were eager to contribute and to learn.

I had observed elsewhere the considerable tendency we all have to believe we are higher up the ladder than is probably the case. People often want to influence others when they are still deeply unsatisfied with their own lives. They get vicarious satisfaction by setting up as a healer, for example, while their own bodies are in a state of imbalance and they are in need of healing themselves. It seems to be a well intentioned but common mistake to want to live other people's lives for them, often by the giving of a lot of unsolicited advice! But the people with Warren knew where they were on the ladder. They had no pretentiousness about them.

In answer to questions, Warren seemed to be able to draw from within himself in such a way that occasionally I thought I heard a master speak. I learnt a good deal from him, but not by any means only about Cabala. It was noticeable that sometimes during his meetings the atmosphere in the room became charged in some way—some good, creative way I thought. It never felt charged with the alien, manipulative power that Pak Subuh and Maharishi had evoked. Afterwards we would eat bread and cheese and drink red wine, according to the ancient Jewish custom of breaking bread together.

Occasionally Warren invited me to stay on and have a late supper with him, if I was spending the night with friends in London. When the others had gone, he would become, not the doorkeeper for a master, (as he liked to describe himself), but an ordinary friend and confidant, with a great sense of humour and an enormous fund of exceedingly Jewish jokes. Between laughter we would eat and talk as equals on all manner of subjects, gleaning from each other. But in his meetings I have always deferred to him with great respect.

The difference between the man and the master is one I have often thought about in recent years, since I became a freelance, sitting in at meetings of many different cults and organizations. There seems little doubt that a lively group, making legitimate demands for assistance towards their own growth, can draw out from a teacher or leader knowledge that is appropriate to

203

the moment, but which he may not have access to in his day to day life. He becomes a channel for higher thought as a result of his own intention and the group desire for enlightenment.

Once at a meeting I asked a question about the inner meaning of the Jews crossing the Red Sea, coming "out of the land of Egypt, out of the land of bondage", words which I had always felt to be a cover for something else. Warren launched spontaneously into an exposition of the hidden meaning behind the Old Testament stories which was rapid, fluent and of extraordinary subtlety and depth. Half an hour later, he was laughing and teasing me after the meeting because I expressed a fear of being mugged if I walked across Green Park so late at night on my way to a woman friend's flat. He lifted down from the wall a Samurai sword that he numbered among his treasures and made a show of buckling it on to protect me with as he said he would accompany me to find a taxi. If I had asked a serious question then I doubt if he could have answered it as before.

Apart from the groups and organizations I had dealings with during those years, I made and cultivated a few personal friendships. One other friend from whom I could also learn, and who was of tremendous help in a crisis that was to come, was the Rev. Alun Virgin, the Bath and Wells Diocesan Adviser on the Paranormal. He was also on the Council of the Churches Fellowship for Psychic and Spiritual Studies. Alun came occasionally to conferences of the Astrological Association. He was quite a competent astrologer and very widely read. He could discuss Rodney's work, Ouspensky and Gurdjieff's writings, Nicoll's and Bennett's books, Warren's work and the researches of James Webb with equal ease. He was another big, burly, bearded man who spilt cigarette ash on his black clerical garb or on the carpet and rarely noticed until his wife came along to clean up after him. We would sit by the Somerset rectory fire exchanging ideas until the early hours while Margaret plied us with cups of tea at intervals before making her way to bed and leaving us to it.

Alun's work on the paranormal had brought him into contact with many apparent hauntings, poltergeist phenomena and the like. He was deeply convinced of the existence of discarnate entities and felt that on the whole they were best treated with considerable caution. He had performed the Church's ritual of exorcism in a number of houses. He had a fund of interesting stories to tell, especially of telepathic communications.

My interest in the underlying pattern of life led me next to study the Tarot, and I Ching, the Runes, and other methods of possible divination. Alun warned me to be very wary and to be sure that I could differentiate between the purely psychic experiences and that which could rightly be described as spiritual. In methods of divination the psychic certainly tends to predominate, and discarnate entities might come uninvited and create havoc in the lives of the incautious, I began to realise. I studied seriously, mindful of Alun's warnings. In the long run I felt that, in spite of certain mysterious elements, divinatory processes appear to bring out into the open the contents of one's subconscious mind—and little more.

Crossing myself and seeking a method of protection from unwanted influence became habitual through the years, though I never felt I could 'profess and call myself Christian', as Alun did. It seems to me that Christianity fits into the great scheme of things, rather than all good thought stemming from the teachings attributed to Jesus of Nazareth. The "dying god theme" as Robert Graves called it in *The White Goddess*, is very old indeed. It seems to represent eternal cycles of death and rebirth, of the willing sacrifice of perfection, in the giving of life that the product of life may flourish. But the cross has a meaning for me of its own. The vertical line seems to me to indicate the descent of the Spirit into matter, and the way back: the horizontal, the lateral movement through time. The bow drawn back, in terms of Maharishi and of the teachings of Shamanism, takes great power from the source. But the way forward for fulfillment of the evolutionary process seems to me to be via the symbol of the cross.

Because I had had a number of experiences of psychokinesis, Charles McCreery of the Institute of Psychophysical Research in Oxford invited me to take part in some experiments. I was asked to work a computer to see whether I could produce more than random or chance results in experiments with numbers and designs. I felt in advance that I could not. Such matters rarely work under laboratory conditions. Most of the day I produced only average results.

Quite late in the afternoon, I suddenly had a sense of

certainty that I knew the next sequence beyond doubt. Rapidly I pressed the appropriate keys. Suddenly my finger appeared to slip and I pressed a key not intended for use in the exercise. The programme immediately disappeared from the screen. McCreery said:

"But pressing that key couldn't cause anything to happen! It *couldn't* clear it". Nevertheless it had. We were left with the tantalizing uncertainty whether I had been 'PK-ing' as they called it, or not. It is certainly a known phenomenon that tape recorders, cameras and other equipment fail to record, jam up or produce no results, when there is an attempt to use them for this kind of experimental purpose. It is as though hobgoblins get into the works. Uri Geller and Matthew Manning both had experiences of this kind when trying to co-operate with investigators. Discarnate intelligences, if such they be, will not be pinned down and examined in this way. If the phenomenon rests in fact within one's self, this aspect is a little inexplicable. Nevertheless the staff at the Institute had experienced it more than once, always when the subject was being moved by the feeling that he or she suddenly knew for certain what was coming next.

I had told McCreery of a series of incidents I experienced in Mexico, and later on my return to this country, when coins had mysteriously appeared, and one in particular which was easily identified by a red mark on its edge, had appeared and reappeared no less than four times in my purse after having been disposed of. It was a phenomenon that continued for several months.

Coins appeared as a rule when seemingly needed for some charitable purpose. But the last occasion was in a restaurant with my daughter. I asked her if she had some small change for a tip. At once something plopped into my lap, as though tossed across the room in an angled arch. It was a sixpence. This was the point at which I somehow, inwardly, ordered it to stop. And it did.

I used to discuss these things with people at the College of Psychic Studies, where I attended meetings for a while. But on the whole, by the time I met the people at the College, I was losing interest in such matters for conversational exchange, and only interested in any scientific explanations that might in due course come along as a result of serious collection and examination of data. I therefore maintained my interest in the Institute of Psychophysical Research for preference.

A degree of intermittent clairvoyance had always existed in me since my childhood, though not then recognised of course for what it was. Once at about the age of thirteen, I looked into teacups at a children's party and exclaimed with sudden certainty that I could tell fortunes from them. With the lack of discretion of one so young, I made a rapid series of predictions at least three of which came true to my knowledge in later years. Then to my small sister, who had handed me her cup, I said quite calmly: "You'll die when you are forty-eight and I shall be by your bedside." When she faded away with a rapid cancer at that age, we both of us recollected the incident quite suddenly, a few hours before she went into her final coma. We had neither of us remembered it till then. Her loss was a sad blow to me. It was the first of a series of events which were again to make a big difference to my life.

16

My daughter had married a materialist who disliked his mother-in-law's interests from the start, and soon effectively prevented me from having any contact with her or with my grandchildren. Efforts to keep the difficult relationship going proved increasingly distressing and ultimately completely abortive. He seemed to feel that studying such matters as astrology was a sign of incipient madness. He forbade me to set up the children's natal charts and told me Ann was afraid of all such matters. The fear stemmed from insecurity in himself and not from my daughter, whose insight in her early years had been most interesting. "How many times do we have to live—before we get there?" she had asked out of the blue at the age of eight. She had recognised Rodney. She had smelt the Subud incense. Now she shut herself off, taking the soft option of obeying her husband's will and conforming to his very limited views.

Then problems suddenly struck my husband. He had been growing increasingly deaf, due to a war wound. His firm made him redundant on these grounds, and the handicap prevented him from finding further work. He was too young to retire, not yet eligible for a pension, and exceedingly alarmed as well as depressed by the situation. From necessity we sold the Sussex house and moved to a small cottage in the New Forest. Here Derry slowly adapted to the new situation, began to write as a freelance and made the best of it. But money was very tight and I could no longer follow my interesting and intellectually pleasing pursuits. It also became increasingly important that I should do people's horoscopes and any other paid work or lectures that came my way to increase our income.

At about the same time, soon after our move, Jamie Webb telephoned, asking me to check up details from my own sources, for a chapter of *The Harmonious Circle*. He sounded unlike himself, rather low and glum. He and Mary had only recently returned from an extended honeymoon in the Middle and Far East. He had sent postcards from the Orient.

"When can we meet?" he asked. "May I come down and see you?"

"Not just now", I told him. "Derry's far from well and things are difficult."

"Will you lunch with me in London soon?"

"I'll give you a ring", I promised.

I had already noticed that Jamie's astrological chart, though fiery and vigorous and tenacious like my own, had an inbuilt depressive tendency and the look of a character that might become progressively turned in upon himself as he became older. Already he had difficulty in finding friends who could keep up with him. He had accumulated an enormous library. He worked at his desk for very long hours, sometimes even falling asleep there from exhaustion. I had warned him affectionately of the tendencies I saw, but he didn't take my comments very seriously.

In a week or so he phoned again, saying he was being 'persecuted' by his publishers and adding wildly that the French Freemasons had got it in for him. I had a dose of flu, and speaking from bed I told him not to be silly. He didn't ring again, and to my great grief later, I didn't find the time to do anything about it. He had always come and gone as he pleased and I had no reason to think he would not just turn up on my doorstep again, if I didn't go to London and get in touch. He had in fact collapsed into total mental breakdown. But because I was no longer moving in our old circles I didn't hear of it. Quite a long time passed before he wrote again.

"My life has just emerged from a nightmare", he said when he was again in reasonable command of himself and able to correspond. "I had a full scale nervous breakdown, with hallucinations, visions and a fine repertoire of subjectively supernatural experiences. Hoist with my own petard, some would say. Despite the undoubtedly hallucinatory nature of many of my experiences, a residue remains which I simply have to take seriously. I can't fit all the altered states of consciousness into one system. Gnosticism and some of the Indian systems

209

seem to provide the best framework. Now all I am interested in is philosophy and religion."

Jamie was writing from Durisdeer in Dumfrieshire, where he and Mary had converted an old kirk into a residence. He had completely fallen out of the lively London circles in which he had previously been such a popular figure. I replied at once, telling him of my own experiences of breakdown, to comfort him. He wrote at great length by return. To my dismay I found he thought I had rebuffed him in his hour of need, just as he was collapsing. He had been in the hands of various psychiatrists and hospitals and was on tranquilizing drugs. He had only escaped E.C.T. by the skin of his teeth, since Mary had rightly refused to sanction it.

"I feel like an engineer whose hands have been cut off", he wrote. He could not work when the central nervous system was dulled by drugs. Without them, his ability to reason normally quickly left him. In the next four or five months we exchanged somewhere near 20,000 words in constant correspondence. Two or three times a week long typewritten screeds would plop through my letter box, and I would answer quickly because of the seeming urgency of the request for my ideas on his new states of mind, and for understanding and support.

He spoke of: "a shattering vision of the wheel of life, the sight of my previous incarnations set up like a great silver millwheel". He had become convinced that there is in the human being "a principle of consciousness which is not merely the result of a congerie of experience". He imagined his own "individualized consciousness" using "poor old Brother Ass (who got well nigh disintegrated two years ago), to manoeuvre around in this rather soupy environment of which Brother Ass is a part. It is rather like being in a deep water submarine and using pincers, grabs, television cameras and artificial light to make contact with the strange world of the seabed."

For some days, he said, he had apparently "seen molecules". He was all together too familiar with the idea "that nature is a Heraclitean flux", quoting from Gerard Manley Hopkins. It was clear to me that he had experienced exactly the same terrifying phenomena of continual change, no stability anywhere, that had driven me almost to the point of suicide fifteen years before.

He agreed with me that, as he put it: "There is no reason to think that the pilgrims of the pit have knowledge which is in essence any different from the riders in the Chariot of the Spirit", and wondered if his breakdown, terrifying and chaotic as it was, might not be a positive, almost evolutionary step in his progress. He had suddenly been "catapulted into a larger universe". But he was pre-occupied with "the sheer horror of discovering one is imprisoned in the coils of cyclical time. I'm convinced there is a way out", he wrote "but we probably only find it at death. I think Rodney Collin was quite right about the importance of dying properly, and I have revised my opinion about the manner of Ouspensky's death."

I tried to give him some ideas about holding the mind steady in a moment of time, as I had learnt to do myself, and to turn him away from his continual preoccupation with the idea of death.

He wrote of his boyhood, of precognitive dreams when he was a teenager, and added that he had always had a private mythology: "that we are most of us participants in something which is a cross between a great adventure and a grand primeval tragedy. My myth puts it in science fictional terms —the crew of a splendid space ship which crashlanded on an alien planet. Immediately they were enslaved by the local inhabitants, and now have forgotten who they were or whence they came. But occasionally something jogs their memories and they remember the times when they flew through the galaxy on high adventures, or something plucks their heartstrings and they recognise, only for a moment, their trapped comrades. Coupled with this is an indescribable happy-sad feeling. Something is calling. And in their hearts is an aching memory of home. And permeating everything is the impression of infinitely long periods of time. The tragedy is infinitely far distant the adventure infinitely long. And we are ageless, simply ageless."

I replied that I had a similar mythology as a child. Being before the time of spaceships it concerned being shipwrecked on an island and enslaved. One was always creeping down to the shore to scan the horizon for a sail. But soon the local inhaitants came and dragged one back to work for them.

We discussed Jung's *Septem Sermones* written semi-automatically after his own breakdown. Jamie commented: "I have never seen why magicians and others wanted to be possessed by the powers. You lose your humanity that way."

It was clear to me that he was going through a long drawn out and quite terrifying self-induced initiatory process. He needed whatever help one could possibly give.

"Its lovely to know I'm no longer alone in the wilderness", he wrote.

Meanwhile Mary, tired of having him mooching about at home unable to be happy or sociable and no longer able to sit in his study and write, began to drive him to take a job, any sort of job, to get him out and about in the world again. To my horror, I found that at her instigation he had taken a parttime job copywriting for a firm of advertising agents in Edinburgh. I thought this quite appalling for a man of his calibre. She appeared not to realise that it was not strictly necessary for him to earn at all. His resources were more than adequate, but he had always liked to live modestly and he had not divulged the extent of his means.

Jamie's letters to me became suddenly extremely stressful and agitated, and his statements increasingly irrational and wild. Having delved into the background of esoteric movements in his own part of the world, he had been attempting to research for a book to be called *Flodden: The Renaissance in Scotland*. But he said "I can't get the pattern of it any more".

This was all so terribly familiar as a result of my own experiences that I became more and more concerned about what might be happening to his mind. I decided to go up and visit him as he had written several times that he so much wanted to see me but couldn't get down because of the copywriting job. However my husband and I would in any case be up in Argyll shortly for our summer holiday, so ultimately I decided to defer it for a few weeks and go over to Durisdeer then instead of making an extra journey. Meanwhile I suggested that it might be a good idea to reduce this enormous correspondence which seemed to be getting out of hand in length and frequency. I thought it might be doing more harm than good.

He wrote once more, and said that he would telephone on the evening before we were to set out to our holiday cottage on Loch Awe, to arrange to meet up there at the earliest possible date.

212

By this time I realised we had established a telepathic contact with each other. Although I hadn't seen the house at Durisdeer, I could sometimes see him at his desk. I felt there was pain in the nerve centre at the back of his neck, a vulnerable area of my own, and of Rodney too. I picked up the pain in my own body. I got glimpses of Freekirk and the surroundings which proved to be absolutely accurate.

Several times in the last stressful weeks, I seemed to hear him crying in the night. Waking, I would sit up, and attempt as best I could to make mental contact with him of a comforting kind. I had not been accustomed to touch him. He was not a very physical type of man, and I don't recollect ever even kissing him on the cheek or putting my arm about him. But now, hearing inwardly the sound of heartrending sobs in the hours of darkness, I stretched out as though to stroke his head and soothe and calm him. Mary told me later that he had moved into a separate bedroom and that he was indeed "always crying" at that time.

On the afternoon before we were to put the car on the night Motorrail for Perth, I suddenly heard his voice. The call was urgent: "Joyce! Joyce!" Stopping my packing, I answered: "Yes, I'm coming."

Almost at once I experienced something inwardly that seemed like an enormous explosion in my head. It was followed by a period of utter silence. He had gone.

I told my husband at once: "Something is wrong with Jamie". He calmed me, saying I must be imagining it. Because Derry thought it all a flight of fancy, I did not telephone, though I almost knew in my bones that he couldn't keep his own intention of ringing me that evening.

All through the hours in the rocking sleeper I worried about him and went over and over the incident of the afternoon. When we arrived at our rented cottage on Loch Awe there had been a telephone message to ring Mary at Durisdeer. Jamie had put his shotgun to his head and killed himself at about 3 pm. the previous day.

We went down to Durisdeer. Mary, distraught, poured out a rather garbled version of events. She led me to his study and dug out from his enormous waste paper basket crumpled letters written to me in the last few days and then thrown away.

"I have no-one but you to whom I can talk of these things......So few people will talk about the really important things, and those who will are usually peddling a proprietary brand of solution not applicable to everyone....."

There was no indication in them that he was about to take his life. It appeared to have been an impulse born of prolonged and increasing despair, and triggered off in the ultimate by no more than a domestic tiff. He had previously said like me: "Suicide isn't a way out". Unlike myself, in my so similar private hell, the gods who shape our ends had sent him on his way, though I had been called back.

Although I had met Mary before, I had never found her easy and I understood why Jamie's parents had been unhappy with the situation. "He was always considering the state of his soul and that sort of rubbish", she said in the brisk sort of tone my mother used to use. "He couldn't talk to me about things like that—I wouldn't let him. I used to tell him to pull himself together and go out and dig the garden or something". Although undoubtedly she had loved him in her way, I found she thought of him as no more than a painstaking researcher. She had no conception of his depths, of his calibre as a historian of ideas, and as a man. She had been unable to give him any deep companionship at all.

When I visited Rosemary and Paddy Dickson, Jamie's mother and stepfather, a little later, I learnt that he had indeed been—like the schoolmaster—'certifiably mad' for a time a few months back. He had run wildly and hysterically from their house one winter night across the estate, and waded waist high through a river, to get to Dunblane Cathedral twelve miles away. There he had banged fruitlessly on the doors to gain admittance.

He had crouched by the fire in the drawing room at Blair Drummond, hunched in the foetal position, repeating the Lord's Prayer again and again, muttering: "What is it all about"? completely unresponsive to word or touch. Only on Largactil, a drug given to the mentally disturbed, did he eventually regain some semblance of normality. Jamie was deeply loved by his parents and the deep distress they felt at their own helplessness was much enhanced by their conviction that Mary was not the right wife for him. "She bewitched him",

Paddy said. "It was as though he were a man possessed."

Back at the holiday cottage on Loch Awe I began to try to come to terms with what had happened. I read the crumpled letters Mary had given me from his wastepaper basket. I realised I hadn't made myself immediately available when he had called on me. Grief overtook me as I walked the hills above the loch. I had lost now the second most beloved person in my life—and in the same way, so it seemed, for Rodney's death had also apparently been by his own will and intention.

Each day I wandered and climbed, passing the sheep and lambs grazing on the uplands, hearing the peewits cry, seeing buzzards circling above. Sitting with my back against a boulder gazing at the wide Highland landscape that Jamie had loved so much, the loch glistening in sunlight far below, I suddenly found myself saying aloud in my misery: "Why didn't you help him?"

Immediately, a voice seeming quite outside myself, replied: "I did." A face appeared briefly before my eyes and disappeared at once. It was dark-haired, dark-eyed, with a steady, penetrating gaze, faintly familiar but seeming very far back in years. I thought of it many times afterwards. I think it is possible that it might have been Rudolf Steiner, but at an earlier age than the photographs I am familiar with. Jamie had been commissioned to write a book on Steiner and had done much of the research before his breakdown. Later Colin Wilson did it instead.

Back home the first thing I did was telephone Warren with the news. I had introduced Jamie to Warren some years back and he had gained much by Warren's steadiness and held him in high regard. Warren reacted with emotion, but seemed to feel the death was inevitable. "He has been lifted out", he said.

Before his breakdown, Jamie had been dabbling in various fields of esoteric knowledge held by guardians of ancient cults—and there is power among those who have higher knowledge and want to protect it from the merely inquisitive. I thought often of his fear of the French Freemasons, and his statement: "They have got it in for me."

Traditionally the Freemasons, although innocuous perhaps in Britain, are among the various holders of the secrets of the Sangraal, the Holy Grail, and the knowledge of a bloodline descending from a union of Jesus and the Magdelene. It has been said it is dangerous to get too close to those who know, and mysterious deaths seem to litter the trail where there have been attempts to bring out into the open knowledge that has been treasured by the few.

Later I came across another enquirer in this line who seemed to have been damaged by his own curiosity. But this is mere speculation, based on my experience of the Maharishi's power to destroy, and Eliphas Levi's warning of the perils of poking a nose into matters of which you understand too little.

Eventually I came to think that the short life span—he was only thirty-four—was possibly completed. He had effectively ceased to live creatively some time before his body died, for as Mary said, the man she married "died two years before he shot himself".

Soon after Jamie's death a series of strange, psychic experiences began to manifest in my own home. I was dozing in my armchair one afternoon when I heard his voice. He said clearly: "Mother". I felt his presence strongly, and sitting up I answered: "Yes, darling", as though to my spiritual son. There was a sense of withdrawal, followed in a minute by: "Go to my mother". I realised I had made a mistake in thinking he was addressing me personally. He seemed to want to use me as an intermediary. Eventually I returned to Scotland and passed on to Rosemary the reassurances of love and devotion and regret at the estrangement that seemed to be coming from Jamie through me, to comfort her in her loss.

I began to feel Jamie's presence more persistently and continually than Rodney's had ever been. He seemed to press in on me as though demanding that I should take on and finish his work for him, a task I obviously couldn't undertake. Eventually I visited Mrs. Wheeler Hopkinson, a much respected medium who works at the College of Psychic Studies, and who lived not far from us. The two long sittings I had with her, and which were recorded, make most curious hearing, and did much to convince me of survival after death. The medium, although told nothing in advance, picked up the name Jamie, his red hair, his tall build, his Scottish ancestry and a good deal about his work and his ambitions.

Personal bits included: "I will come to you in the quiet of

216

your home, when you are working at night, with your feet up on that long footstool. I will come at special times......Look for the inspirational thought—it may come from me. Get my books. Mary doesn't understand them. Go on writing. You'll write creatively again. But your work will change......."

Eventually Jamie's presence seemed to become so strong, overwhelming in its pressure, in my own house, that I began to feel concern about what I was experiencing. I couldn't free myself of the sense that he wanted something from me: that the more I did—such as travelling back to Scotland to see his parents—the more he would demand. The voice through Mrs. Wheeler Hopkinson also became more vigorous, pouring out more and more information on matters of which I had no knowledge myself previously. Most of it turned out to be true.

But gradually I began to feel there was something amiss with this phenomenon. It seemed I was slowly being taken over. This was not the whole Jamie. It was bits and pieces of him. It was part of his mind. Perhaps it had reality. But it was not complete. In fact I began to wonder whether it was something of an automatic nature, the repetition of 'thought forms', something no longer living and advancing onwards.

I began to say, "Move on, Jamie. I love you, I remember you, but I can't do your work. Move on."

"Make a replica of me", came the voice through the medium. "Put the photo back on the wall where I can see it." I had in fact removed his photograph from my study wall in an effort to free myself from obsessive grieving. "There's love there. Think joyfully....I'll help you with your work.....I often watch you setting up those charts....You are so like me....Here are red roses for you from the spirit world......I shall re-incarnate. Not yet, but there's a duty......"

The mixture—the hotchpotch of messages that seemed possibly genuine and the trivia and absurdity of some, struck me as extraordinary and puzzling. The words "I shall re-incarnate. There is a duty", had considerable reality for me, in that they echoed Rodney's oft-repeated statement that he expected to remain within reach "until the consummation of the world". He felt he had work to do, and so did Jamie. And of course it tallied also with my own early childhood experiences of an urgent thing that had to be remembered, something one had promised once, and had to do. But "red roses from the spirit world?" this could not be 'real'.

Eventually I drove over to Somerset to consult Alun Virgin. He was the best possible person to advise me in my extraordinary predicament. "All this is a known phenomenon", he said. "I have heard this 'make a replica of me' phrase before. You are quite right to stop it. Don 't do it any more. We must release you from this. You have reached a state of psychic saturation. Would you like me to say a requiem for him? We could do it in the church tomorrow morning."

I was surprised to find the Church of England has a somewhat obscure form of service which asks for "all entities to go each to his rightful place", and requests that the soul of the departed be released from this world's coils and freed from all further need to linger here. Alun gave it to me to read and approve, and I agreed. I jibbed, however, at the inclusion of a sentence intended to 'seal off' the dead from the living, so that the ones who loved the departed soul should no longer be troubled.

"There's a Karmic link between Jamie and me", I told Alun. "We must not be sealed off from one another, in case he can't find me again the next time round." He agreed to omit the sentence from the service.

In the morning Alun, Margaret his wife, and I walked to the little village church at West Huntspill where he was rector. Here he lit the candles in the side chapel, and said the requiem slowly and with deep sincerity, and we repeated all the prayers together. I had no idea whether it would do anything to help the situation. But suddenly, at a certain point, as I knelt head in hands, I had a strange and most convincing sense that something had happened on an inner plane of life, and that whatever remained of that well beloved young man had indeed been set free to go its way.

This was in 1980. Since then, the essence or the Spirit or whatever it may be that is the highest form of Jamie, has visited me at home from time to time, and his remembered voice has echoed in my ears. I hear him, as I hear Rodney on occasion, always unexpectedly, never at will. Sometimes a comment or a statement has especial significance. Sometimes a little precognitive clue, like the word 'crossbow' long ago, reaches me.

One day quite recently, sorting through old photographs of people who have departed long ago—Madame K., Ernest Lenney, Elsie Abercrombie, Rodney and Janet, Jamie, I sighed and said to myself: "All dead. All dead. All gone. I'm all by myself." Inside me Rodney's voice answered on an indignant note: "*I'm* not dead!" I knew I had not imagined it. In some sense it is surely true that there is no such thing as death.

17

Just as Jamie's voice through Mrs. Wheeler Hopkinson had predicted, my work began to change, so that I gradually found myself conducting workshops and seminars on a variety of subjects. The people who came were mainly of a younger generation than myself. But the voice had also said "you'll write creatively again". However the whole field of creative ideas remained closed to me and the stream that had been dammed or diverted so long ago, still did not open up. I continued with my long, careful horoscope analyses, and my considered astrological and philosophical articles. The doors of the emotions, which had opened so joyously to Jamie and with such anguish at his end, were again locked and barred. I sought the company of older friends of like mind, but no-one touched me deeply any more.

I had corresponded for some time with Colin Wilson, but had never met him. I knew him as the author of *The Outsider, New Pathways in Psychology, The New Existentialism* and other important books. Then one day he invited me to go and stay with him and his wife in their Cornish clifftop home.

He had been asked to write a Foreword to Jamie's *The Occult Establishment*, by a small publisher called Richard Drew, who liked to think of himself—not quite truthfully, Paddy and Rosemary said—as Jamie's 'best friend'. He lived not far from them in Perthshire and had been at Harrow at the same time as Jamie.

The two writers had never met, though they had corresponded, so Colin drew on my knowledge of Jamie, and I showed him extracts from our letters for this purpose. But *The Occult Establishment* was published without Colin's interesting and valuable Foreword* in the end, for Mary vetoed almost all of it on the grounds that she didn't want the details of Jamie's 'illness' talked about. The book quickly went out of print. It is therefore already unobtainable by researchers in this country and the American edition is unavailable now. Mary's copyright prevents its re-appearance through another publishing house. Scholars have to borrow copies of this really rather important and exceedingly erudite volume from esoteric libraries.

I found that Colin and Joy Wilson live in warm, comfortable haphazard style in Cornwall—ten thousand books lining almost every room from floor to ceiling, good classical music, boys, dogs, the continual coming and going of visitors. In my rather low state I found the household a relaxing and happy one. Perched above a Cornish cove, its grounds command wide views over sea and sky.

With their golden labradors Rosie and Ben beside me, on my first visit in 1981 I walked the clifftops and the lanes and byways of the little harbour village, sorting out my thoughts a bit as I went, straightening my back and beginning to hold up my head again. Colin, a self-disciplined man who keeps his daily routine intact and has an enormous output of books and articles, had welcomed me with genuine warmth and kindness. In the evenings by a log fire we would all drink wine together, and later, supper trays on laps, watch television and indulge in intermittent conversation which was always relaxed and natural and good. We discussed a wide field of ideas concerning the nature of life, the human mind, esotericism and the paranormal, always coming back to Colin's positive and optimistic view of mankind's evolutionary possibilities and the use of the will towards this end. He also encouraged me vigorously to write again, and turned my attention in that direction. The comfort I received in Colin's home remains with me as an example of great generosity to a comparative stranger. His chief attribute is his openness to all ideas. His boundless enthusiasm for life means that he gives and gets in equal

* It was subsequently published in *Light*, the magazine of the College of Psychic Studies, Vol. 102, No. 2.

measure, for it is certainly a basic law that one gets out of life in the same measure as one puts into it.

Sitting in Colin's orchard I wrote the opening chapter of this book. Rosie and Ben were there still, lying beside me in the long grass, panting in the heat. Ben walks more slowly now, taking himself down at a leisurely pace to bathe at the harbour instead of romping ahead over the clifftops and showing visitors the way to his secret coves and beaches, as he did when I first visited the Wilsons. But then, I walk more slowly too, and stop and lean on gates or sit on stiles and think: and I use a walking stick in the more scrambly places.

I've been fortunate in my friendships through the years. The only thing lacking was a partner on the Way, for my kind husband, in spite of his fraternal link with Rodney Collin, has been a supporter in life rather than in esoteric thought.

The Way is essentially lonely, I incline to think, and must surely continue through many incarnations. The yearning for someone with whom to travel seems like a lateral movement rather than a movement forward—but it is a part of human nature to yearn for it. Companionship along the Way is a joy and comfort at times of trial and testing, of course, but it is probably not essential. Obviously, we yearn towards one another because we are part of the same Being, the Being known as Mankind. We may help, enlighten or love each other. But *inwardly* most people seem to travel always on their own.

The question whether the Way can be entered by human love, by the man/woman relationship, is one I often ponder. It appears to me to be a legitimate first entry, in that in the ecstasy of sexual union a man and woman may get the initial glimpse of something beyond the norm of their existence. There is a Jewish tradition that the divine creative activity, like that of human beings in procreation, is a joyful dialectic between male and female elements. This coming together is known in Cabalistic terms as the marriage of the king and the matrona. It irradiates a divine light called the Schechinah. Wherever the divine creative forces are at work, there also is the Schechinah—which was lost at the Fall and can only be regained in moments of rare exaltation: one being when complete love and harmony exist between man and woman.

Coleridge wrote: "So closely are the human and divine

creativity linked that if the Schechinah is recovered between human beings, God himself is affected. He is given a joy He would not otherwise possess."*

But many men nowadays yearn towards women from the belief that somehow they can enter the Way through a woman's influence, or through a woman's loving submission to them. The idea of conquest seems to be is inherent in this though, and the Way does not open to the conqueror! Any strong woman becomes aware of this phenomenon, which is part of the age and the more apparent now that women themselves do not seek a lord and master in the opposite sex.

It is surely part of the *Paradigm Shift*, to use Fritjof Capra's term—the slow changeover from the long dominant male principle to the female, of which the strident demands of bra-burning women's libbers were the first and extremist lunatic fringe. The feminist movement is gaining momentum in this age, of course. But in the ultimate, the male and female principles will surely be seen in balance, neither dominating, neither subservient—though alternating dominance and subservience on each side are part of the ever-changing interplay between the principles. The man/woman relationship only reflects these great principles: the attempt at dominance by one side has no more permanency or reality in itself than the attempt at a 'partnership' of equals or the evolution of an androgyne.

By nature the male must enter the female and be reborn by this means in perpetuity, and she must receive and give birth to him again and again until the end of time: in her womb, at her breast, in her vagina she bears and sustains him. But she can't find his true centre for him, the point of balance which enables him to move forward on the Way. That he must do for himself.

There is perhaps another feminine role too, and it is epitomized in the words 'Stabat Mater Dolorosa', and the Pieta: the woman who must be helplessly acquiescent at the crucifixion, ready to receive the Beloved, at the end and at the beginning. But not all women are required to play that agonisingly inactive part.

If a woman receives a man with the wish to claim and control

* *Coleridge, the Visionary* by J.D. Beer.

223

him, she achieves no more than he does if he holds and takes her with a desire to conquer and despoil. Much greater delicacy and sensitivity are really needed on either side, than most of us achieve in our human partnerships. The small personal relationships of men and women must surely reflect and carry the great archetypal principles, as the world moves on into the new age, where the individual becomes increasingly responsible for his own development and makes his contribution, like a small, light-holding droplet of water on the evolutionary wave.

There is a tradition of Shamanistic practice that two initiates may work together, the male partner working from his 'female shield' and the woman from her 'male shield'. A very powerful partnership may ensure. But this is a rarity indeed. Having a half memory, I sometimes wondered if I should eventually meet someone who fulfilled this role for me. I have long been aware that I work from the 'male shield' in this way. The dim recollection of the partner who used the female shield had been with me since the time of puberty. It was the same type of memory as that of my brother, but of course I had never heard of these esoteric ideas about partnerships. None of the young men I met before or during the war were anywhere near it, so the dim and nebulous memory didn't develop in me very strongly, in my youth. Anyway, it was a joy the gods didn't grant me.

In later years I used often to think, fortunate are those who find a true partner with whom to travel, unfortunate those who think they can't or won't move on alone.

Increasingly alone inwardly now, though often among friends, acquaintances and astrological clients, I found myself more and more inclined to silence and to prayer. I had travelled by way of the simple 'listening to God' technique, to psychological exercises, esoteric practices of a transcendental kind, and intellectual efforts to get back to creativity, over the span of nearly half a century. In much of this I had followed the paths trodden by Rodney, whose only practice at the end had been that of prayer.

But unlike Rodney, who became devoted to the idea of the Christos, I don't pray regularly to Jesus Christ or the Madonna, or attempt as a rule to invoke known saints or deities. Invocation of any kind seems to me to be quite a dangerous practice—one may arouse lower discarnate entities and not the gods! I attempt to contact an inner part of my own being, to which I normally have little access, or no access at all: The Overself, the Dweller in the Innermost or whatever one may choose to call it is my objective. But with eyes open again after prayer and in day to day living, I see God present in every living thing. Whether one seeks God immanent, the kingdom of God within one's self, or God transcendent, one still seeks communion with the Creator as he permeates the whole universe.

My experience has been that it is perfectly possible, if one wants to, to contact a source of power, and that apparently miraculous results may ensue. And this can come about just the same whether one asks to speak to God the Father, or invokes St. Jude, who reads the Personal Column in the Daily Telegraph! Or by requiring assistance from one's mentor—in my case Rodney Collin—or from some other loved one beyond the grave. One doesn't know who hears. But often one knows something or someone does.

When people address themselves to God, they may get help from lower down the hierarchical scale than they imagine. I believe we possibly link in with a genuine influence or being, but not actually at the ultimate level that the earnest so often believe in. We contact whoever hears and recognises us.

As Rodney once said to me: "The only true helplessness is when a man is unaware of the need for help. When true help comes, it is incommensurate with anything we can do for ourselves". But true help seems to come by grace, not as a swift answer to pleas.

Possibly the most powerful source of all, if it can be contacted is, as Rodney believed, the Trinity of Beings that form the first manifestation of the Absolute. To go beyond that, into the ineffable, the immutable, the unchanging, attributeless source of all, is to go into the silence: into the void: into Ain Soph Aur, Ain Soph, Ain,—Limitless Light, Endlessness, the Void—the three outer universes of Cabala, which lie by tradition beyond Kether the Crown of the Tree of Life. I do not think practical help for living, or aid for those who are in this earthly realm can be attained from doing this often, for in the end the soul 'wants out' and there is no longer any purpose seen in living in this world. To go so far is to cultivate the will to death, before one's time is up. Here is the 'bliss consciousness' and one gets hooked on it, and gradually contracts out of life.

I have had many strange experiences of apparent results of prayer when help is needed. I rarely pray for myself, because I incline to think that the 'I want' element creeps in rapidly and one does not know what in fact is one's real requirement. One occasionally succeeds in changing outer events, only to find that nothing beneficial has been gained.

There is obvious reality behind the German fairy tale of the couple who were granted three wishes. As they sat pondering how to use them for the best, the old man said: "I'm hungry. I wish we had a sausage". A sausage appeared on the plate before him. "You fool!" cried his wife. "You've wasted one of our wishes. I wish that sausage were on the end of your nose." The third wish had inevitably to be used to get the sausage off her husband's nose on to the plate again and eat it. Usually we don't know what to wish for, what to pray for for the best. Even prayer for others is by no means sure to bring anything advantageous in the long run, though if undertaken with love and with humility it does sometimes seem to reach them like a healing touch, bringing a sense of peace. But I confine myself to a prayer that so and so may be helped, no more. It is easy to intrude on someone else's preserves in a manipulative way, meaning well but increasing the chaos in a troubled life by trying to change things for the better. There is an ancient tradition that one should never pray for someone without their permission, lest one interferes with their true needs. Though sounding a bit extreme, I think this could be very wise advice!

I rarely pray on my knees. I don't take to the 'miserable sinner' attitude. I think those who observe us from the inner or the higher realms should be looked in the face, not boldly, but not shrinkingly either: simply with quiet dignity. My father once told me: "After you say your prayers, get up and start living as though they had already been answered. That way they will be". This is surely the meaning of Goethe's well-known words about commitment:

Until one is committed there is the chance to draw back;

226

always ineffectiveness. Concerning all acts of initiative (and creation) there is one elementary truth, the ignorance of which kills countless ideas and splended plans—that the moment one definitely commits one's self then Providence moves too. All sorts of things occur to help one that would not otherwise have occurred. A whole stream of events issues from the decision, raising in one's favour all manner of unforeseen incidents and meetings and material assistance which no man could have dreamed would have come his way. Whatever you can do or dream you can, begin it! Boldness has genius, magic and power in it. Begin it now.

While I was thinking so much about prayer, and commitment, and pursuing my solitary inner life and my increasingly full outer one the gods provided one further and unexpected turn to my last active years.

Once long ago, at an Ouspensky meeting, a young girl said: "If only we could be always in love, we should achieve the higher things much more easily! All the colours are brighter and everything is much more vivid and alive for me, now that I am in love".

I was the one appointed to make the notes at the meeting, and transcribing them the following day, I paused and pondered on the possible reality of the comment. It occurred to me that I had never really been in love. In spite of all my adventures, my two marriages and my many contacts in life, I had experienced only passing delight in a few brief amorous adventures, and then returning rapidly to controlled and self-disciplined living. I had ridden my horse on a short rein for many years, and continued to do so as a matter of course. Probably me father's puritanical views always influenced me in my behaviour. But in fact I had never met anyone who made the colours brighter and everything more vivid and alive.

Here I tell a story without an ending. In my late sixties, too late it seems for fulfillment in this life, my eyes looked into those of the man who works from the female shield—and recognised him, as I had recognised Rodney and Jamie, in different circumstances, long ago. It did not surprise me at all to realise that his face, his height, his build, his blue eyes and his bearing

227

were much the same as my own, and that of Rodney. In looks we could easily pass as being of the same family, the same blood. Even the lines on our hands, that palmists use, turned out to be almost identical. Our minds worked in the same way. The affinity was deep. This relationship was not fraternal.

Fate had conspired to bring us into one another's presence by a series of coincidences of the kind Jung describes as 'synchonicities'. Far more than chance lay behind the meeting. I had met several men who work from the female shield—it is not uncommon. But this was the beloved, remembered one.

Within a few hours I knew for the first time what the girl in the Ouspensky meeting had meant. All my senses awakened with a joyous ease, so that the world was as full of beauty and wonder and glory as it used to be when I knelt among the grasses as a child and sang softly to myself. This was the way the gods had chosen, it seemed, to undam the creative stream that had been for years untappable. "I believe I can write a book again"! I told myself with astonishment.

We must surely live many lives, and for all possibilities to be fulfilled, the timing must be right. For months I thought: It will come right somehow, and be fulfilled, in spite of the obvious difficulties that come with a late love, well past the prime of life, when people have bonds and obligations in the world. I rode through the days with a free rein, like a perpetual gallop across the springy turf of the Downs on an early summer morning.

Eventually I realised that this third, deeply remembered relationship was possibly not due for fulfillment this time round at all. Many problems exist. But at least I have seen and touched and heard the presence of the once known partner, for reassurance that the Way is long and that I do not tread it quite alone. This time I didn't shed tears for a death, for a loss, but for a joy withheld. At least now the doors are open again, the lifeblood flows through me as though stemming from eternal things, and I have been handed the keys of the treasury. I lost no time in tumbling the gold out into the market place of life, by writing with a free, creative pen. And when I feel a sense of yearning, I remember William Blake's words of wisdom:

> He who bends to himself a joy
> Does the winged life destroy.

He who kisses the joy as it flies
Lives in eternity's sunrise.

So the third of the Karmic links has been made. Somewhere I
have a 'brother', somewhere a 'son', and still on this planet earth
which I must tread for another decade or so, is the beloved one
whom I was permitted to glimpse once again, as a last benison,
perhaps, before my departing. So now I return to my work with
a steady will.

'The Work' is a term appropriated by Gurdjieff, but it is in
fact very old. People who have come across esotericism in this
life incline to feel the Work simply means being in a group,
listening to what Gurdjieff or Ouspensky or any other teacher
had to say, doing psychological exercises, observing disciplines
and trying by this means to develop themselves.

But in fact the Work is an ever-changing, ever-moving,
ever-developing response to the times. It moves strongly
through all creative people: is negated by those who are
destructive in their attitude to life.

The minute anyone grasps what the Work is, in its true sense,
he is in it. He can't go back, nor does he desire to retreat
—although he soon sees that he has not entered upon a flowery
path or been given the keys to paradise. He has set his foot on a
stony way, but he is impelled by his own self to continue.

The words in *A Cloud of Unknowing*, "this is the shortest
Work that a man may do", surely apply to this first recognition:
the step forward, with courage born of hunger, into the
unknown future. Shakespeare says it simply enough in: "This
above all, to thine own self be true. And it will follow as the
night the day, thou canst not then be false to any man."

As long as an aspirant glimpses the truth inherent in this
aphorism and yet hesitates, thinking of money, family, personal
vanity, he is like the young man of the gospel story who went
away sorrowful because he had great possessions. Many people
hover on the threshold, moving back and forth over the years,
never quite able to dare the final bound. Those who have seen
the prize, but counting the cost, turn away repeatedly, tend by
tradition to go eventually into the downward spiral of creation,
back whence the flesh came, back to the foundations of life on

229

earth, instead of taking the heritage of Man to which the angels beckon.

As the teachings of both Buddhism and Hinduism indicate, everything we do in life is for happiness. All our actions, our plans, our intentions spring from this desire. But the happiness of wordly achievement is of course ephemeral and vanishes as we grasp at it. Yet when the true idea of the Work is seen we have our hand within reach of that which is never-changing; the eternal, which runs via the creative stream in artists, and in ordinary men. To make. To do. To be—according to the highest that we may perceive in our silent vigils or behind the hurly-burly of our everyday lives—that is the Work. It is always creative, for in making and doing you put yourself in direct line with the Creator. Even in making simple things, requiring skill of hand and eye and disciplined attention, there is happiness. In its denial there is always grief.

But the Work is inevitably lonely in its essence, whatever the outward form may take in the individual, because everyone does it innerly, for himself, and no-one else ever knows exactly what one is doing. "The Way is very long", Rodney once said to me. "You find it in one place, among one set of people, lose it there, and find it again somewhere else." I have always enjoyed group work, and listening to scholars and to teachers. But as Joan Halifax the anthopologist has said: "If you are rightly motivated you can study with the meths drinker under the bridge and you will get nectar. You need not even discard the charletans".

Gurdjieff commented that every little man thinks that only Jesus Christ himself is good enough to be his teacher. But you can learn from the most ordinary people, the most ordinary circumstances—once you have the key that opens all doors.

I tend to think of Systems and Ways as climbing frames. Seeing children in a playground surrounded by great trees, I watched the young feet and small hands learning to take hold, to test for safety and to advance by simple, regulated steps and guidelines. One day they would venture out in the wild woods, where none of the branches conform to regularity or expectation and safety is by no means guaranteed, but by that time they would have learnt to grip, to balance and to hold.

The idea that Systems are like maps to show the land ahead

230

has less reality for me, though it is frequently given as an analogy. But after all, maps must at least all agree which is the north, and which is the way to Birmingham or New York. Thinking of Systems and Ways as maps appears to me to lead to the common tendency to be forever comparing one thing with another: to want to fit the planets and the Signs of the Zodiac on the Tree of Life or into the Major Arcana of the Tarot: to compare Gurdjieff's Ray of Creation with something out of Alice Bailey or from Arthur Young's *Reflexive Universe*. To analyse Fritjof Capra's *Turning Point* and Peter Russell's *The Awakening Earth* looking for points of sympathy or divergence. One can work with numbers, using the Gematria, and play endless games in which one thing is seen to tally with another—only not quite. This seems to me to lead round in circles of argument. Without the understanding that what one has to do is learn to move *for one's self*, progress can be exceedingly slow and tentative throughout a whole life span.

The climbing frames are good. Like the masters, they exist to be grown out of. In the end, everybody has to make his own way into the jungle of ideas, and to some the years in the wilderness may be long. Learning to endure the arid deserts, the slough of despond, even to travel through the valley of the shadow of death, requires endurance. Apparent signposts often turn out to be just mirages, and if followed lead you back again whence you came. Truth lies within the seeker. Once you begin to take responsibility for your own development you are on the Way. But as Krishnamurti said: "Truth is a pathless land".

For me, the way leads, not to the darkness of the Himalayan caves, or into the jewelled realm of the elementals who rule the mineral kingdom, the waters and the fire and the air that wreaths the earth. I look now continually towards the Sun. But I am wary and awake to the unexpected, for as the Mexican Indios say: "He who is abducted by the Sunbird must look at the Thief!"

In truth the Way is always your own. In solitude and with an inward promise, you make the first step, even if it is over a precipice of time and circumstance, saying "for this I give myself". And miraculously you are caught in the arms of Fate and turned to face reality.

231